Treasures from the

MAP ROOM

Treasures from the MAP ROOM

A Journey through the Bodleian Collections

EDITED BY DEBBIE HALL

Bodleian Libraries
UNIVERSITY OF OXFORD

First published in 2016 by the Bodleian Library
Broad Street, Oxford OX1 3BG

www.bodleianshop.co.uk

ISBN: 978 1 85124 250 4

Text © the contributors, 2016
Images, unless specified on pp. 213–17 © Bodleian Library, University of Oxford, 2016

Cover design by Dot Little at the Bodleian Library
Designed and typeset by Laura Parker in Sirenne Text MBV
Printed and bound by Great Wall Printing Co. Ltd., Hong Kong on 157gsm matt art

British Library Catalogue in Publishing Data
A CIP record of this publication is available from the British Library

CONTENTS

BARNAGASO

DOARA

Magadoxa

This Scale Contaneth Two Hundred Leagues

MELINDE

QVILOA

MOSAMBIQVE

SVFFALO

ACKNOWLEDGEMENTS

The editor would like to thank many the many people who have helped to make this book possible, in particular Nick Millea, Stuart Ackland, Tessa Rose and John Mackrell (retired) of the Bodleian Map Room, Michael Athanson for scanning so many maps, and Paul Holloway for retrieving them. Curatorial staff in other Bodleian departments were also enormously helpful, especially Alan Coates, Lucy Evans and Francesca Galligan of Rare Books. Other current and former Bodleian staff and readers have written articles for the book and their contribution is gratefully appreciated.
A full list of authors can be found on page 211.

INTRODUCTION

A Map for All Reasons

THROUGH THE CENTURIES, MAPS HAVE ALWAYS HAD A POWERFUL appeal. A good map can give a sense of encompassing a landscape – a visual, artistic and scientific portrait of a place or situation at a specific moment in time. This applies equally to early printed maps with lavish decoration, bird's-eye views or functional modern publications, detailed plans of a town or estate or even a depiction of the whole world.

The majority of the maps included in this book are printed and were published for general consumption, though a small number are in manuscript; most are European in origin. Until the nineteenth century, most printed maps were produced in books or atlases. The main printing technique used was intaglio engraving on copper, although steel was also used and some very early printed maps were made using woodblocks. From the mid-nineteenth century a wider range of printing techniques and machine-made paper ushered in the era of mass production. Hand-drawn maps may date from before the era of printing, or have been made thus because a large number of copies was not required or, in the case of maps with content that was secret for military or trade reasons, desirable. Manuscript maps can have a unique beauty and some are highly decorative.

The maps in this book represent a broad range of different examples, organized by theme to enable us to see parallels between maps produced in very different eras and places and to put them into a wider context than their historical one. Maps have been produced for practical reasons, to help travellers by land and sea. They have been made to show what we know about the whole world and the skies above, or to demonstrate detailed knowledge of some specific part or aspect of our environment. Maps have been made to establish ownership of land, from an international empire to a country or a single estate, and to express pride in that ownership. They are essential tools of war, and have been for hundreds of years. Maps of towns and cities have a special appeal and have their own chapter in this book. More recently, maps have been made for recreation, as more people have the opportunity to enjoy the landscape. Finally, maps have also been made of fictional places and to represent imaginative or artistic interpretations of real locations, providing a tangible guide to places that do not actually exist. All of these themes are illustrated by maps from the Bodleian's collections, which are rich in maps both individually produced and included in larger works. The diverse range reproduced here, including many of the milestones of published cartography, comes from the collections of this single institution.

Maps in the Bodleian Library

A library is a repository of knowledge, and the gradual development of human knowledge of the Earth and skies is demonstrated by the cartographic as well as the written collections of the Bodleian. One of the Bodleian's strengths is the number of collections put together by individuals and subsequently acquired by the Library. Even where collectors of books and manuscripts were not specifically interested in maps, atlases and printed works containing maps were often acquired alongside texts. For example, Sir Henry Savile (1549–1622) established a collection of mathematical books – added to by holders of the Chair of Astronomy that he founded (including Sir Christopher Wren) – which includes early maps of the stars and works on surveying and navigation; this was acquired by the Bodleian in the 1880s. In 1834 the Library received on his death the book collection of Francis Douce, who had a wide range of interests and bequeathed over 19,000 printed volumes, including some significant early atlases, and hundreds of manuscripts. Of particular significance is the antiquary Richard Gough, whose bequest to the Bodleian (received in 1809) included thousands of volumes, and whose interest in topography meant that significant collections of maps and topographical views were amongst them. The famous fourteenth-century Gough Map of Great Britain, the very first item featured in this book, is one of the Bodleian's great treasures and is named simply for the man who donated it.

Not only do these named collections often include important rare and early works, but the individual interests and quirks of the collectors have meant that the library holds some unusual and ephemeral material that not everyone would have thought worth preserving; Richard Rawlinson's collection of copperplates is a case in point, as is John Johnson's collection. The latter forms the basis for the Library's collection of printed ephemera and contains many maps, including unusual items produced on cloth, as propaganda or as souvenirs.

Some significant military mapping has been acquired more recently. Donations from the Ministry of Defence have formed an important source for the Map Room's collections for many decades, including trench maps from World War I and both allied and captured enemy mapping from World War II and subsequent conflicts. This includes many maps not commercially available or otherwise hard to obtain in the United Kingdom. Countries that the United Kingdom has colonized, invaded or fought wars against are particularly strongly represented.

The collections have continued to grow, in many cases owing once more to the generosity of donors who have given material or, alternatively, donated money towards its purchase. The extraordinary medieval Islamic Book of Curiosities was acquired earlier this century. The earliest known maps of the continents in Hungarian arrived within the current decade, as did a manuscript map by General Gordon thought to be lost and surviving only in reproduction; both were donated. Richard Ballam's collection of toys and games, which includes material with a geographical or cartographical theme, has just been donated at the time of writing. Although maps have formed part of the Bodleian's collections from early on, they have been collected actively only since around 1800. Since 1801 the most numerically significant acquisition has been the printed maps of the Ordnance Survey (OS), received under the Legal Deposit arrangement, which has existed in some form since 1610. Initially this meant that all books entered at Stationers' Hall had to have a copy deposited in the Bodleian. This was not particularly effective for the 150 years or so following, but the Library has now long exercised its right to claim a copy of any publications produced in the UK or the Republic of Ireland, including, of course, published maps. The coincidence of the beginning of the OS publishing history and the Bodleian's more active approach to map collecting was a happy one. By 1882 it was reckoned that the Library was receiving between three and four thousand sheets a year from the OS and the Hydrographic Office (publisher of Admiralty charts) alone, all received on Legal Deposit. As a result the Library has a very comprehensive collection of maps of the British Isles, including virtually all OS maps and an enormous range of commercially published examples. This includes maps of other parts of the world published within the United Kingdom and Ireland. More lightweight mapping, such as tourist maps, which an academic library might not think worth purchasing, can prove unexpectedly interesting to future generations, as much for the social history it illustrates as for its cartographic content.

The state of world mapping has changed beyond all recognition in the past hundred years. At the beginning of the twentieth century topographic mapping was available only for very limited areas of the world, mainly western Europe, North America and South Asia. Access to geographical information via satellite imagery is now at unprecedented levels, and publication of paper maps continues to flourish.

CHAPTER I

Travel and Exploration

THE MOST FUNDAMENTAL PURPOSE OF A MAP IN THE MODERN AGE is to help us find our way, so the association of maps and travel seems obvious. However, although maps have been in existence for thousands of years, and examples of route maps exist from much of that time, until fairly recently maps of this kind were rare. It is interesting to appreciate what a recent innovation the road map is. In the majority of pre-industrial societies, most people made only local journeys or followed routes they knew well for which no map was required. For those who did travel further afield, written or spoken directions were often all that was available. Such early route maps as do exist are the exception rather than the rule.

It is worth making a distinction between maps about travel and maps for travel. The famous Peutinger Table, one of the earliest road maps, was probably made in the fourth or fifth century CE and showed road networks throughout the Roman Empire. The original is lost but later copies survive, the earliest made in the thirteenth century and held in Vienna; it is named not for the original cartographer (unknown) but for a former owner, Konrad Peutinger. An extract is shown overleaf. It is unlike anything else from the period and it is not known how the map was used. The same is broadly true of the two fourteenth-century travel maps featured in this chapter, the Gough Map of Great Britain and a map of the Holy Land. The latter may have been used as much for spiritual as physical travel, enabling the viewer at home to share the experience of pilgrimage. Similarly, the Selden map of China, also

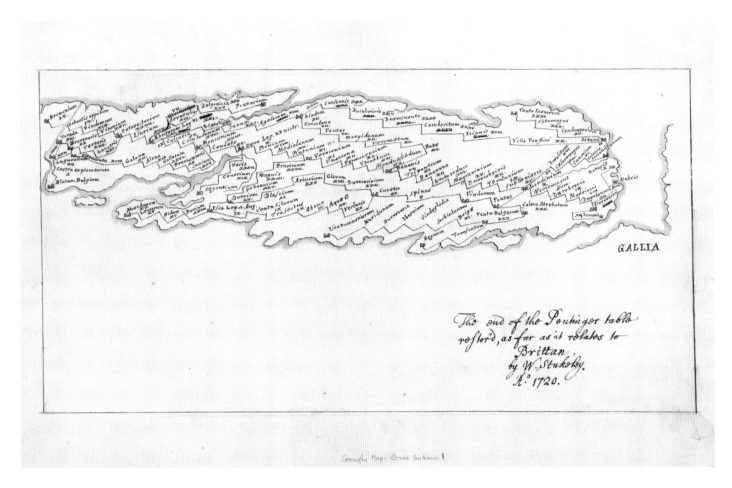

An extract from the Peutinger table redrawn in 1720 by William Stukely.

featured here, is thought likely to have been made for use in a merchant's home rather than carried at sea.

Before the striking innovation of John Ogilby's atlas of the roads of Britain in 1675, many maps did not show roads at all. Ogilby's atlas was too large to be conveniently carried on the road and may have been designed to be consulted in advance, when planning a journey. The idea was widely copied, with many smaller road atlases being published through the late seventeenth and early eighteenth century. The inclusion of roads on maps increased through the eighteenth century, and was standard by the nineteenth. With the invention of the bicycle and the car, ever increasing numbers of people could cover large distances independently, and the market grew exponentially. American road maps (of which millions were issued free by fuel companies) are particularly iconic; a lovely example from the 1930s begins this introduction.

This portolan chart, produced in Venice in 1559, was part of an atlas covering the eastern
and southern Atlantic Ocean and the Mediterranean Sea.

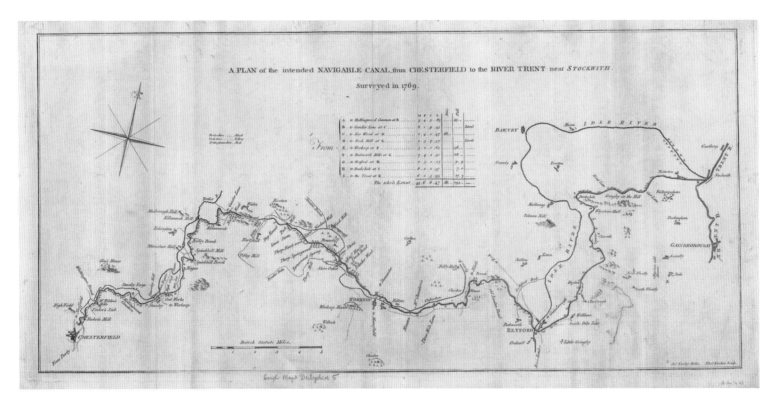

This planned route for the Chesterfield Canal is one of many maps made to show proposed canal schemes in the late eighteenth century.

Both the roads and the maps that portrayed them improved during this period; we now take it for granted that road maps are reliable, widely available, and utilitarian.

It is unsurprising, then, that some of the early maps in this chapter were created for travel on water. This arguably has a longer cartographic history than land travel. The earliest sea charts, known as portolan charts, cover the Mediterranean and surrounding areas. Examples survive from the thirteenth to the seventeenth centuries, after which they were largely superseded by printed sea charts and atlases. The highly decorated example shown on the previous page is from an atlas of portolan charts by Bartolomeo Oliva, a founder of a family of three generations of chartmakers who worked in Majorca, Italy and southern France, producing charts of this type from the mid-sixteenth to the late seventeenth century. From the fifteenth century European exploration to find new lands and new routes to existing trading partners such as China was dominated by maritime activity, and the movements of people, goods and ideas resulting from this age of discovery changed the world irrevocably. This chapter includes a fifteenth-century atlas that may have played a role in Columbus's first voyage to the Americas, and sea charts of different eras. From the nineteenth century navigational charts began to be produced by official government agencies, such as the United Kingdom Hydrographic Office, which still publishes Admiralty Charts today, and equivalent bodies elsewhere.

Maps for inland navigation are perhaps more easily overlooked. This chapter includes sketches for an early chart of part of Lake Victoria in Uganda. The Gough Map gives prominence to rivers; this is echoed nearly 500 years later in Walker's 1830 map of Great Britain, also included in this chapter, showing canals and navigable rivers and the industrial products conveyed on them, though by this time railways were also of increasing importance for both industrial and passenger transport. The intervening period had seen many schemes to improve rivers and make them more navigable; by the eighteenth century these were increasingly succeeded by the construction of new canals for the movement of goods, a leap forward in terms of reducing the cost of transport. One of the maps associated with proposed canal schemes is shown here. The Chesterfield Canal was proposed in the 1760s, built in the 1770s and heavily used for over half a century; nearly two hundred years after its construction restoration began and parts of it are now open for recreational use.

The Gough Map of Great Britain

Dating from the late Medieval era, the Gough Map is the oldest surviving map of Great Britain showing a recognizable coastline and depicting a relatively faithful geographical representation of settlements and rivers. The manuscript is drawn in pen, ink and coloured washes on two skins of vellum, and measures 115 × 56 cm. In 1809 the map was bequeathed to the Bodleian by Richard Gough (hence its name), along with the rest of Gough's topographical collection of maps, prints, books and drawings. Nothing is known of its provenance except that it was bought by Gough at a sale of the antiquarian Thomas Martin's manuscripts in 1774 for half a crown (12 ½ pence).

Once the reader is aware that the map shows east at the top, then the familiar outline of Great Britain quickly becomes apparent. Rivers are given strategic importance, with the Severn, Thames and Humber predominant, and even the loop of the Wear at Durham readily evident. Almost two hundred rivers are marked. Other physical features are identified by signs, for example a tree locates the New Forest. Scotland assumes an unfamiliar shape, and almost certainly was mostly unknown to the cartographer, although the Clyde and Forth are clearly identifiable. Over six hundred towns are shown. The lettering for London and York is coloured gold, while other principal medieval settlements, such as Bristol, Chester, Gloucester, Lincoln, Norwich, Salisbury and Winchester, are lavishly illustrated. Around 4,700 km of routes between towns are marked in red on the map, with distances included in Roman numerals, also marked in red – best seen on the network radiating out of London, and also along the Welsh coast.

Although the identity of the mapmaker is unknown, it seems clear that the text on the Gough Map is the work of many hands, spanning from the late fourteenth until well into the fifteenth century. There are visible differences between recorded details in Scotland and England. The text written by the earlier scribe, for example, is best preserved in Scotland and the area north of Hadrian's Wall, whereas text written by later scribes is found in southeastern and central England. The buildings in Scotland do not have windows and doors, unlike those in the revised part of the map, where most have both windows and doors. Closer inspection of the rivers reveals that those south of the Wall tend to have a dark bounding line along their banks; north of the Wall this is not the case, giving this part of the map an unfinished look.

The Gough Map is considered to be a copy of an earlier map. It shows significant local knowledge of Lincolnshire and southeast Yorkshire, which leads to speculation that further versions may have been made and held regionally. The earliest compilation date for a Gough Map prototype is likely to be around 1280, in the reign of Edward I. So, was the Gough Map an official compilation for government use, perhaps amended for local use on this Bodleian exemplar?

The Gough Map's mysteries may not remain impenetrable much longer. In early 2015, a group of scientists from Oxford, Durham, Boston (Massachusetts) and Madrid gathered at the Bodleian Library for a week of intense data gathering. It is hoped that a combination of 3D scanning, hyperspectral imagery and Raman spectroscopy will shed some light on the secrets held on the map since the late Middle Ages.

MS. Gough Gen. Top. 16

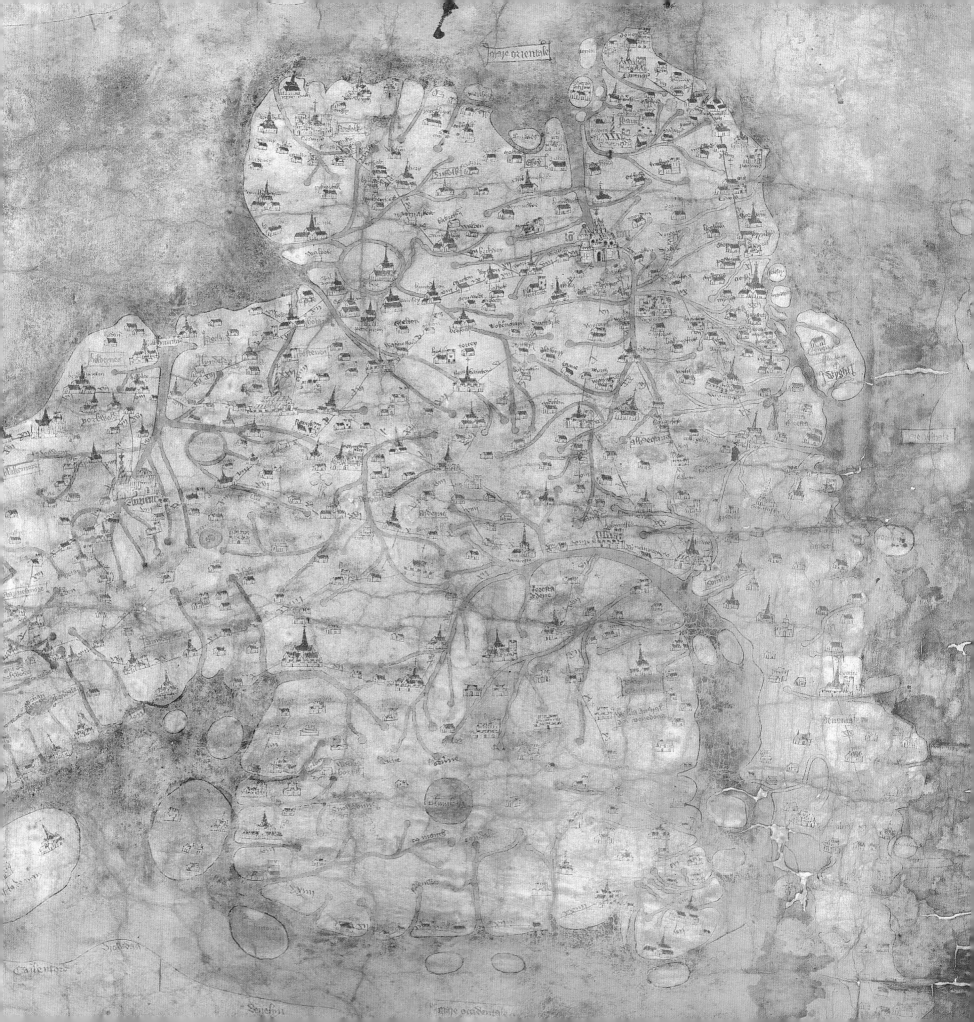

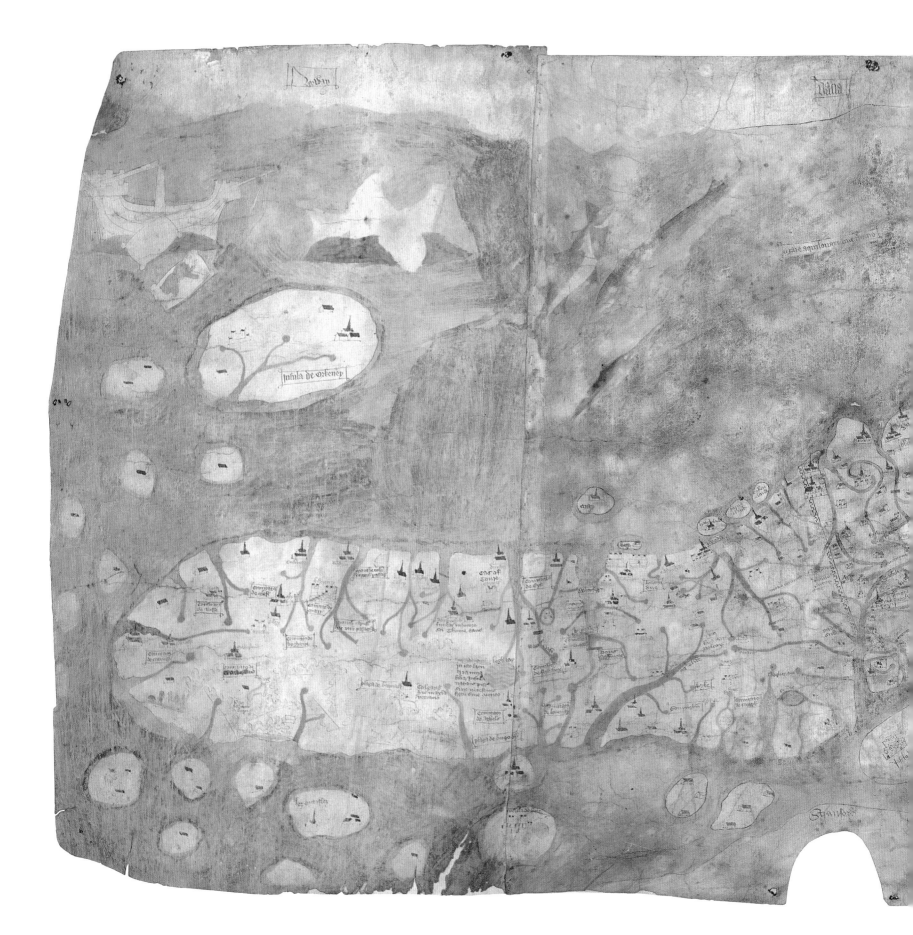

A virtual journey to the Holy Land

This manuscript map is made up of three parchments, measuring together 41 × 212 cm. With the east at the top, it shows the land from Damascus and Sidon in the north (left) to Beersheba and Hebron in the south (right); and from the Jordan Valley in the east (top) to the Mediterranean shoreline in the west (bottom). The extract here shows the left part; the inland sea in the centre is the Sea of Galilee. The map is dated to the fourteenth century on the basis of palaeographic examination.

The map suggests a fertile country, full of rivers and green tracts of land. Varied forms of architectural structures represent cities and sacred places. No roads are depicted. The spaces between the painted elements are filled with numerous inscriptions containing geographical details or referring to biblical traditions attributed to the various sites. A few sites associated with biblical traditions are indicated by pictorial symbols. Six jars within a square frame stand for the miracle at Cana (John 2: 1-11), for example. By showing the land planted with references to past sacred events, the map offers the observer an image essential to the simulation of the experience of pilgrimage in situ – an experience that involved a constant movement between past and present, between sacred and earthly geography.

A list containing fifty-two entries recording distances in miles between pairs of sites is written on the left side of the map. Lists of distances are not commonly found on medieval maps and MS. Douce 389 is the only surviving map of the Holy Land that shows such a list. This one appears to be a synopsis of a twelfth-century treatise depicting the Holy Land as a sacred topography (*Liber Locorum Sanctorum Terrae Jerusalem* by Rorgo Fretellus). Considering that it does not record any particular itinerary but includes references to sacred sites – with special emphasis on the cities of Jerusalem, Nazareth and Bethlehem – the list was apparently meant to enhance the viewer's spiritual experience of wandering in the biblical land.

This list of distances associates MS. Douce 389 with the fifteenth-century English pilgrim William Wey. In a manuscript describing his two pilgrimage voyages to Jerusalem (MS. Bodley 565), Wey mentions a map of the Holy Land. He makes two lists of places that appear on that map as well as a list of distances, similar to the one that appears on MS. Douce 389. This similarity led to the assumption that Wey copied the list from MS. Douce 389 or a map that resembled it.

The association of MS. Douce 389 with William Wey is most significant for our understanding of its cultural context and functionality. MS. Bodley 565 contains William Wey's testament, in which he mentions a 'chapel made in the likeness of the Sepulchre of Our Lord in Jerusalem' – that in all probability he established in his priory at Edington in Wiltshire – and several objects that he displayed there and was willing to donate to the priory. These included devotional paintings, vestigial mementoes brought from the Holy Land (stones from various *loca sancta*, measurements of sites, and wooden models of churches in Jerusalem and Bethlehem), a *mappa mundi* and the map of the Holy Land. Evidently, a map like MS. Douce 389 would have been used in fifteenth-century England – and was by Wey – as a purely devotional image and in the context of monumental evocations of Jerusalem in the Catholic West.

MS. Douce 389

Old World to New World

Claudius Ptolemy (fl. 146–c.170) composed his *Geographia* in Alexandria in around AD 160. He provided coordinates for 8000 places, tied into a grid of longitudes and latitudes – an extraordinary achievement for the time. It is not known if he ever made the maps his work describes, but his description survived as a set of instructions for making maps of the known world. The earliest datable maps found with the text are by Maximus Planudes (c.1260–1310). Ptolemy's work was unknown to Europeans for centuries, but it survived in Arabic manuscripts and was translated from the Arabic into Latin by Jacopo d'Angelo (c.1360–1410) in 1409/10. At about the same time, the maps were redrawn with Latin inscriptions, and later revised by Nicolaus Germanus (fl. 1451–6), a German Benedictine. He aimed to follow Ptolemy's instructions and his maps must be close to those Ptolemy himself might have compiled.

The European rediscovery of Ptolemy's work coincided happily with the development of printing in the West, and Ptolemaic atlases are amongst the earliest printed books. A version with the maps engraved on copper was produced in 1478, but the woodcut version shown here, produced in Ulm, has a unique charm. The Ulm editions are based on Germanus's third revision of the maps, dating from c.1468. Germanus added modern maps of Italy, Spain, France and Palestine, and extended the world map to include more of Africa and Scandinavia. In the present edition the map also gives the name of the man who cut the block from which it was printed,

a 'Johannes woodcutter from Armsheim'. As classical knowledge was recovered and more widely disseminated, it began to be integrated with modern knowledge. Ptolemaic maps continued to be included in atlases even after the European discovery of the Americas made it clear that their geography was obsolete.

This particular copy has an intriguing link with the European discovery of the New World. Printed in Germany, and containing the first printed modern map of Spain, this volume belonged to King Ferdinand and Queen Isabella of Spain, whose coat of arms is in the book. Ferdinand and Isabella supported Columbus's voyage across the Atlantic. Although Ptolemy's locations were amazingly accurate for their time, his calculation of the Earth's circumference was an underestimate. Columbus, who owned a 1478 edition of the *Geographia*, believed the distance to China to be less than it was, partly on the basis of this. As Ptolemy's *Geographia* demonstrates, the understanding that the world was round was nothing new even in Columbus's day. But would Columbus have planned to travel west to China, and bumped into the Americas on the way, without this misconception of the distance involved? Would Ferdinand and Isabella have backed the venture if they had not also owned a copy of the book that supported his theory?

The book was presented in Burgos on 25 August 1492 to Francesco Capello, Venetian ambassador to Spain. It was bequeathed to the Bodleian, with the rest of his collection, by Francis Douce.

Arch. B b.19

The Selden Map of China

This was one of the first Chinese maps to reach Europe. It came into the Bodleian in 1659 from the estate of the London lawyer John Selden, who must have acquired it by 1653 at the latest, as in a codicil to his will dated that year he describes the map and an accompanying compass as having been 'taken both by an englishe comander'. Perhaps Selden acquired it from an East India Company trader who took it from another European, Japanese or Chinese vessel in the lawless conditions of the South China Sea, but the East India Company records make no mention of it.

Striking in both size and appearance, the map was kept on permanent display in the Anatomy School and is noted in a list of the School's contents that was prepared by its keeper, the antiquary and diarist Thomas Hearne, in 1721. Although it was never lost sight of, its importance lay undiscovered until January 2008, when it was examined by the American scholar Robert Batchelor, who noticed two features that distinguished it sharply from all extant Chinese maps that had been produced hitherto.

The first was that it is not just a map of China, but of the whole of east and southeast Asia. Earlier and most later maps depicted China not only as the centre of the known world, but as occupying almost its entire area. China occupies less than one half of the area of the Selden Map, which is centred on the South China Sea, with an equal area depicting the Philippines, Borneo, Java, Sumatra, Southeast Asia and, notionally at least, India. The depiction of China itself was not the purpose of the map, and was copied from a standard printed map of the period. The second was the presence of shipping routes with compass bearings radiating from the port of Quanzhou on the coast of Fujian Province to all the areas covered by the map, which thus charted the commercial world as no map, whether European or Chinese, had done before. It was the earliest surviving example of Chinese merchant cartography, unique in not being a product of the imperial bureaucracy. It indicates the extent of China's intercourse with the rest of the world at a time when it is generally supposed to have been isolated.

A third feature of the map became apparent during the course of the conservation work that was undertaken following this discovery. When the old backing was removed, the main sea routes, identically drawn, were found on the reverse, showing not only that this was a first draft, but that the map was being drawn by systematic geometric techniques. It is the first known Chinese map to have been produced in this way, and its techniques of obtaining voyage data from a magnetic compass and calculating distances from the number of watches are without Western parallel.

Unfortunately, it is not known exactly when and where the map was drawn, or who drew it and for what purpose. Recent scholarship suggests that it was probably produced in the early seventeenth century by a Chinese mapmaker, as Chinese sources are used for the place names on the map and also the shipping routes; the compiler was probably based in Southeast Asia, as the map's depiction of that area was to remain the most accurate for another two centuries. It is elaborately decorated with landscapes and plants, and was almost certainly produced for reference in the house of a rich merchant rather than for use at sea.

MS. Selden supra 105

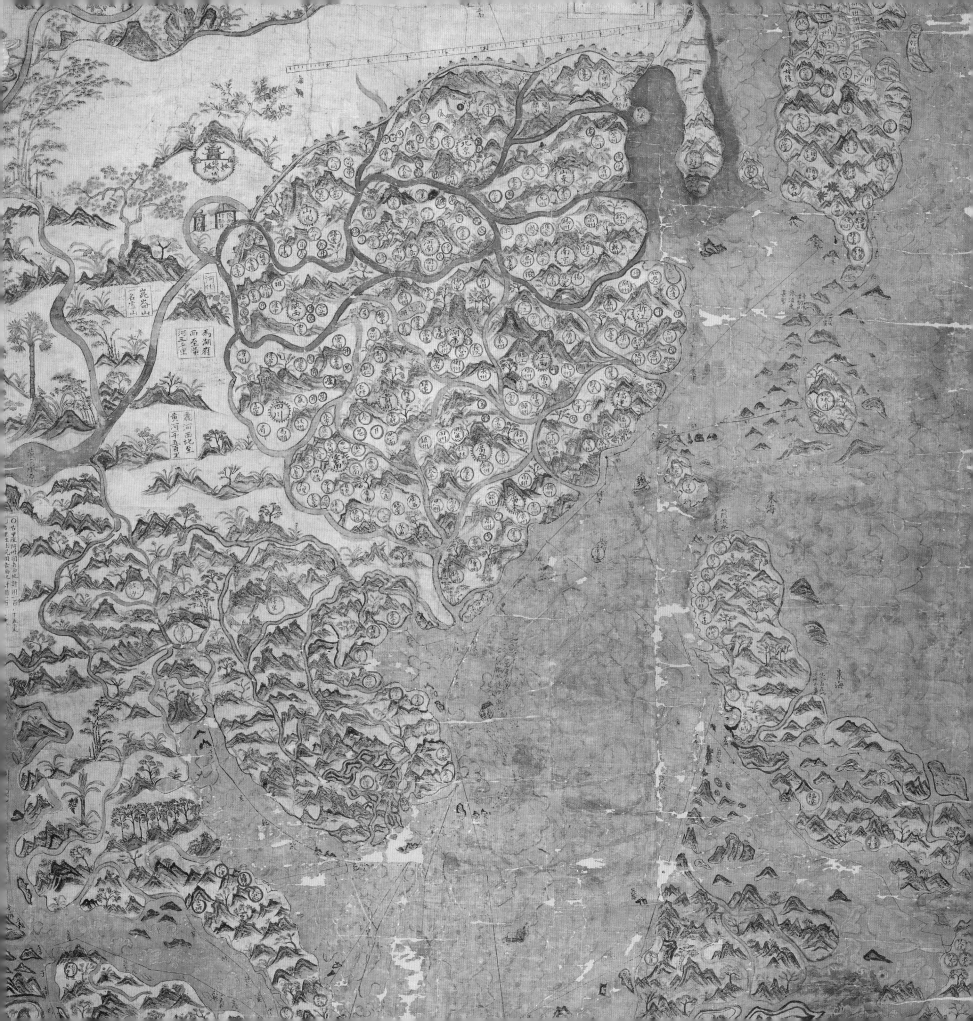

The first road atlas

This road map, taken from John Ogilby's *Britannia* of 1675, was a revolution in mapping when it appeared, and was copied, plagiarized, improved and revised for many years afterwards. In the seventeenth century it was usual for maps of medium scale (such as Speed's county maps, discussed on page 68) not to show any roads at all. There existed only road books, which listed the places en route from one town to another every few miles; on arriving at a town or village on the list, the traveller could ask directions to the next one. Ogilby's distinctive strip maps were a considerable advance.

Ogilby himself was a remarkable man, who had had many varied careers – including dancing master, Deputy Master of the King's Revels in Ireland, theatre manager, soldier, translator and publisher – before embarking on his final and most successful venture, as a mapmaker, in his sixties. He began by surveying the burnt centre of London after the Great Fire of 1666, having perhaps used his contacts at court to obtain the commission. He was assisted by his wife's grandson William Morgan (he had married a wealthy widow in middle age); Morgan eventually inherited Ogilby's business, published several maps and was appointed His Majesty's Cosmographer in 1681. With others Morgan and Ogilby completed a plan of London which Morgan was eventually to publish in 1676; on twenty sheets, it was the most detailed and accurate plan of London ever made at that time. Ogilby then produced several volumes of a multi-volume atlas of the world, in conjunction with Dutch mapmakers. His plan

for a detailed survey of Britain was never fully realised, but the volume produced (misleadingly titled *Britannia: volume the first*) was an extraordinary innovation: the first national road atlas of Britain, it covered 7,500 miles of road. Four editions were produced within two years of its initial publication.

The maps were produced in strips showing only the area around the road. The road was depicted in detail, showing whether it was enclosed, with small plans of the towns it passed through, hills and gradients, minor cross roads with their destinations, and landmarks such as windmills (one can be seen bottom right). Each strip bears a small compass rose, since precise differences in direction could not be easily accommodated in the strip-map design. Liberties were occasionally taken with precise routes and orientations of sections of road, and there are errors, but it was still a remarkable work for its time. The maps are at a scale of one inch to a mile, unprecedented for many of the areas covered, and the small plans of towns are often sufficiently detailed to be useful to historians looking for early depictions of these places. Distances are given in statute miles and furlongs, at a time when measurement was by no means standardized, and are generally quite accurate. There are notes about the surrounding landscape on the maps themselves and descriptions of the routes on the intervening text pages.

Ogilby died the year after *Britannia*'s publication, at the age of seventy-six, having completed a work for which he will be long remembered.

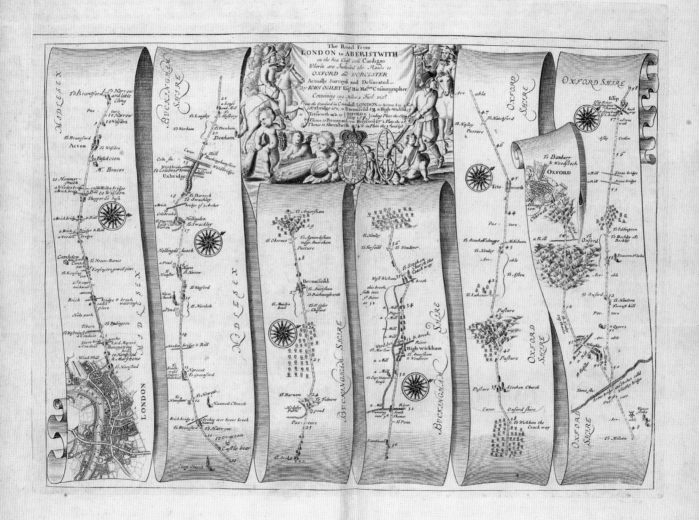

The Road From
LONDON to ABERISTWITH
on the Sea Coast of Cardigan
Wherein are Included the Roads to
OXFORD and WORCESTER
Actually Survey'd and Delineated
By IOHN OGILBY Esq.r His Ma.ties Coßmographer

John Smith's Virginia

This famous and beautiful map of the Chesapeake Bay area in Virginia was first published in 1612, along with a written description of the region, by John Smith, Governor of Virginia. Smith had an extraordinarily adventurous life. The son of a yeoman farmer, by the time he was in his early twenties he had travelled widely in Europe by land and sea, become a mercenary soldier in the Austrian army, been promoted to captain, taken prisoner, sold into slavery, escaped and returned to England. He then sailed to Virginia, one of the first to establish a permanent English colony there and part of the governing council from his arrival. Smith was one of the founders of Jamestown, shown towards the left-hand side of the map, conspicuously coloured in red amongst the greens and browns of the landscape. His discipline and strong work ethic were influential in the successful establishment of the settlement.

Smith spent a great deal of time exploring and mapping the area. A number of small crosses are marked at various points on the map, and a note at top right explains their significance: 'To the crosses hath bin discovered, what beyond is by relation.' He appears, then, to have been scrupulous in recording how much of the map was based on his own exploration. The choice of a cross as symbol may also be of significance.

The most striking feature of the map is the illustration of a native American, in traditional attire, who looms over it on the right and may be holding up the banner bearing the word 'Virginia'. There is also a smaller illustration of Powhatan, a local chieftain, showing how he appeared when Smith, having been captured while exploring the area, was 'delivered to him prisoner'. Smith developed and encouraged reasonably cordial relationships with local tribes, realising that the colonists' survival depended on them, and his relationship with the chieftain's daughter Pocahontas is legendary. These two illustrations are considerably bigger than the royal coat of arms in the centre of the map. Smith named many of the local native tribes and marked over 150 local villages on the map. Indeed, it is for the evidence relating to native American tribes that this map and its accompanying text have long been particularly valued by historians and anthropologists. To whom is Smith implying that the land belongs?

The map was engraved by William Hole, who also engraved the maps for Michael Drayton's *Poly-Olbion*, featured later in this book in the 'Imaginary Lands' chapter; some similarities can be seen in the pictorial representation of trees and hills. It is oriented, rather unusually, with west at the top. This makes sense in the context of British exploration of the Americas; for explorers arriving from the east, west was ahead. This map was used as a basis for many more of the same region in succeeding years; this is its first state, appearing in a manuscript narrative.

Smith left Virginia in 1610, partly as a consequence of an injury resulting from an accidental explosion, and, although he never returned, his subsequent writings did much to promote and encourage its colonization.

MS. Ashmole 1758 13v-14r

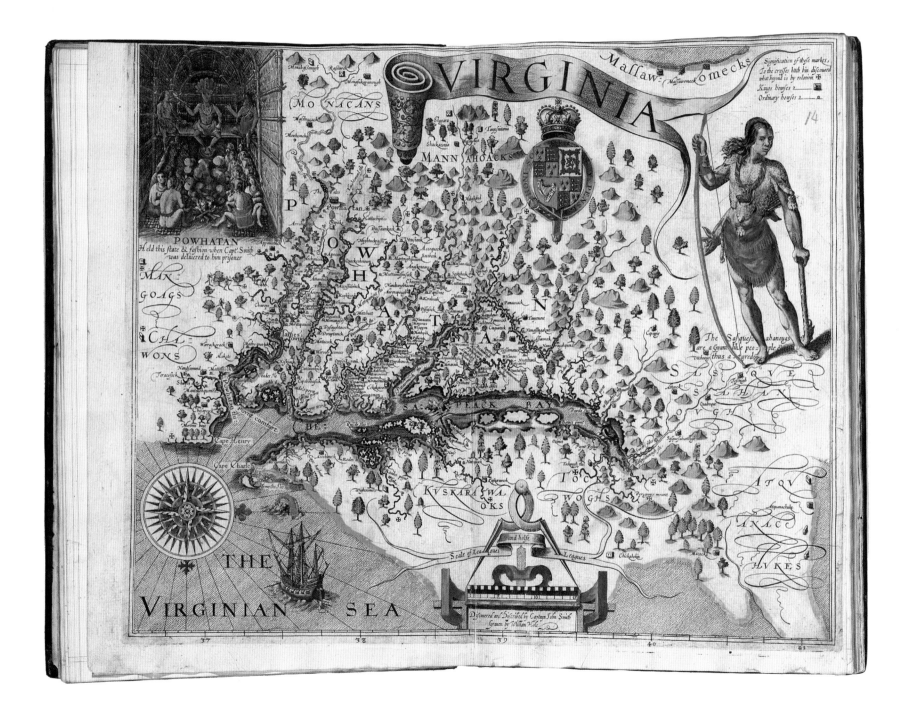

From the Thames to the Indian Ocean

This lovely coloured chart by John Thornton is a fine example of a portolan. Portolans were early sea charts, drawn by hand, usually on vellum. They have a distinctive style with very accurate coastlines, a great deal of coastal detail and some exaggeration of bays and headlands. Typically there are many place names written at right angles to the coast and little inland information. They have clusters of rhumb lines (lines of constant bearing) representing sixteen points of the compass. The style reflects the navigational methods used, where mariners either hugged the coast or navigated across short stretches of open sea by compass bearing. It is interesting to compare this chart to the much earlier portolan in the 'Pride and Ownership' chapter.

John Thornton was a prolific mapmaker, producing both manuscript and printed sea charts. Based at the Minories in London, he was a member of the Thames School of Chart Makers, so called for their places of work on the north bank of the River Thames; this was close to the London docks and hence to a large number of potential customers. They were also known as the 'Drapers' School', as many were members of the Drapers' Guild; they were too small a group to have a guild of their own. Thornton was hydrographer to the East India Company and also to the Hudson Bay Company,

so his mapmaking stretched around the globe. He worked at a time of transition, when manuscript charts were being superseded by printed charts of different type; he is known to have produced about forty manuscript charts as well as numerous printed maps, including those for John Seller's *Atlas maritimus* in 1675; he made terrestrial maps as well as maritime charts. By the time the present chart was made, he was already involved in the printed map trade, and his later manuscript charts may have formed the basis for printed ones published in the early eighteenth century. His business was taken over by his brother Samuel in 1706, two years before he died.

The chart shown here is a late and fairly small-scale example of a portolan, probably produced for decorative rather than navigational use. The decoration is very elaborate, with many colours and gold leaf incorporated into features like the major place names and scale bar. It is mounted on hinged boards so that it can be folded concertina-style and stored like a book (which has probably helped its long-term preservation); this is typical of charts of the Thames School. The tip of Australia is labelled 'Dutch discovery' – the first intimation of a whole new continent, in the last days of a medieval style of mapmaking.

Map Res. 117

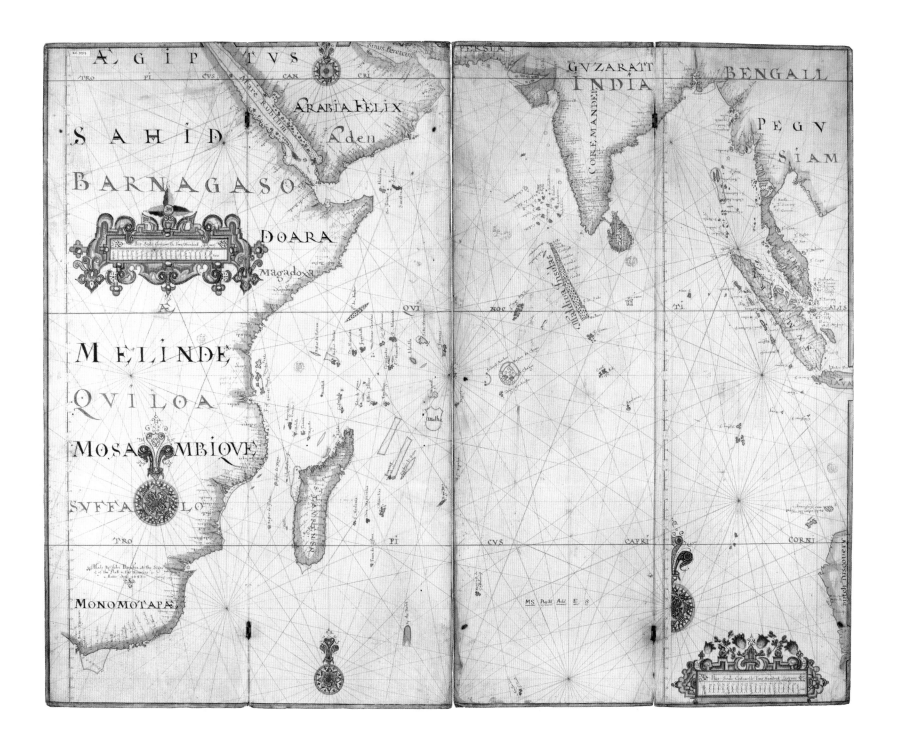

ÆGIPTVS

PERSIA

GVZARATT

BENGALL

INDIA

TRO   PI   CVS   CAN   CRI

ARABIA FELIX

Aden

PEGV

SIAM

SAHID

BARNAGASO

COREMANDEL

DOARA

Magadoxa

MELINDE

QVILOA

MOSAMBIQVE

QVI

NOC

TI

ALIS

SVFFALO

TRO   PI   CVS   CAPRI   CORNI

MONOMOTAPA

MS. Pepl. Add. E. 8

Early Sydney

When setting out on a journey to chart the 1769 Transit of Venus (featured in this book in the chapter 'Knowledge and Science') Captain James Cook was also tasked with locating the southern continent 'Terra Australis Incognita', whose northern coast had been partially mapped by earlier Spanish and Dutch navigators. After measuring the transit of Venus from Tahiti the *Endeavour* continued its voyage of exploration, journeying westward towards New Zealand and then on to Australia's east coast, never previously encountered by Europeans. Cook landed at the soon-named Botany Bay in April of 1770 and then travelled north, running aground on the Great Barrier Reef on the way, before finally claiming the land for King George III and naming it New South Wales.

Defeat in the American War of Independence caused the British Government a number of problems, one of which was the loss of a place of settlement for convicted criminals. Despite the logistical problems involved in transporting a large number of convicts halfway around the world, a fleet of eleven ships set sail in 1787 destined for Botany Bay, under the command of Captain Arthur Phillip. These ships, known as the 'First Fleet', landed in early 1788, but soon realised that Botany Bay was unsuitable for settlement and relocated to Sydney Cove in late January of that year.

This map, one of the earliest known maps of the area, is taken from a book, *The Voyage of Governor Phillip to Botany Bay ...*, and shows the first settlement at Sydney Cove, Port Jackson, at what is now the Rocks and Circular Quay area of Sydney, in July 1788. It shows the layout of the colony early in its existence but does not show any prison or jail, the idea being that the transportation itself was sufficient punishment. A passage in the book describes the layout of the first settlement:

Lines are there traced out [on the plan] which distinguish the principal street of an intended town, to be terminated by the Governor's House, the main guard and the criminal court. In some parts of this space temporary barracks at present stand, but no permanent buildings will be suffered to be placed, except in conformity to the plan laid down.

As well as telling the story of the voyage of the First Fleet to Australia, the book, published in London in 1790, includes numerous illustrations of the local flora and fauna (see 'The Kangooroo'), as well as scenes of Aboriginal life. There are also tables at the start of the book listing the ships in the voyage, the names of the captains and officers of the ships and the number of convicts on board (600 men, 250 women).

THE KANGOOROO.

Published as the Act directs June 1 1789 by J. Stockdale.

20675 c.4

34

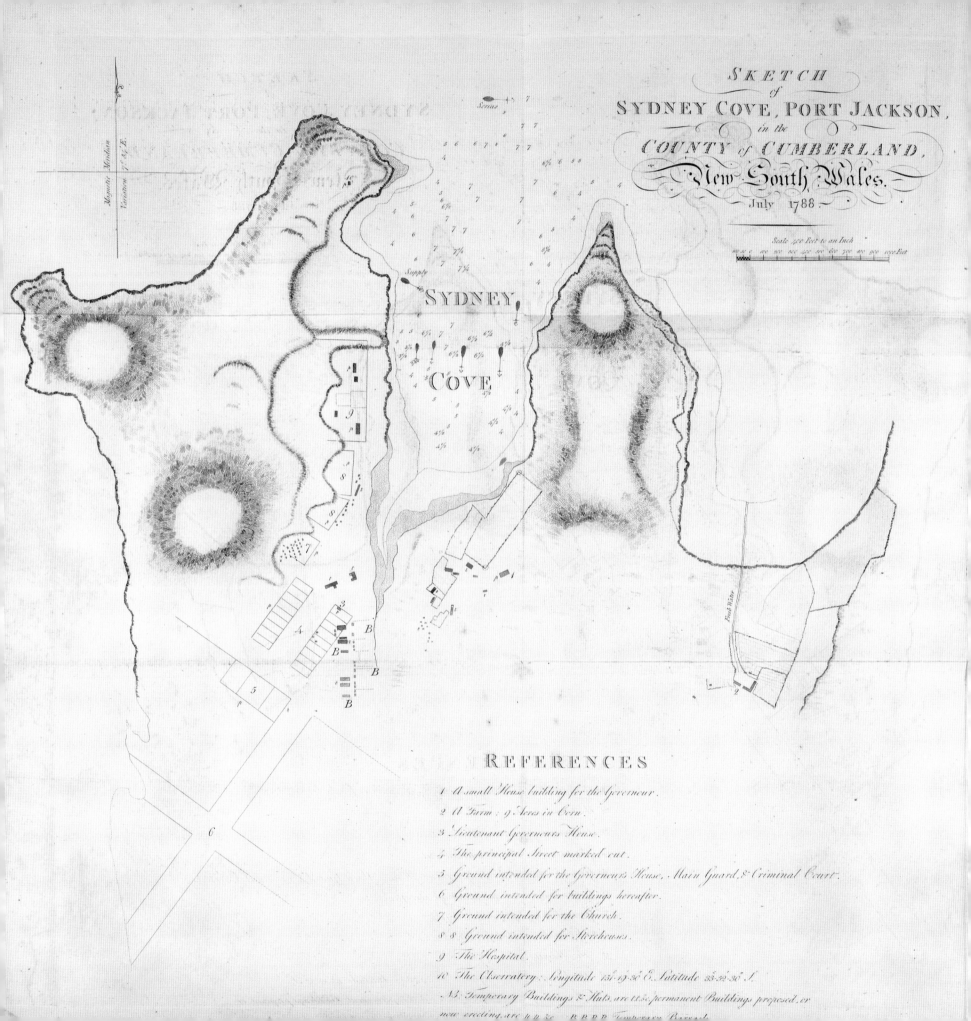

SKETCH
of
SYDNEY COVE, PORT JACKSON,
in the
COUNTY of CUMBERLAND,
New South Wales.
July 1788.

Scale 450 Feet to an Inch

SYDNEY

COVE

Sirius

Supply

Fresh Water

REFERENCES

1 A small House building for the Governour.

2 A Farm: 9 Acres in Corn.

3 Lieutenant Governour's House.

4 The principal Street marked out.

5 Ground intended for the Governour's House, Main Guard, & Criminal Court.

6 Ground intended for buildings hereafter.

7 Ground intended for the Church.

8 8 Ground intended for Storehouses.

9 The Hospital.

10 The Observatory. Longitude 151.19.30 E. Latitude 33.52.30 S.

N.B. Temporary Buildings & Huts, are thus; permanent Buildings proposed, or now erecting, are thus; B B B B Temporary Barracks.

Travel without roads

This enormous, beautiful map, dating from 1830, shows a vanished Britain. It is a transport map, showing (according to the elaborately engraved title) 'the inland navigation, canals and rail roads with the situations of the various mineral productions throughout Great Britain'. It illustrates a land whose natural resources for industry were still key to its economic activity, and whose transport of those resources was mainly done by water or railway; transporting heavy goods on the poor roads of the day was an uncertain and expensive business. There are very few roads shown, only the most major being featured. But every canal and river is shown, the latter divided into navigable and non-navigable. Schemes to improve rivers had been increasingly common since the seventeenth century, and in the eighteenth century the construction of artifical canals for water transport grew enormously. The network of railways and tram roads is also portrayed, and some navigational information (water depths, rocks, buoys and anchorages) is shown around the coast – domestic transport by sea was still important for coastal areas.

The map was produced by John Walker, a surveyor based in Wakefield, and published in both Wakefield and London. Wakefield was an agricultural market town whose prosperity was built on corn and wool, but coal mining became increasingly important there through the nineteenth century. The railway had yet to arrive in 1830, but the river and canals had long been important.

The industrial products shown are largely those of the land; stone, ironstone, sand, clay, chalk and lime are all shown, and the fuller's earth of Somerset. Some are relatively exotic, such as the marble of north Dorset and the copper of the southern Lake District. Some are well known resources, such as the porcelain clay and tin of Cornwall, but others (manganese and antimony in the same region) are more unexpected. Symbols such as : for lead, ♀ for copper and ♂ for ironstone, identified in the legend, are used to save space. East Anglia, still predominantly agricultural, has far fewer mineral resources, although 'stone' and lime are fairly ubiquitous.

The map is striking for its size and beauty. The hand colouring stands out, the counties being shown in six colours. The fineness of the engraving (by Franks and Johnson of Wakefield) is even more amazing when viewed close up. In particular, the way that text (of varying sizes for different levels of information) is intertwined with cartographic information is a masterpiece of planning and artistry – where canals and railways cross the enormous letters of 'ENGLAND', for example. Relief is shown by hachures, short lines following the direction of the slope, and the scale of about 1:400,000 (about six miles to the inch) is a relatively large one for a map showing the whole of Great Britain. Northern Scotland is shown as an inset at a reduced scale, with 'Scotland continued' engraved, rather charmingly, on a cloud.

(E) C16 (138)

SCOTLAND
CONTINUED.

GERMAN OCEAN

Map
of the
INLAND NAVIGATION,
CANALS,
and Rail Roads, with the Situations of the various Mineral Products
throughout
Great Britain,
FROM ACTUAL SURVEYS
Projected on the Basis of The Trigonometrical Survey made by order of
THE
HONORABLE THE BOARD OF ORDNANCE,
by
J. Walker Canal and Mineral Surveyor Wakefield,
accompanied by
A BOOK of REFERENCE, Compiled by JOSEPH PRIESTLEY, ESQ.
of the Aire and Calder Navigation.
Published by EDWARD NICHOLS, Bookseller Wakefield &

A violent landscape

With the eruption of its volcano in August 1883, the landscape of the island of Krakatoa changed in an instant. Over two thirds of the island disappeared in the explosion, unleashing a tsunami that killed at least 36,000 people in the immediate area and created waves of sufficient power to register on tidal readings as far away as the English Channel.

This map, *Sunda Strait* ..., is an inset on a larger chart of parts of Java and Sumatra published by the Hydrographic Office of the Royal Navy. It shows the narrow passage between the islands of Java and Sumatra and the volcanic islands of Krakatoa, Beeze and Zebooko. An extract from a later Admiralty Chart (below) shows the changes to the landscape the eruption caused.

Established in 1795, the Hydrographic Office was tasked with providing reliable nautical charts for the ships of the Royal Navy. At first this was achieved by collating existing charts and then reprinting these and other sources in new maps. This way of producing charts was soon found insufficient to supply the needs of a navy charged with the protection of an expanding empire, and by 1821 the Office was producing its own Admiralty

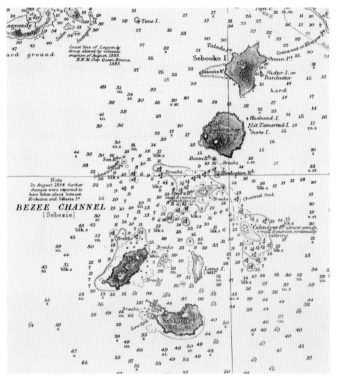

Charts, which were often the product of officers from the Hydrographic Office setting out to explore new lands and uncharted coasts, taking readings and forging links with local people. This inset map of the Straits is a copy from an earlier Dutch chart. The Straits were an important passage between the Indian Ocean and the Java Sea and then on to China, and were a key area of Dutch control during the time of the Dutch East Indies. Dutch influence in the area dates back to the late sixteenth century and was driven by the opportunities for lucrative trade, especially in spices. While the inset is copied from a Dutch government chart, the main chart is 'Compiled from the most recent British & Dutch Government surveys'.

Charts such as this contained detailed information of sailing conditions, including depths, obstacles and compass roses, for navigational readings of oceans and seas throughout the world. The present chart was published in 1867 and the Hydrographic Office continues publishing charts like it today. Early charts can be a valuable source of historical information on changing ports and coastal towns or, as in this case, changes to the physical landscape itself.

Admiralty Chart 941a

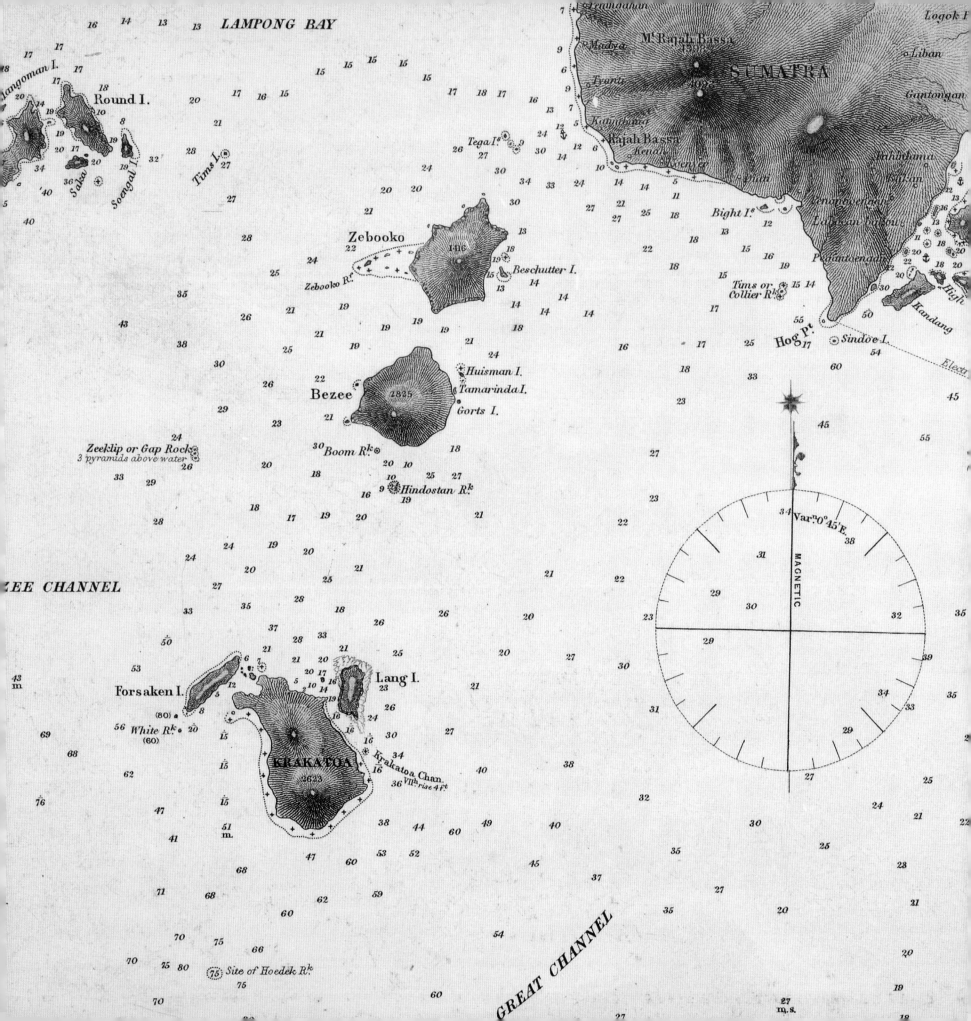

Gordon's route to Khartoum

'The road from Suakin to Berber is through an arid mountainous country, as far as Ariab it is sparsely covered with dwarf trees of stunted growth.' So writes General Charles Gordon in a letter to his friend Lestrange in 1874. This letter, and a series of tables listing travel times and stops on his journey to Khartoum in 1874, is included in a detailed and precise manuscript (hand-drawn) map, designed for those following in his footsteps.

Gordon travelled from Cairo to Suakim on the Red Sea coast by steamer and then from Suakim to Berber on camel, making records of times, distances and topographical and local conditions along the way. This journey is picked out with a dotted line on the map. On reaching Berber, Gordon continued to Khartoum by steamer down the Nile.

Exploits in the Crimea and then in China had forged a reputation and garnered awards and titles for Gordon, but it was his time in Africa, and the nature of his death, that gave him heroic status amongst his fellow Victorians. Gordon was employed in 1874 by the Egyptian Khedive to become the Governor of Egypt's Equatorial Provinces (now part of South Sudan), where his main aim, in which he had considerable success, was to put an end to the slave trade. In 1877 he became Governor-General of the Sudan, a post he held for just over two years before returning exhausted to England.

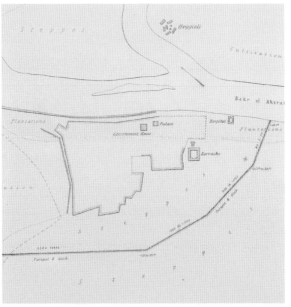

The inset map below is from a plan of Khartoum made by the Intelligence Branch of the War Office in March 1883. By this time an uprising by Sudanese forces loyal to Muhammad Ahmad al-Mahdi, a military as well as religious leader, had begun to take control of large parts of the Sudan and Gordon was charged by the British government to return to the region and organize an evacuation of British and Egyptian troops and nationals. With characteristic stubbornness he attempted to hold Khartoum against the attacking forces. By May 1884 Khartoum was under siege. Protests from the British public forced the government to organize a relief force but it arrived too late to save Gordon, who was killed on the steps of the Palace on 26 January 1885.

This map was reproduced by the famous London map-maker Stanford's in 1885. It was one of many such items produced after Gordon's death, when he was regarded in Britain as a hero and a martyr. Stanford's reproduction did not include the letter Gordon wrote on the map, but did include all the travel information – times of journey, wind conditions and stations. The location of the original had been a mystery until it was generously donated to the Bodleian in 2014.

MS. E4:1 (19)

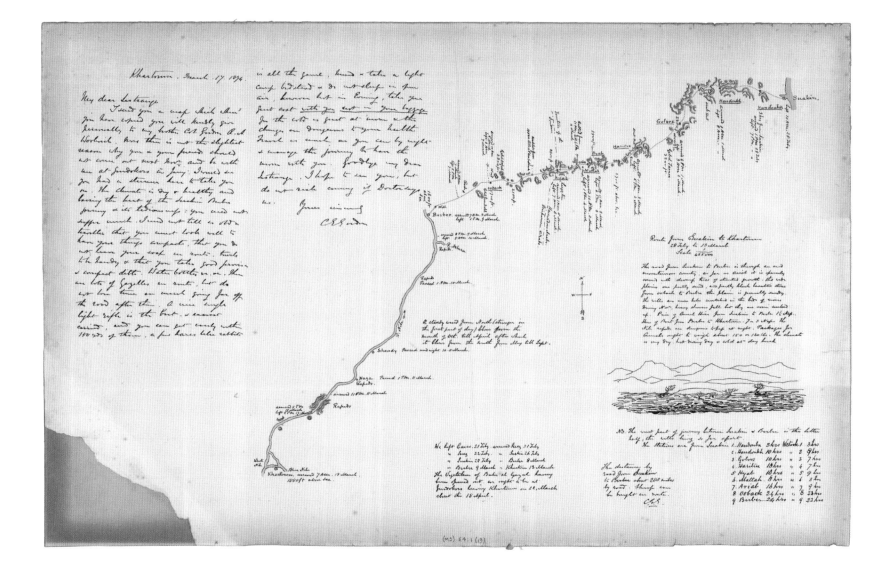

Khartoum, March 17, 1874.

My dear Lestrange

Yours sincerely
C E Gordon

Route from Suakin to Khartoum
Scale

1. Handouba	3 hrs	Wells	1	3 hrs
2. Handouba	10 hrs	"	2	9 hrs
3. Golors	10 hrs	"	3	7 hrs
4. Haritin	10 hrs	"	4	7 hrs
5. Hyat	10 hrs	"	5	9 hrs
6. Mellah	8 hrs	"	6	8 hrs
7. Ariab	16 hrs	"	7	9 hrs
8. Ooback	24 hrs	"	8	33 hrs
9. Berber	24 hrs	"	9	33 hrs

C.E.G.

Navigating Africa

This manuscript survey of the Sese (or Ssese) Islands in Lake Victoria in East Africa – one of a set of three – gives a glimpse of the difficulties of the surveyor's job. The other two of the set are only in pencil; the one shown here is partly finished in ink. They show carefully drawn outlines of the islands and shore of the lake, with bearings between survey points and depth measurements across the water. Surveying was carried out using trigonometry – taking bearings from two or more points towards the same landmark, and using geometry to calculate its position. When done carefully, it was a remarkably reliable method. It is interesting, therefore, that on the most finished, inked plan, the part of the paper not filled by the map is completely covered in dozens, maybe hundreds, of tiny pencilled sums. In the heat of Africa, without a calculator, someone was laboriously making a very accurate map. The separate sketches cover overlapping areas; Entebbe and the surrounding area, for instance, is shown in some detail on one map, but indicated by only a rough outline on the most finished plan. The different surveys would be pieced together to make the final chart.

The plans are undated, but national surveys of Uganda – of which the Ssese Islands are part – did not begin until 1950. Colonial traders and administrators were confronting a landscape for which conventional scientific mapping did not yet exist. The British Admiralty had published surveys of Lake Victoria, however, including a survey of Entebbe Bay, by a Commander B. Whitehouse, as early as 1907, acknowledging the importance of this enormous lake as a waterway. The presence of depth soundings indicates that the finished maps were intended for navigational use, so they were probably surveyed for this purpose at the time when Uganda was a British protectorate. These maps have a handwritten note on the back, apparently much later, attributing them to a 'G.C. Whitehouse Esq.'. They came to the Bodleian Map Room from the Bodleian Library of Commonwealth and African Studies at Rhodes House, along with other early African surveys. That they have been preserved despite being very much working documents makes them both intriguing and unusual. Another map from the same source also covers the Ssese Islands, *Archipel de Sésé, echelle 1:260,000 par le Père Leonard des Pères Blancs*. This states that it was 'copied by B. Whitehouse 20.8.00'. On very thin, translucent paper, it is a copy or possibly a tracing of a French original apparently made by a missionary (the Pères Blancs still exist, now also known as the Missionaires d'Afrique). Along with these careful sketches, this simpler, less detailed map may also have been one of the source documents for the finished chart.

Everything is drawn with great delicacy and precision. Place names, camps and features are shown in detail and, although these are pencil-and-ink sketches, they are far from rough; everything is represented with scientific accuracy. There is one intriguing little sketch which may indicate a personal idiosyncrasy on the part of the surveyor: a drawing of a hill side indicates 'Top tree' and then, half way down, 'My tree'. There is also a slightly larger sketch of 'My tree', showing its unusual shape. This may have been simply to identify a landmark, but it is tempting to think that the surveyor had some attachment to the tree.

752.11 t.1 (24)

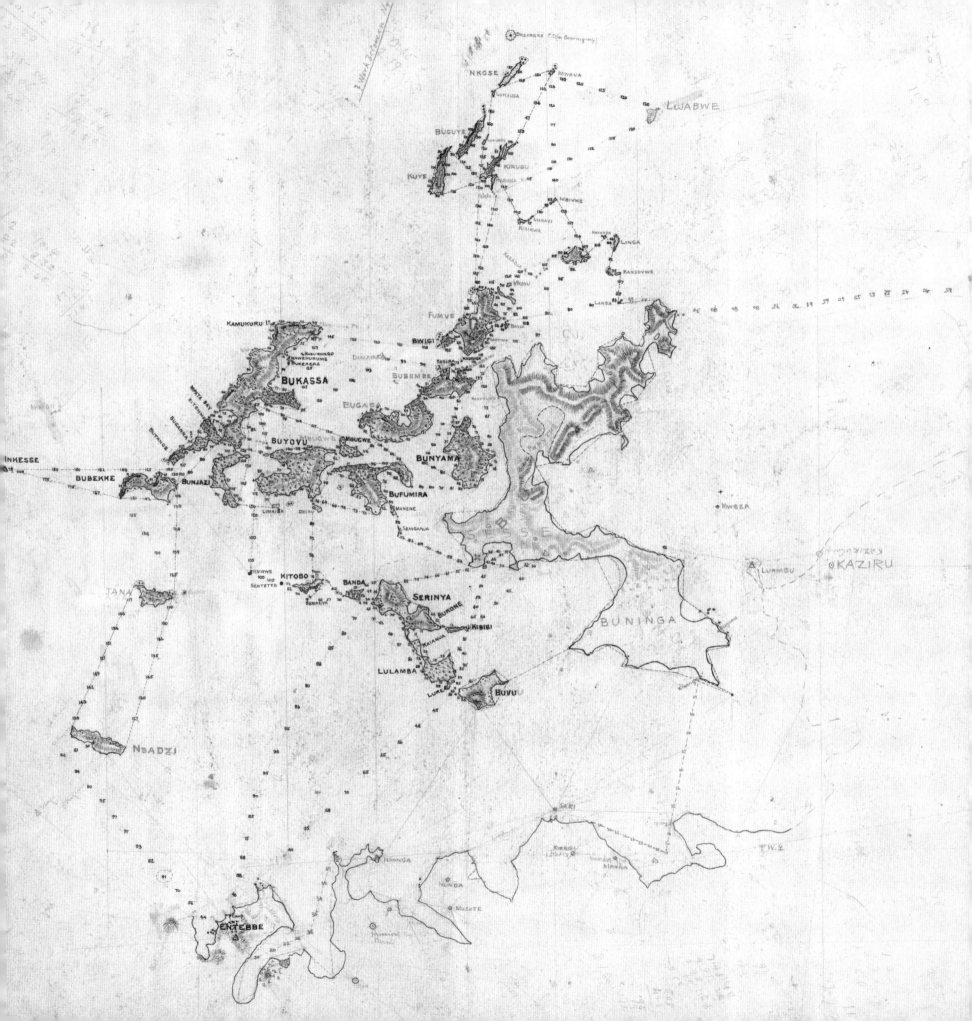

ICH DIEN

CIRCLVS

Davis Streightes

GOENLAND

ISLAND

Slepe Sanderson
Londen Coast
Lord Dauells

ISLAND

EVROPE

NOVA ALBION

VIRGINIA

THE
MIDLAND   SEA

TROPICVS   CANCRI

AFRI

GVINEA
GVIANA
PERV

AMER=
ICA

VA GVINEA

TROPICVS

EQVINOCT

William Kip
Sculpsit.

This belongeth to ye page 116

That the west shoare of America trendeth
somuch to the Eastward, it may appeare by M.
Fullers observation thereof in Mr Candish his Voya=
ge about the world. The coast of Tartarie and of the
South continent we found thus laid forth in a fayre,
large ancient sea chart, which we referre to the
triall of a further discoverie

The numbers scatteringly dispersed here and
there in this sea chart, signifie the variation of
the compasse The letters E and w shewe whether it be East or west. The other letters following
signifie the observers names: as D.Davis, k Ren-
dal H. Hall, L. Lynschet, c candish, ca Iohn de

CHAPTER 2

Knowledge and Science

A MAP IS A SYMBOLIC REPRESENTATION OF KNOWLEDGE ABOUT the world or universe derived from scientific observation. It also shows what aspects of that knowledge are considered important. Some of the earliest surviving maps represent the whole world, drawn not for practical use but to try and understand the nature of things. Long before satellites enabled us to photograph Earth, early mapmakers tried to represent the world as a whole.

In the sixteenth century, Gerard Mercator planned an atlas of all the known world and universe – a project that came to fruition long after his death. He also designed his often-misunderstood conformal world map projection, which progressively exaggerated the areas and distances towards the polar regions but showed all longitude and latitude as parallel lines crossing at right-angles. This imparted directional accuracy – an attribute much valued by mariners; an early example is illustrated opposite. As navigational aids and mathematics developed, the Mercator projection became and remains the standard on which to plot position and a straight-line course.

The development of mapmaking shows how geographical knowledge was passed on. Each cartographer consulted the work that was available to him and this occasionally crossed the line of plagiarism. Mistakes were passed on too; California was famously depicted as an island on many seventeenth- and eighteenth-century maps; the misconception arose in the 1620s and lasted for nearly a century. This geographical 'fact' was copied on hundreds of maps long

FACING

A world map on the Mercator projection, published in Edward Wright's *Certaine errors in nauigation* in 1610, which explained the mathematics behind the idea.

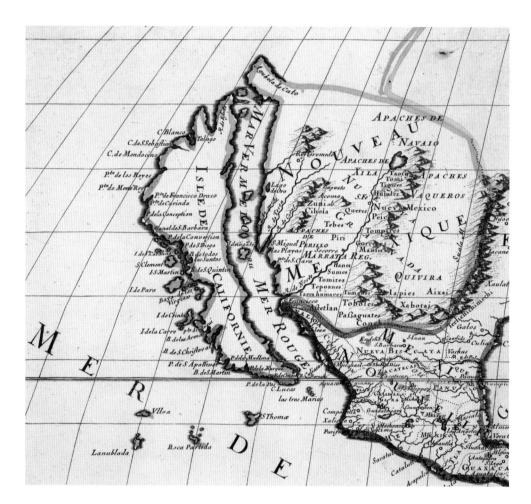

This extract from a 1669 French map by Nicolas and Guillaume Sanson shows California as an island, typically for maps of the period.

after reports had confirmed that California was part of mainland America. Map production techniques also encouraged the re-use of information; most printed maps from the fifteenth to the early nineteenth centuries were printed using the intaglio process, engraving the image in reverse on a copper plate. In many cases the engraved plates were revised and re-used, perhaps with a different publisher's details added; the cost of copper and the expense of the original engraving made this a prudent approach. In other cases geographical information was manually copied. Matthaeus Seutter's maps of the continents – including the title cartouche – were copied by Péter Bod, but were engraved in a different language for a very specific purpose (Bod's Africa is reproduced in this chapter). The great seventeenth-century English mapmaker John Speed was open about the fact that

This extract from the first edition of the OS County Series sheet covers
Stratford and the River Avon.

he had derived information from existing works, including those
of Christopher Saxton, to create his cartographic masterpiece *The
Theatre of the Empire of Great Britaine*. Examples of the county maps of
both men are also included in this chapter.

Arguably, the roots of British national surveys can be traced back to
Saxton and the publication in 1579 of the first county atlas of England
and Wales. The Crown supported this largely privately funded project
as Queen Elizabeth I's ministers realised that a national survey could
bring administrative benefits.

Maps of the regional and administrative divisions of most European
countries became increasingly available through the seventeenth and
eighteenth centuries, until the implementation of full national surveys

Part of a set of French educational cards, including regional maps
and information, published in Paris in the 1820s or 1830s.

– the first being Cassini's survey of France, undertaken in the 1740s.
Other countries followed suit, with the Ordnance Survey's first published maps of parts of Great Britain dating from the very early 1800s.
Perhaps unsurprisingly, the Bodleian's holdings are particularly strong
in maps of Great Britain, and the Oxfordshire region is well represented. As a result of Legal Deposit legislation the Bodleian's collection
of Ordnance Survey maps is all but complete. The very large-scale maps
of the OS 'County series', showing individual trees, fields and buildings,
and covering the whole of the British Isles from the late nineteenth century onwards, remain one of the library's most popular cartographic
resources; the extract reproduced on the previous page shows part of
Stratford-upon-Avon in the 1880s. They continue to be revised (on a
metric system, to modern standards and in digital format) to the present
day.

This chapter also illustrates some of the novel methods devised for passing on geographical knowledge. Edward Quin published an extraordinary visualization of human history. Games, playing cards and jigsaws – such as the one of India dating from the 1850s in this chapter – have long been used to make geography fun and accessible to children. Opposite is an early nineteenth-century set of educational cards representing the *départements* of France, with a map, facts and illustrations for each district. As knowledge of the world grows ever larger, packaging it for consumption becomes more important.

Cartographic representations are not confined to the terrestrial globe. This chapter also contains maps of the heavens. Each map or chart is a mere snapshot, fixed in time. When viewed together, however, they reveal how our ability to map land, sea and sky has led to ever more comprehensive coverage, and to the accurate mapping that we today take for granted.

The Book of Curiosities

This rectangular world map is unlike any other recorded ancient or medieval map. Drawn with ink on paper (32.4 × 49 cm), it is a copy made around 1200 of a map produced in Egypt between 1020 and 1050. The scale bar (or graticule) is testimony to the circulation and use during the medieval period of maps employing mathematical techniques. The map also differs from all earlier ones by being a stand-alone map – that is, one that does not illustrate a historical or theological narrative and which conveys information independent of a related text. It is, moreover, the earliest world map to be annotated with names of cities (395 in number) rather than simply names of regions or countries.

To a modern reader the layout of landmasses appears unfamiliar. As is common in Islamic maps, south is at the top, where the graphic scale is placed. The 'Mountain of the Moon' – considered by medieval Arabic writers to be the source of the Nile – is represented at the centre of the scale by a semi-circular mountain from which ten streams diverge, five on either side, pouring into two circular pools, which in turn feed into one lake before emerging as the River Nile. In the lower right quadrant, opposite the long North African coast, the European landmass is represented, with the right half dominated by an overly large Iberian peninsula. Italy and Greece are to the left, though only Italy bears labels, while Constantinople is behind a brown masonry wall on the left side of the European continent.

The Indian Ocean occupies the upper left quadrant. Jutting into it are two peninsulas, the larger representing Arabia, the smaller one subsuming Persia with India. The two highly stylized and complicated river systems between and below the two peninsulas are the Euphrates and Tigris. To the left (east) of the Indian/Persian peninsula, another river flows into the ocean, with the nearby curved coastline representing China. Along the left-hand margin, a brown landmass labelled 'Island of the Jewel' represents the easternmost limit of the inhabitable world. The map also depicts, in the lower left corner, a gate in the legendary wall constructed by Alexander the Great to enclose Gog and Magog. From this barrier a river flows inland toward the circular Caspian Sea. All the cities on the map are indicated by simple red dots of uniform size, with the single exception of Mecca, distinguished by a yellow horse-shoe-shaped symbol.

This rectangular world map constitutes the entire second chapter (titled 'On the Depiction of the Earth') of Book Two ('On the Earth') in an anonymous eleventh-century Arabic treatise whose title, *Kitāb Gharā'ib al-funūn wa-mulaḥ al-'uyūn*, translates loosely as *The Book of Curiosities of the Sciences and Marvels for the Eyes*. Though not giving his name, the author provides quite a lot of information about himself, and, from references to various events, it is possible to place the composition between 1020 and 1050 and define the location as Egypt, then under Fatimid rule. This map, and the treatise containing it, was unknown to scholars until offered for sale at Christie's in London in 2000; in 2002 it was acquired by the Bodleian Library.

MS. Arab. c. 90, fols 24a-23b

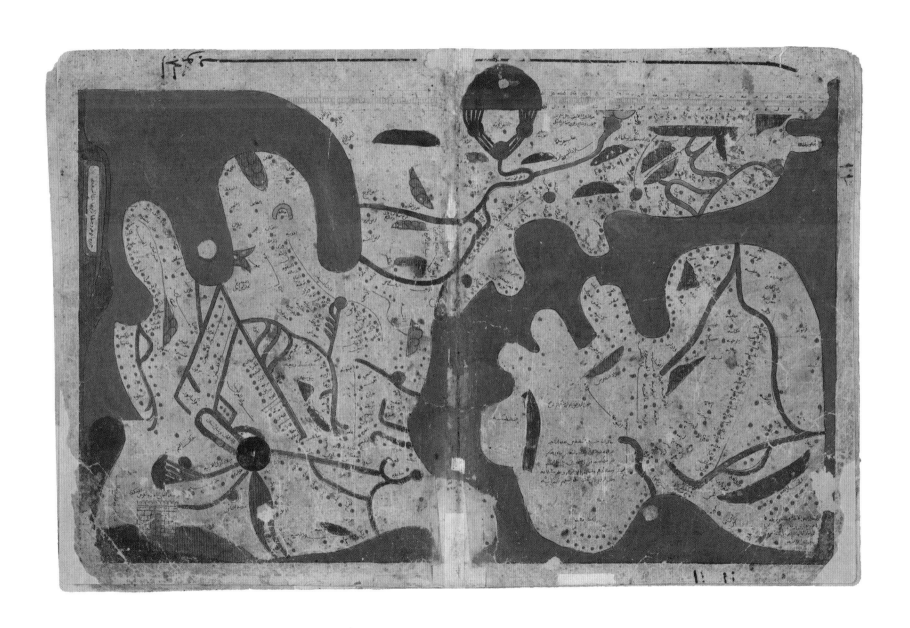

Gerard Mercator and the first atlas

Gerard Mercator (1512–1594) was an influential publisher of maps and globes whose contributions to cartography were to change it forever. His name was originally Gerard de Cremer, but it is the latinized form under which he published by which he is remembered. Born in Rupelmonde, near Antwerp, he worked as an instrument maker, surveyor, cartographer and engraver. He was a successful producer of wall maps and particularly terrestrial and celestial globes through the 1540s and 1550s. In 1568, while in the service of the Duke of Jülich, Kleve and Berg, he published a plan to write a cosmography – a multi-volume work covering all aspects of creation. It would cover the geography of the world with maps ancient and modern, with history and chronology, and maps of the heavens. He completed only a few parts of this ambitious project, but he proposed publishing it under the title 'Atlas', a new term for a volume of maps that has been used ever since, and his planned conception of what an atlas should be, with comprehensive geographical coverage of the world, was innovative. Five volumes of his atlas were published between 1585 and 1595; the last volume, under the title *Atlas, sive Cosmographicæ meditationes de fabrica mundi …* was published by his son Rumold after his death. The volumes produced contain maps of parts of Europe, and the final 1595 volume included continental maps by Mercator's sons and grandsons.

Mercator's work continued to influence atlas production for many years after his death. His atlas plates were sold to Jodocus Hondius in 1604, and two years later Hondius and Cornelis Claesz published an edition of Mercator's atlas with new maps to cover areas not previously included and new text, bringing it considerably closer to the complete atlas Mercator had envisaged. The wonderful map of Iceland included here is taken from this 1606 edition; it was drawn by Mercator and bears his name. The mountains are shown in dramatic relief, including an erupting volcano in the centre, and there is a terrifying sea monster top left. This was to be the first of many editions and versions of the atlas. Hondius's successors, including his son Henricus and son-in-law Jan Jansson, went on to publish many of them, adding to and updating it as time went by. In 1630 the plates were sold to a competitor, Willem Blaeu, but Hondius and Jansson commissioned copies of some of the maps so that they could continue to sell them.

Mercator commanded enormous respect; Ortelius (for whom see overleaf) described him as 'the Ptolemy of our time'. His maps were unprecedented in their high standards and scientific accuracy, and his planned vision of a book encompassing the whole of creation was inspirational for others. But it is specifically his means of representing the world that is best remembered today – his map projection. This was created with the mathematician Edmund Wright in 1569. Mercator had the inspired idea of creating a cylindrical projection in which the lines of latitude became further apart towards the poles, thus keeping the shape of the land consistent. This was crucial for navigation as it enabled mariners to plot a straight course across the map, and follow a line of constant compass bearing (rhumb line) to their destination. It took some decades for the benefits to be fully understood by mariners, but the projection has been used for navigational charts ever since; an example appears in the introduction to this chapter. It has the incidental effect of exaggerating the size of landmasses in high latitudes.

Map Res. 105

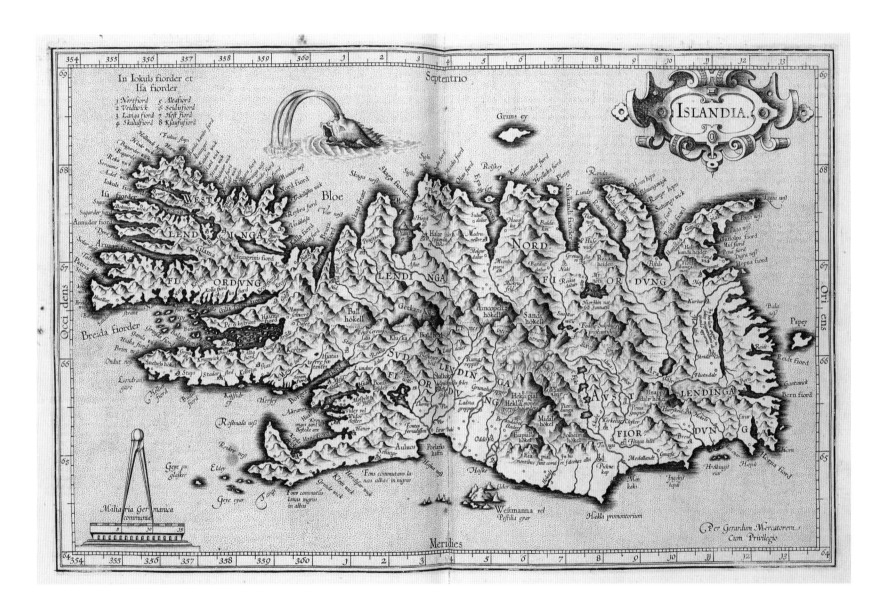

ISLANDIA.

Septentrio

Meridies

Occidens

Oriens

In Iokuls fiorder et
Isa fiorder

1 Nortfiord   5 Alttafiord
2 Veidiwick   6 Seidufiord
3 Langa fiord   7 Heft fiord
4 Skulufiord   8 Ksaufusfiord

Miliaria Germanica
communia

Per Gerardum Mercatorem
Cum Privilegio

Abraham Ortelius and his *Theatrum*

Abraham Ortelius was born in Antwerp on 4 April 1527. Although he was of German descent (his family originated from Augsburg), his father Leonard Ortels had also been born in the city. Having lost his father at the age of ten, the young Ortelius was taken in by Jacobus van Meteren, his maternal uncle, who became guardian to his sister's three orphans, Abraham, Anne and Elizabeth. Working first at colouring maps with his sisters, at the age of twenty he became a member of the Guild of St Luke as an illuminator of maps (*afsetter van kaerten*). Ortelius was fascinated by classical history, and became an enthusiastic collector of ancient coins and medals. As a young man he travelled to the various cities of Europe, including those of Italy and France, sometimes in the company of his friend and later rival Gerard Mercator.

Ortelius is recorded as a cartographer for the first time in a letter dated 22 September 1563, in which he is addressed as '*Domino Abrahamo Ortelio, Cosmographo Antverpiensi amico suo*' by his friend and fellow numismatist János Zsámboky (or Johannes Sambucus), a Hungarian historian at the Imperial Court in Vienna. Ortelius may already have been working on his masterpiece, the monumental *Theatrum Orbis Terrarum*, which he first published on 20 May 1570. This first edition of the *Theatrum*, containing fifty-three uniformly sized maps, was so popular that it had to be re-issued four times in that year. As demand grew, some thirty-four separate editions in seven different languages (fifteen Latin, four French, five German, three Spanish, two Italian, one English, four Dutch) were published, the last one in 1612, some fourteen years after Ortelius's death. The Latin text editions were prepared for scholarly study,

the editions with vernacular languages for the average reader. Occasionally maps without text on the verso are seen; these were sold as individual copies, some to be inserted into composite atlases, and are very rare. One exceptional first edition can be found in the library of Oriel College, Oxford, into which, at the request of the client, blank pages were inserted at the time of publishing (they carry the same watermark as the maps) so that the Latin text could be translated into English. In between the continually enlarged editions, additional maps appeared in separately bound *Additamenta* volumes, of which twelve were published. The last edition of the *Theatrum* in 1612 contained a total of 128 maps.

Although Ortelius's *Theatrum* was the first world 'atlas' in which readers and scholars could study a collection of maps in a single bound volume, it is conjectured that he did not name it as such out of respect for Mercator, who first used the term. An estimated 8,175 copies of the *Theatrum* were printed, out of which about a quarter survive, mainly in private and national libraries or academic institutions, while individual maps from 'butchered' atlases are treasured by map collectors worldwide.

Ortelius died a wealthy man: the *Theatrum* brought him fame and fortune. He never married, and on 28 June 1598, after a fruitful life, he died aged seventy-one at his house on the rue de Couvent, a fashionable part of Antwerp. He was buried in the crypt of St Michael's Abbey – sadly laid waste during the French Revolutionary Wars and demolished in 1831. His bones have been scattered and his grave lost. His *Theatrum Orbis Terrarum*, however, is a permanent memorial to this most remarkable man.

Douce O subt. 15

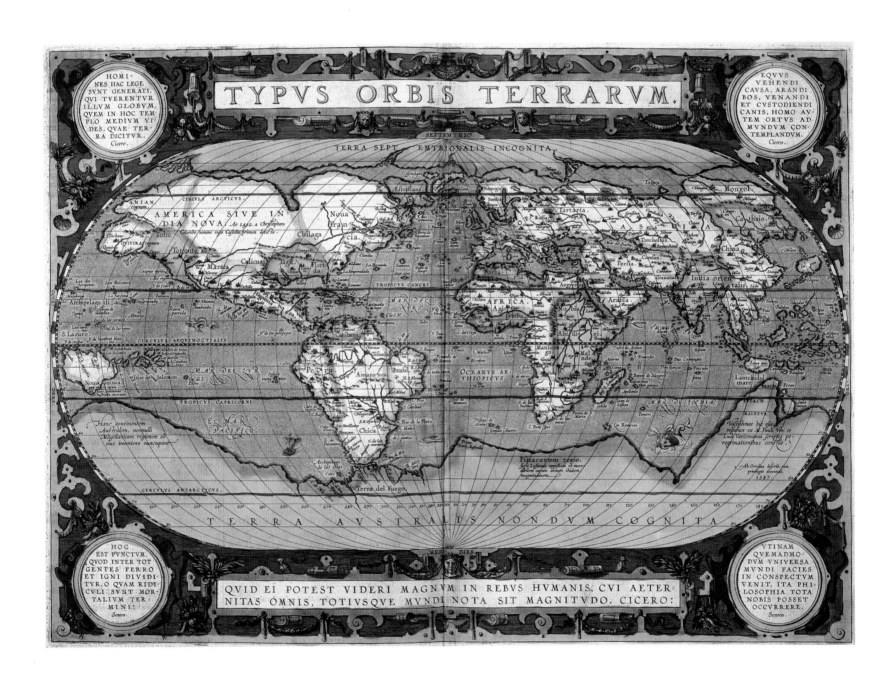

Mapping the Moon

The famous Italian philosopher, astronomer and mathematician Galileo Galilei published the first map of the Moon in 1610, in his book *Sidereus Nuncius*. He produced his map after improving on the design of the telescope, which had first appeared in the Netherlands two years earlier. Galileo's maps were small and did not name any of the Moon's features.

The rapid advance in telescopes after 1610 was matched in the quality of maps of the Moon published after Galileo, but it was only in 1645 that any nomenclature was introduced, with the publication by Michiel van Langren of his *Selenographia Langreniana*. Van Langren named the features on his map after European royalty and the philosophers, scientists and mathematicians of the time and before, as well as religious figures and saints. Van Langren's names did not last long, though. Johannes Hevelius two years later used classical terms for the Moon's features, believing that using the names of contemporary scientists would cause jealousy amongst those left out. This scheme did not last very long, either. A new work, published in 1651 by Giovanni Battista Riccioli, called *Almagestum Novum*, used the same scheme for naming as Van Langren, but limited it to those who had contributed to the science of astronomy in the past up to Riccioli's age. Some of Van Langren's names are still used, though often moved to a different feature, and many of the names on Riccoli's map are still in use today.

Riccioli printed two maps of the Moon in his book. The first shows the features without names, while the second has the names included. Riccioli writes, above one version of the map, that 'People do not inhabit the Moon, neither do souls migrate there'. Above the other he states that the map is partly based on previous maps of the Moon by cartographers such as Van Langren, Hevelius, Divini and Sirsalis, but wants to ensure that people recognize his as being the best, stating that his has been 'corrected and augmented' by his own observations, using the 'best telescope from many phases'. The phrase 'many phases' was important for early cartographers. Deciding on which phase of the Moon to copy would have an effect on how much information could be noted. The brightness of a full Moon tends to hide much detail on the lunar surface, so the best maps were produced after taking drawings of the different phases and creating a composite picture. Van Langren used thirty different drawings to create his final map; Hevelius made forty.

This Bodleian copy of the *Almagestum* was originally owned by Sir Christopher Wren. According to a note on the title page, Wren gave his copy to Sir Henry Savile, who founded the Savilian Chair of Astronomy in Oxford University in 1619. Savile donated his collection to the University and the collection was given to the Bodleian in 1884.

Savile F 5

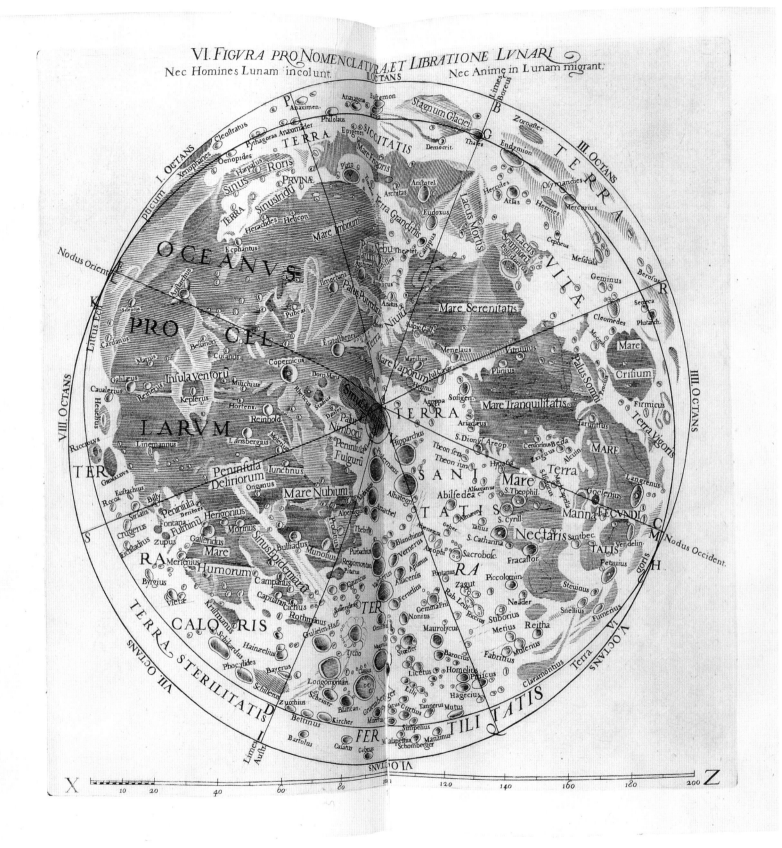

A map of the heavens

Evidence that humans have studied the stars and recorded what they saw can be found in the tomb paintings of the ancient Egyptians, in clay tablets from Mesopotamia and in the layout of prehistoric monuments in Europe and throughout the world. Greek cartographers began to map out the locations of stars and to plot constellations using scientific reasoning to try to get a sense of the order of the cosmos. The works of such figures as Hipparchus and, particularly, Ptolemy, in the second century CE, that, after rediscovery and translation by Islamic scholars into Latin, were crucial in the study of astronomy in Renaissance Europe.

Amongst a large number of astronomical works from the sixteenth and seventeenth centuries held in the Bodleian is Andreas Cellarius's *Atlas Coelestis seu Harmonia Macrocosmica,* first published in Amsterdam in 1660. Cellarius was a Dutch mathematician and cartographer who was rector at a school in Hoorn. Like other atlases of the time, Cellarius's work is a mixture of the classical and the modern – classical with the inclusion of maps of the signs of the Zodiac and the layout of the planets according to Ptolemy, modern with the inclusion of maps showing the theories of the Solar System by astronomers such as Nicolaus Copernicus and Tycho Brahe and planetary motion around the Earth, the phases of the Moon and the Sun's journey in the sky. Gerard Mercator had set out nearly a century earlier to publish a

series of atlases which were to include all available knowledge of the Earth (see page 52). The first of his atlases, the *Chronologica,* appeared in 1569, and after his death his work was continued by his son. Jan Jansson, publishing the *Harmonia Macrocosmia* in 1660 as the concluding part of a multi-volume atlas of the world's geography and history, finally brought this idea to fruition.

We show here a page from the *Macrocosmica* of Copernicus's heliocentric world view. A heliocentric view differed from perceived wisdom up to that point, which stated that the Earth was at the centre of the Solar System and that all other planetary objects orbited around it. Copernicus believed instead that the Sun was the centre around which all objects revolved. Another of Copernicus's theories was that, as well as revolving around the Sun, the Earth also revolved on its own axis, which explained the movement of the stars in the sky and the change from night to day. This theory went against religious beliefs – which held that the Earth, at the centre of the cosmos, was stationary – and it was widely ridiculed at the time. Surely people would fall off the Earth if it were true?

The map shows the Sun at the centre with the planets revolving around it. There are four versions of the Earth, each tilted slightly to show the different seasons. Note North America with California as a separate island, as it was commonly believed to be at the time.

Vet. B3 a.3

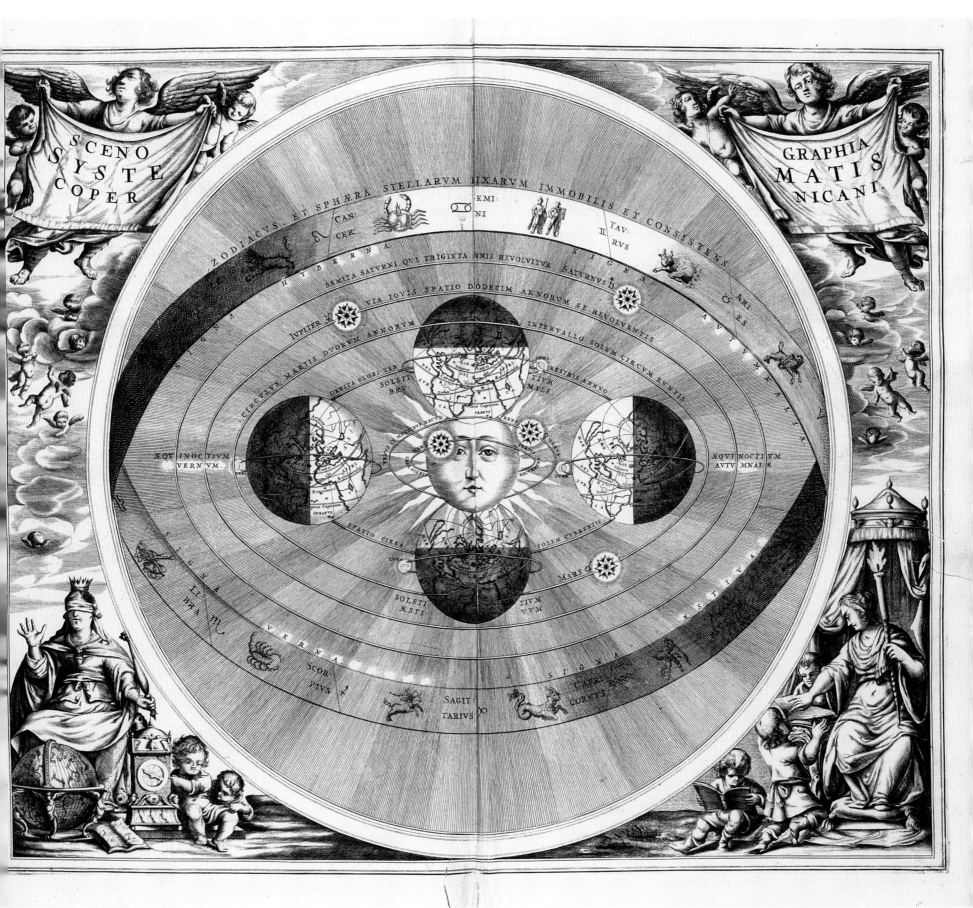

The transit of Venus

This *Mappemonde*, by Joseph Nicolas de L'Isle – official astronomer to the French hydrographic office, the *Dépôt des cartes et plans de la marine* – is one of the most important maps in scientific history. Created at a time of great international conflict – with most of Europe involved in the Seven Years War, France and Britain fighting for control of the New World and the Indian subcontinent, and armies fighting on the American, European and Asian continents as well as the high seas – the map was designed to bring together the scientists of these warring nations to measure the transit of the planet Venus across the face of the Sun in 1761. On the basis of these measurements the distance between the Sun and Earth, and from this the size of the Solar System, could be established.

To get the most accurate measurements of Venus's transit, readings were to be taken in as many places and as far apart from each other as possible. Scientists were sent to the extremes of the northern and southern hemispheres with an array of expensive and delicate equipment, the most important being a telescope to observe and an accurate clock to measure the time. They risked illness, hostile local populations, hazardous travelling conditions and attack by enemy forces, as well as bad weather at the time of the transit making it impossible to make any readings.

This double hemisphere world map shows with its use of colours where the transit would be at its greatest. The red zone covers the area where the total transit is visible: '*Ceux qui verront la durée entire, sont teints en rouge*'. The blue and yellow zones are parts of the world where only the start or end of the transit would be visible, though readings from these zones would still be useful as astronomers could measure the time it took for Venus to 'enter' or 'exit' the Sun.

Transits of Venus occur with an eight-year interval followed by a gap of 105 years. As the results of the 1761 observation were not accurate enough to give a reliable measurement, scientists set out again in 1769 to record the next transit. This time more reports and observations were made and a distance of 153 million kilometres between the Earth and the Sun, only 4 million kilometres from the accepted distance today of 149 million kilometres (93,000,000 miles), was agreed on.

De L'Isle's map helped bring together the scientists of warring nations from the Americas, from Britain and France, and from Scandinavia and Russia to take journeys over land and sea to achieve something truly remarkable. They endured great hardship and showed true dedication, and one of the major puzzles of the Solar System was finally solved.

(E) B1 (198)

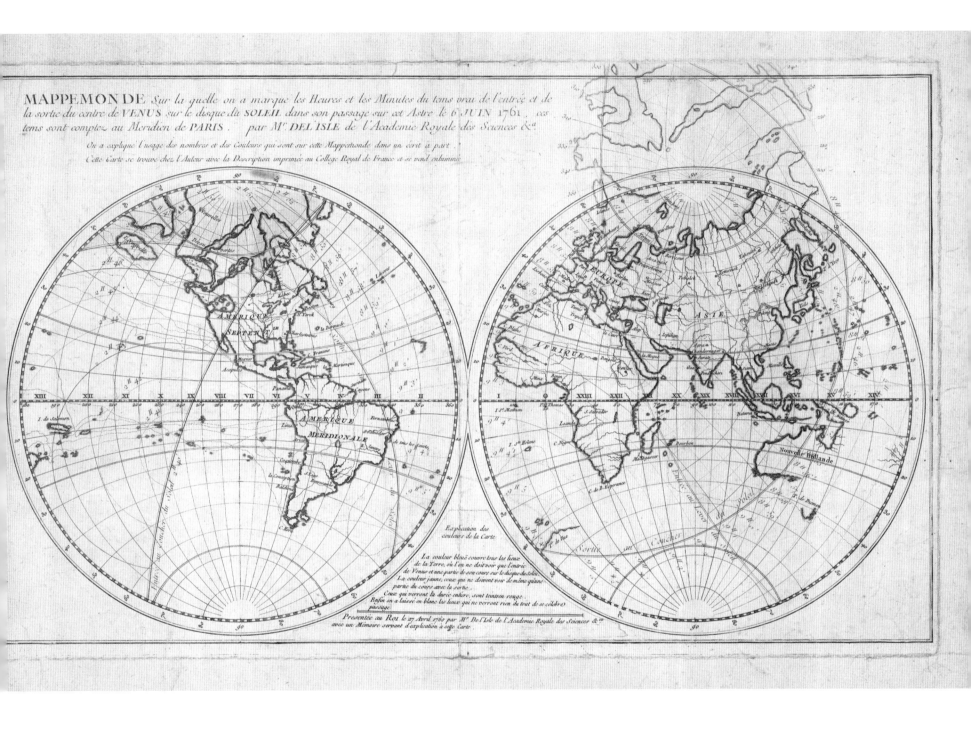

MAPPEMONDE

MAPPEMONDE *Sur la quelle on a marqué les Heures et les Minutes du tems vrai de l'entrée et de la sortie du centre de VENUS sur le disque dit SOLEIL, dans son passage sur cet Astre le 6 JUIN 1761, ces tems sont comptez au Meridien de PARIS. par Mr. DEL'ISLE de l'Academie Royale des Sciences &ᵃ.*

On a expliqué l'usage des nombres et des couleurs qui sont sur cette Mappemonde dans un écrit à part.
Cette Carte se trouve chez l'Auteur avec la Description imprimée au College Royal de France et se vend enluminée.

AMERIQUE SEPTENT.

AMERIQUE MERIDIONALE

EUROPE

ASIE

AFRIQUE

Nouvelle Hollande

Explication des couleurs de la Carte.

La couleur bleue couvre tous les lieux de la Terre, où l'on ne doit voir que l'entrée de Venus et une partie de son cours sur le disque du Soleil. La couleur jaune, ceux que ne doivent voir de même quand partie du cours avec la sortie. Ceux qui verront la durée entiere, sont teints en rouge. Enfin on a laissé en blanc les lieux qui ne verront rien du tout de ce célèbre passage.

Presentée au Roi le 27 Avril 1760 par Mr. De l'Isle de l'Academie Royale des Sciences &ᵃ avec un Mémoire servant d'explication à cette Carte.

Péter Bod's lost continent

In 1998 an unknown map of America came up for sale at a London dealer. It was exceptional in neither its size nor its appearance, and carried no publisher's marks or engraver's signature. It showed California as an island and western North America as uncharted territory. The cardinal points were in Hungarian, as were all the features. The cartouche depicted a Native American in feathered headdress, and the dotted lines on the map denoted … something. As research trying to identify the map yielded no fruitful results, it seemed that the mystery would remain unsolved.

Over two centuries earlier an octavo book had been published by Johann Rudolf Imhoff, the Basle printer: its title read *Az Isten Vitézkedő Anyaszentegyháza állapotjának, és világ kezdetétül fogva a jelen való időig sokféle változásinak rövid Historiája* (The history of God's heroic church with its many changes from the Creation to the present time), with an additional '*négy fő mappával*' (with four maps) almost as an afterthought. A chance browsing in the British Library catalogue under the name of Péter Bod revealed that one of these four maps corresponded to the unknown map of America. The book, in Hungarian, had the date at the bottom of the title page, 'CIƆIƆC LX' (1760).

Péter Bod was born in Transylvania in 1712 in the village of Felsőcsernáton (Cernatul-de-Sus, Romania). He was sent to the famous Calvinist college at Nagyenyed (Aiud), where he subsequently secured a bursary to the university at Leiden in 1740. Apart from the Classics, he attended lectures on astronomy, anatomy, theology and rhetoric, and studied Arabic, Hebrew and Syrian. His three years there were spent diligently and his professors gave him glowing references.

In 1743 Bod returned to Transylvania, his books transported in barrels weighing 700 kg. It took three months to reach Olthévíz (Hoghiz), his first ministry. After six years, he received an invitation from the wealthy parish of Magyarigen (Ighiu) to become their pastor. He took up his duties on Christmas day in 1749 and soon began his ecclesiastical history. The manuscript was ready by autumn 1753, but Bod needed an engraver for the maps. An opportunity came in 1759; his former pupil Count József Teleki embarked upon a European study-tour. Arriving in Basle, the count found a printer for the book and an engraver for the maps and an agreement was reached in February 1760 for an edition of 500 copies. Unfortunately, the engraver had difficulties in cutting the plates in an unfamiliar language, delaying the publication. Teleki showed his annoyance by writing, 'Im-Hof is ready with the printing of Sire Bod's Ecclesiastical History, but the engraver working on the plates keeps lying'. Eventually the book was printed and delivered via a Vienna agent, about fifty copies at a time.

Of the 500 copies printed, only sixty-three survive. The British Library has a copy, and, through a generous donation, the Bodleian. Of the surviving copies only about half still have their four maps, on which Péter Bod decided to 'take the reader along the dotted lines'. These maps of 'Europa', 'Asia', 'Amerika' and 'Afrika' are not only extremely rare but are the first maps of the continents with Hungarian toponyms and terminology. The cartouche of the map of 'Afrika', on which a native tribesman with spear and arrow leans against a block of stone, with a rather docile leopard and a ferocious-looking anaconda in front of pyramids and a palm tree, is simplified from Seutter's map of Africa, whose atlas was Bod's source.

Christopher Saxton and the first county map

Yorkshire-born Christopher Saxton's main achievement was to create the first national atlas of English and Welsh counties, which appeared on completion in 1579. The volume contained a map of 'Anglia …' (including Wales) followed by thirty-four county maps, of which the map of Norfolk was the earliest to be produced, making it England's first printed county map. Saxton received patronage and assistance from Thomas Seckford, Master of Requests to Queen Elizabeth, financing the project. By 1575 the queen authorized Saxton be given assistance wherever he went on his county survey, although by this time the Norfolk map had been finished. Survey work on Norfolk had commenced around 1570, and the map was completed by 1574, surveyed and drawn by Saxton and engraved by the Dutchman Cornelis de Hooghe, Norfolk being the only county for which Saxton used de Hooghe's services.

The key to Saxton's success was that his mapping was not derivative. There were no maps at this level of detail available in the mid- to late sixteenth century. Such an enterprise had simply not been previously attempted. Saxton started afresh, and it is believed that his county maps were constructed by triangulation, involving him and his team going out 'into the field' and connecting prominent points in the landscape using geometrical techniques, rendering his maps far superior in accuracy to anything previously produced in England. His county maps were quickly appreciated for their significance for the overall governance of the country. During their production phase, Lord Burghley, chief advisor to the queen, and Lord High Treasurer from 1572, acquired copies of proof versions, which he duly annotated.

The Norfolk map measures 33.5 × 49.5 cm. It shows the whole county, with towns represented by a church and buildings, and villages marked with a church; administrative divisions (known as hundreds) are identified (only five Saxton county maps do this); and hills, woodland, rivers and bridges are clearly marked. A scale bar of ten miles is included at the bottom right (giving a scale of 1:185,000), along with Saxton's name. Saxton lists all thirty-one Norfolk hundreds in a panel at the top right corner, using alphabetical notation to mark each of these administrative units on the map. In many ways the Norfolk map can be regarded as experimental, this feature being a prime instance, as Saxton did not employ this cartographic device at any other point in the atlas.

The example illustrated here is the second state of the Norfolk map, which appeared in 1577. In the intervening three years, Saxton added the royal coat of arms, seen at the top centre, as well as Seckford's arms with the '*Pestis patriae pigrities*' motto. There were also corrections to three settlements: in the south of the county, Caston was corrected to Easton; West Herlinge was added; and in the west Wallington was also squeezed into position. This Norfolk map appeared with many amendments in further editions of the atlas over the next two centuries. Saxton's maps were not superseded as the basis for geographical representation of England and Wales until the nineteenth century, when the Ordnance Survey launched its national mapping programme in the form of the one-inch map. In the interim, mapmakers such as Speed, Blaeu and Jansson clearly drew inspiration for their own county maps from Saxton's remarkable output.

The sixteenth century is considered a time of cartographic revolution in England, and Saxton has been described as the father of English cartography.

Map Res. 76

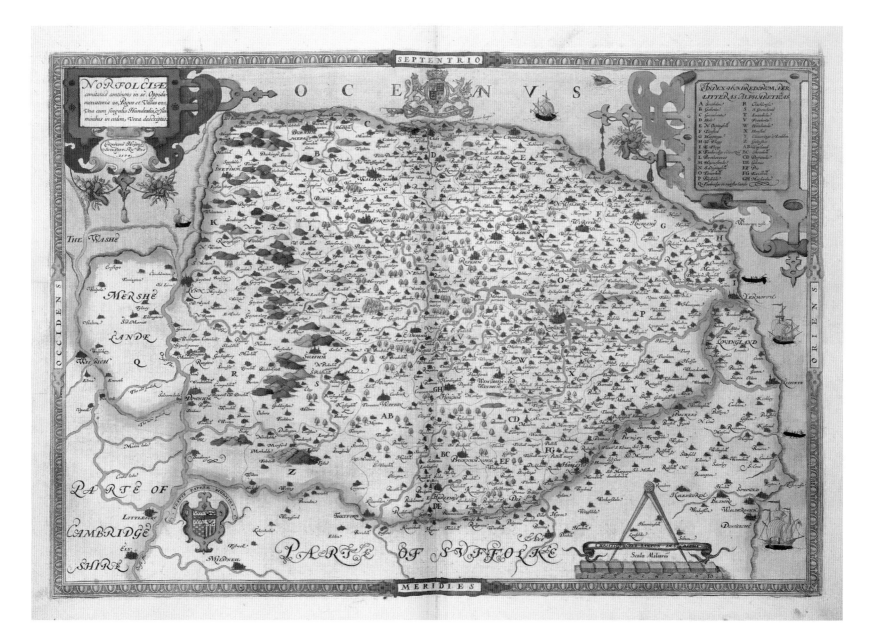

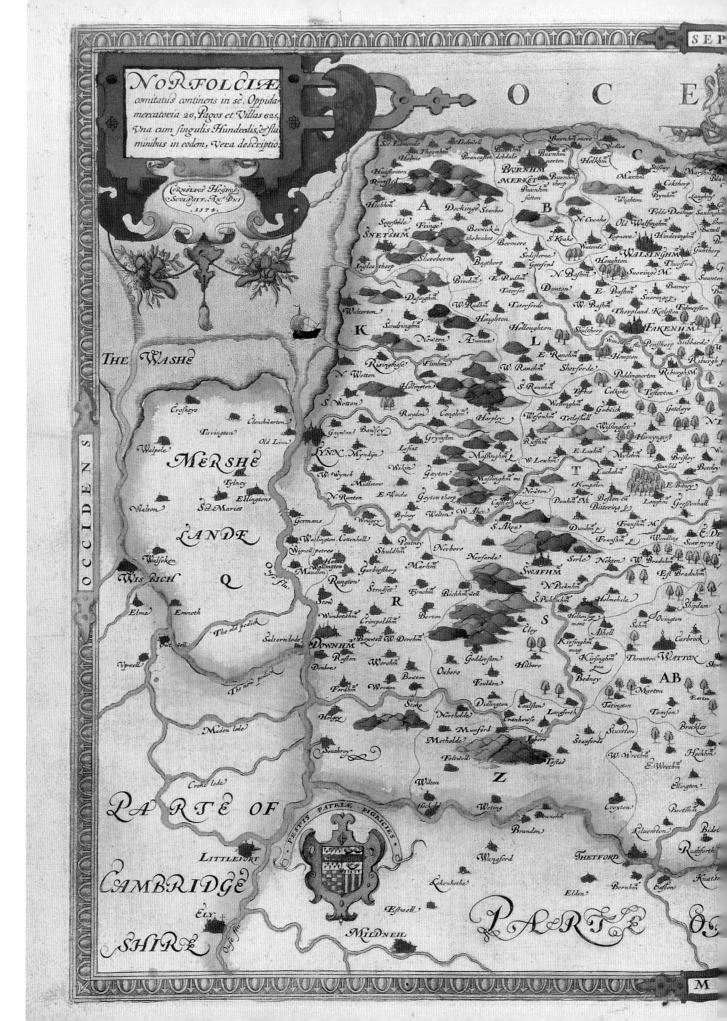

NORFOLCIÆ
comitatus continens in se. Oppida
mercatoria 26, Pagos et Villas 625,
Vna cum singulis Hundredis, & flu=
minibus in eodem, Vera descriptio.

Cornelius Hogius
Sculpsit. An° Dni
1574

O C E

THE WASHE

OCCIDENS

MERSHE

LANDE

Q

WISBICH

THE WASHE

PARTE OF

LITTLEPORT

CAMBRIDGE

ELY

SHIRE

PESTIS PATRIÆ PIGRICIES

PARTE

MILDNEIL

BVRNHM
MERKET

SNETSHM

A

B

C

WALSINGHM

K

L

FAKENHM

T

LYNN

S

R

SWAFHM

DOWNHM

AB

WATTON

Z

THETFORD

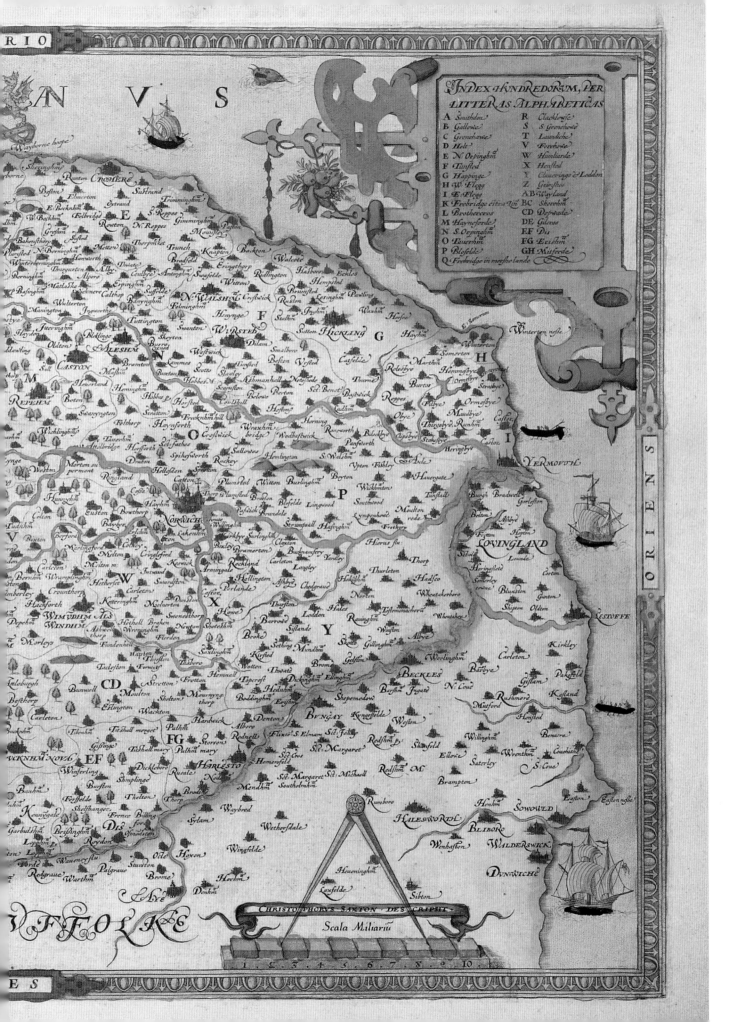

History and geography: John Speed

This is one of the county maps of John Speed, a man remembered as one of the greatest English mapmakers. His county maps have been valued by collectors ever since they were first published in 1612. Speed's first love was history and antiquities and his mapmaking developed alongside his studies of these. The work for which he is most famous, *The Theatre of the Empire of Great Britaine*, was conceived as a companion volume to his *History of Great Britain*. The *Theatre* was a county atlas; after some introductory maps of the whole of Great Britain (past and present) there follow maps of each county with text on the verso. For each one there is a page of historical and geographical descriptive text, then a map across the double plate, and on the next page an alphabetical list of places in the county. It has been observed that both the title and the format of the *Theatre* are reminiscent of Ortelius's *Theatrum* (see page 54).

Speed's early career was as a tailor; he was a member of the Merchant Taylors' Company. In 1598, after publishing a map of the Holy Land, he benefited from the patronage of Fulke Greville, through whose influence he was granted a sinecure that enabled him to pursue his interest in history. This interest shows in the decoration of his maps; British counties come in unrectangular shapes and Speed used the blank areas around their edges for illustrations. As well as coats of arms there are often pictures of local antiquities, Roman coins, monuments (such as Stonehenge) and vignettes of historic battles with a brief account of events. The map of Warwickshire, for example, has a picture of the Battle of Wolney of 1469, with a description of how King Edward IV was taken prisoner. The map of Leicestershire includes an illustration of the Battle of Bosworth, the last great battle of the Wars of the Roses. Cambridgeshire shows surveyors using enormous compasses to measure a map scale. Castles and portraits are found throughout. Nearly every county map has at least one accompanying town plan or view.

It is not known how much original surveying Speed did. Some of the town maps were copied from existing maps, but many were surveyed for the first time. The county maps in the *Theatre* were derived largely from revisions of existing maps such as those of Christopher Saxton, John Norden, William Smith and Robert Cotton. Speed admitted this, famously declaring, 'I have put my sickle into other men's corne'. Yet he put the information he collected to such good use, and his maps are so beautifully designed, composed and decorated, that he deserves full credit. The maps were expertly engraved in Amsterdam by Jodocus Hondius, and the atlas was first published by Sudbury & Humble in London. Many more editions were published throughout the seventeenth century, until long after Speed's death.

Map Res. 74

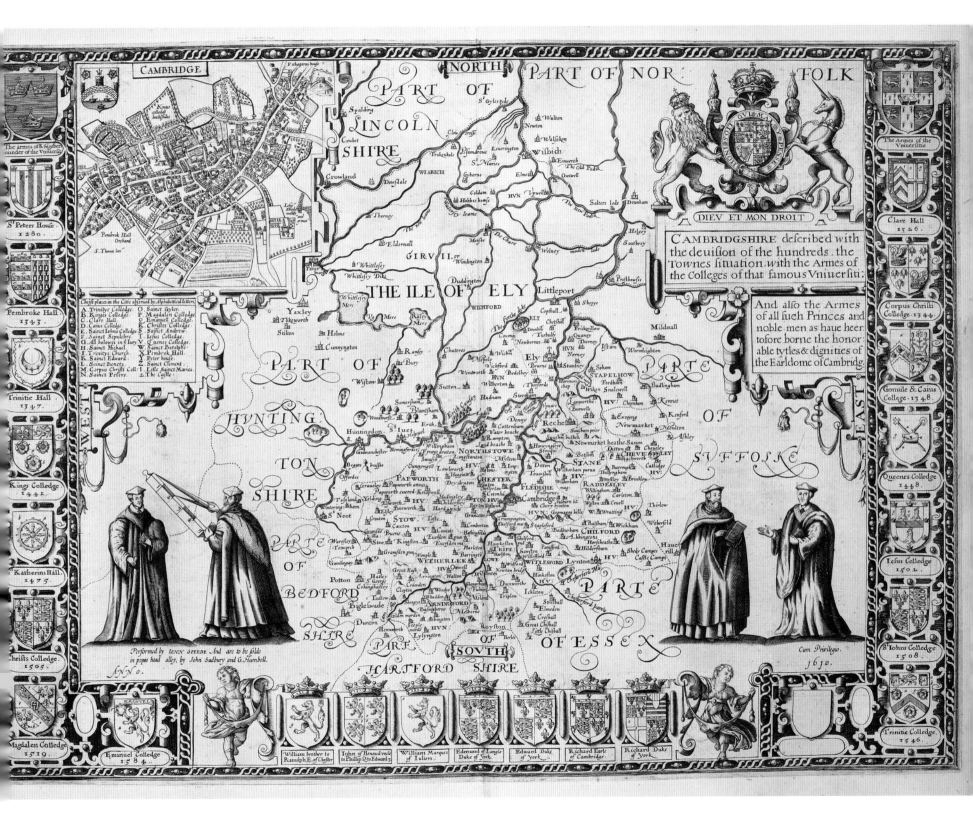

CAMBRIDGE

NORTH

PART OF NOR: FOLK

PART OF LINCOLN SHIRE

DIEV ET MON DROIT

CAMBRIDGSHIRE described with the deuision of the hundreds. the TOWNES situation. with the Armes of the Colleges of that famous Vniuersiti:

And also the Armes of all such Princes and noble-men as haue heer: tofore borne the honor: able tytles & dignities of the Earldome of Cambridg.

GIRVII. or Winlington

THE ILE OF ELY

WICHFORD

Chiefe places in the Citie obserued by Alphabeticall letters.

A. Trinitie Colledge.   O. Saint Gyles.
B. Kings Colledge.   P. Magdalen Colledge.
C. Clare Colledge.   Q. Emanuell Colledge.
D. Caius Colledge.   R. Christes Colledge.
E. Saint Johns Colledge.   S. Saint Andrew.
F. Saint Sepulchre.   T. Iesus Colledge.
G. All belowes in S Iury   V. Quenes Colledge.
H. Saint Michael.   W. Saint Botolphe.
I. Trinitie Church.   X. Pembrok Hall.
K. Saint Edward.   Y. Peter house.
L. Saint Benets.   Z. Saint Clement.
M. Corpus Christi Coll.   1. Litle Saint Maries.
N. Saint Peters.   2. The Castle.

PART OF HVNTING TON SHIRE

PARTE OF BEDFORD SHIRE

PARTE OF SVFFOLKE

PARTE OF ESSEX

WEST

EAST

Performed by IOHN SPEEDE. And are to be solde in popes head alley, by John Sudbury and G. Humbell.

ANNO. 1610.

Cum Priuilegio.

SOVTH

PART OF HARTFORD SHIRE

The learned Dr Plot

Dr Robert Plot was a remarkable man. In 1683 he became both the first Keeper of the Ashmolean Museum in Oxford, the world's first university museum, and Oxford University's first Professor of Chemistry. In 1674, under the patronage of Dr John Fell, who was both Dean of Christ Church, Oxford, and Bishop of Oxford, he had begun to collect and study natural artefacts, and this led him to publish in 1677 *The Natural History of Oxford-shire,* a book which set the standard for the recording of natural history in Britain. Its author was ever after referred to as 'the learned Dr Plot'.

The book was planned as the first of a series of such volumes covering the counties of Britain; sadly Plot only had the resources to complete Oxfordshire and Staffordshire. A second edition of *The Natural History of Oxford-shire* with additions by John Burman, Plot's stepson, was published in 1705.

The *Natural History* was illustrated with thirty-seven engravings of minerals and fossils, including one of a dinosaur femur, which Plot believed was that of a long-extinct giant. They were produced by Michael Burghers, a Dutchman who became Oxford University's engraver after the death of his predecessor, David Loggan. Burghers also engraved Plot's map, which was folded into the front of the *Natural History.*

The map is strikingly decorative. It is engraved in a very clear style and is relatively accurate; Plot was rightfully proud of it. He says in his foreword:

To the READER … though I dare not pretend the Map of Oxford-shire, prefix to this Essay, is so accurate as any I shall make hereafter, yet I dare promise the Reader, it far exceeds any we had before; for beside that it contains all the Market Towns, and many Parishes omitted by Saxton, Speed, &c. it shews also the Villages, distinguished by a different Mark and Character, and the Houses of the Nobility and Gentry, and others of any magnitude within the County; and all these with their Bearings to one another, according to the Compass.

The border of the map consists of 172 coats of arms – 148 of them of the gentry, with reference numbers linked to their houses shown on the map. It also shows the coats of arms of eighteen colleges, of the University and the City of Oxford, and of Banbury, Woodstock, Henley, Burford and Chipping Norton. In the elegant title cartouche Plot says:

To the Right Reverend Father in God IOHN [Dr John Fell, his patron] by divine permission Ld. BISHOP of OXON THE MAP OF OXFORDSHIRE being his Lordship's Diocess, newly delineated, and after a new manner, with all imaginable Reverence is humbly dedicated by R.P. L.L.D.

In addition to major houses, the map shows towns, villages, rivers, woods, parks, hills, churches and windmills. It is one of the earliest county maps to show a few roads. Although a 1593 English Act of Parliament in defining the statute mile said 'A Mile shall contain eight Furlongs', Plot says:

As for the Scale of Miles, there being three sorts in Oxford-shire, the greater, lesser, and middle Miles, as almost every where else; it is contrived according to the middle sort of them; for these I conceive may be most properly called the true Oxford-shire miles, which upon actual Dimensuration at several places, I found to contain for the most part 9 Furlongs and a Quarter.

This is a somewhat cavalier attitude to the mile but is compensated by the delightful group of figures and surveying instruments surrounding the scale of 'The Miles of OXFORD-sh', which helps complete a truly beautiful map.

Douce P 19

THE MAP OF OXFORDSHIRE

To the Right Reverend Father in God JOHN by divine permission BISHOP of OXON

THE MAP OF OXFORDSHIRE being his Lordship's Diocess, newly delineated, and after a new manner, with all imaginable Reverence is humbly dedicated by R.P.

PART OF WAR=WICK=SHI=RE

PART OF NORTHAMP=TON SHIRE

PART OF BVCK=ING=HAM SHI=RE

PART OF GLO=CES=TER SHI=RE

PART OF BERK SHIRE

EXPLICATION OF THE MARKS

A CITY and Bishops seat	C. Church.
A Mercat towne	G. Great.
A Parish	L. Little
A Village	Le. Long.
Ancient houses of KINGS	M. Middle
Ancient fortifications	N. North
Religious houses	Ne. Nether
Ancient ways	S. South
Ancient Baronies	V. Vpper

The Armes of the Gentry within, but out of OXFORD=shi.

The Miles of OXFORD=shi. whereof about 60 equall a degree

OXFORD

Michael Burghers Sculp.

Birth of the Ordnance Survey

Like many national surveys, the Ordnance Survey of Great Britain has its roots in war and the threat of invasion. One of the meanings of the word 'Ordnance' is artillery, something that it is easy to forget when consulting a modern OS walking map. The fear of Jacobite rebellion in Scotland led to the creation of a detailed survey of the country in the 1740s and '50s, directed by William Roy. This was for military purposes and was never published, being kept only as a manuscript copy (which survives in the British Library). After its completion, Roy proposed that it should form the beginning of a national survey, but it would be many years before his suggestion was put into effect.

By the end of the eighteenth century, surveys of parts of southern England had been carried out that would in time form the basis for the national survey. Roy was employed in the 1780s by the Royal Society to carry out the triangulation to determine the relative positions of the observatories in London and Paris, making astronomical observations more accurate, in a spirit of international cooperation and scientific enquiry. The base line he surveyed on Hounslow Heath was eventually used for the OS triangulation, a network of points that would cover the whole country. The main motivating force for the national survey, though, was anxiety about a possible Napoleonic invasion on the south coast.

In the 1780s the Board of Ordnance Survey commissioned a survey of Plymouth from William Gardner. Again this was unpublished and survives only in manuscript. Gardner went on to produce a detailed military survey of Kent. From 1801 engravers were employed by the Ordnance Survey in the Drawing Office in the Tower of London, and the first one inch to the mile sheets were prepared for publication; an extract from the very first published sheet, covering parts of Kent and Essex, is shown opposite. It would take until 1873 for this series – known as the 'Old Series' – to cover the whole of England and Wales, and another twenty years before Scotland was covered. The Ordnance Survey's first published one-inch sheets are things of beauty. Relief is indicated by hachuring, the engraving is very fine, and the maps show a remarkable amount of detail for their scale. Until this point, the best mapping available for most of the country had been individually produced county maps, varying in scale and quality and without the topographical accuracy of the OS maps. Now for the first time the whole of Great Britain was accurately mapped, at a consistent scale, with good representation of relief, to standard specifications. Much larger scale surveys, organized by county, were also under way by the mid-nineteenth century.

The one-inch maps went through many incarnations, with new editions produced to different designs throughout the late nineteenth and early twentieth centuries. The 'Popular Edition' of the 1920s and '30s, as its name suggests, brought OS maps to an ever increasing audience. Maps were produced at a wider variety of scales; some of the illustrated covers used to promote maps for walking and recreation appear on page 167. After the end of World War II, metric scales were used and 1:50,000 maps replaced the slightly smaller one inch to a mile (1:63,360); the larger 1:25,000 scale was introduced around the same time and remains very popular.

C17 (26) [1]

What lies beneath

The mapping of the rocks below the Earth's surface is a comparatively recent science compared with the history of cartography as a whole. The earliest attempts to map the rocks and minerals of the Earth date from mid-eighteenth-century France. The cartographer Philippe Buache, who had a great interest in the structure of the Earth and in bathymetry, made two mineralogical maps to illustrate a geological paper by Jean-Étienne Guettard in the *Mémoires de l'Academie Royale des Sciences*, published in 1751; these have a fair claim to being the first ever geological maps. A few other small-scale geological maps followed within the next few years, produced in France and other European countries and covering parts of Europe and North America. By the 1770s the use of colour to distinguish different rock types had been explored; the first geological maps used symbols.

William Smith's famous map *A delineation of the strata of England and Wales, with part of Scotland ...*, published in London in 1815, marked a new development. It was the first nationwide geological map, and Smith's understanding of the relationships between the geological strata across the whole country was unprecedented; he is now regarded as the father of English geology, although it took years for the value of his work to be recognized and for the accolades he deserved to be heaped on him. An official geological survey of Britain was established under Henry de la Beche in 1835 as part of the Ordnance Survey, and became a separate civilian organization in 1845. Initially covering both Great Britain and Ireland, it carried out detailed geological surveys of the whole of the

British Isles at a scale of one inch to the mile (1:63,360), as illustrated here. It would take many decades to produce geological mapping of the British Isles at such a large scale. This sheet shows part of Achill Island, off the west coast of Ireland, in County Mayo, and was published in 1871. The deep yellow colour shows quartzite, and it can be seen from the hachures showing relief that this is on the higher ground; pale yellow indicates peat. Melaphyre, basalt and dolerite (not distinguished) are shown in purple, and pink indicates granite. The use of colour for rock types on geological maps renders them particularly attractive as well as making them easier to interpret. Early hand-coloured examples like this one are often more beautiful than one might imagine from their scientific purpose; even modern printed versions are generally very colourful compared with general purpose maps.

The British Geological Survey (as it is now called) continues its work to the present day, as does the Geological Survey of Ireland, which has long been a separate organization. Geological surveys are extremely time-consuming and produced only for specialist consumption, so geological mapping is generally less detailed and widely available than maps produced for general use. However, geological surveys are often incentivized by the possibility of financial gain, since they may reveal where valuable minerals are likely to be found. In some African countries today, Earth science mapping is being pursued more actively than standard topographic mapping.

C19 (31) [62]

Dark clouds of ignorance

This historical atlas shows the world in a series of maps of different periods, each one showing only the 'known' world, the remaining parts being covered by dark clouds. The first map portrays the time of Noah's Flood, dated precisely to 2284 BC; a tiny gap in the clouds reveals the rivers Euphrates and Hiddekel flowing through the garden of Eden, and little else. Each successive map shows a slightly larger mapped area as the clouds withdraw, up to a contemporary map of the peace of 1828, after the Napoleonic Wars. There are twenty-one maps, of which the first eight are BCE and the one shown opposite (*Empire of Charlemagne, AD 814*) is the twelfth, just over halfway in the series. Throughout, the known world appears sunlit and tranquil, surrounded by threatening storm clouds that gradually recede as the light of knowledge pours in. The atlas is the only known published work by Edward Quin, a London barrister of Irish descent, who died in his early thirties; he both wrote the text and designed the maps. The first edition of the atlas (from which these maps are reproduced) was not published until after his death.

The idea of mapping the world as known to (European) civilization and showing the rest shrouded in cloud appears almost laughably Eurocentric to the modern reader. The areas covered by cloud in the early maps were occupied, and must have been known to their inhabitants if not to outsiders, and to show them as if they did not exist until 'discovered' by Europeans seems appallingly arrogant. Quin did point out, however, that the clouded areas existed before they were known to 'civilised human beings'. And his understanding of the world was typical of his time; his maps make explicit a view of history which would then have been commonplace. Other nineteenth-century cartographers produced atlases of 'ancient geography' or of the world 'as known to the ancients'. Arrowsmith, for example, published at least two maps entitled *Orbis veteribus notus* within ten years of Quin's atlas appearing, which fail to acknowledge the existence of areas outside Europe, North Africa and South Asia. Quin's atlas shows the world as it was known to its intended audience and their ancestors; the clouds in the earlier maps can perhaps be seen as an acknowledgement of geographical ignorance. The maps are also redeemed by their beauty; the fineness of the engraving (by Sidney Hall in the first two editions), the drama of the clouds gradually withdrawing to reveal a delicately coloured world, make their popularity unsurprising; the atlas ran to five editions.

Each plate is accompanied by a few pages of narrative text, recounting the main events of that period in history, beginning with an account of the deluge and subsequent population of the Earth (from biblical sources). The most important or dramatic events throughout are italicized (presumably for easy reference) – for example, 'Carthage again became sufficiently powerful to excite the jealousy of the Romans, and *in 146 BC it was burned and razed to its very foundations*' – considerably enhancing the dramatic effect.

The cloud motif was not widely copied elsewhere. It had previously been used in a German school atlas, though there is nothing to suggest Quin ever saw this, and there was some reproduction of Quin's maps in the United States for educational purposes. The plates were redrawn by William Hughes from the third edition onwards, along the same lines but slightly less dramatically. Both Hall and Hughes were highly regarded and prolific engravers who engraved maps for many other atlases, but nothing else quite like this.

2023 b.9

Assembling India

The jigsaw puzzle was invented as an aid in the teaching of geography. It was one manifestation of the educational revolution taking place in the second half of the eighteenth century: learning was to be a pleasure rather than a chore, and children's attention was engaged imaginatively to encourage their interest in acquiring knowledge. To this end various games, toys and cards were produced for use in the classroom.

In the 1760s the London printmaker and dealer John Spilsbury, previously apprenticed to Thomas Jefferys, who had been appointed Geographer to King George III in 1760, had the idea of pasting a map of the world on a thin mahogany board and cutting or dissecting it into pieces. He sold the dissected maps in a box with a pictorial lid, for children to reassemble, either under the guidance of a tutor or parent, or simply as a pastime, thus instilling the names and the disposition of the different countries. It was part of a series which included jigsaws of the continents (divided into countries or states) and Great Britain (divided into counties). For twenty years maps were the only subjects of such dissections, but then others adopted the idea for different types of images, both educational and entertaining. By the time of this jigsaw of India, dissected maps comprised only a fifth of all such puzzles.

The map used here by John Passmore in making this puzzle was G.F. Cruchley's *New Map of India, the Seat of the Mutinies*. It was very topical. The Indian rebellion began in May 1857, when the sepoys (native soldiers) in the army of the East India Company mutinied in Meerut.

The uprising soon spread through central India and the upper Ganges plain until it was defeated at the end of June. The towns where mutinies took place are underlined in red on the map.

This puzzle was thus a tool to teach both the geography of the subcontinent and its tumultuous current affairs, which were to lead to the demise of the East India Company and the inauguration of the British Raj, with Queen Victoria assuming the title of Empress of India twenty years later in 1877. Educational games like this one were expensive and only available to the children of the wealthy – children (sons at least) who may well have later found employment in helping to administer the British Empire. Knowledge of the events in India at this time was deemed an essential part of the education of such children.

The earliest dissected maps comprised large, simply cut pieces, with little of the complex interlocking effect which we are used to today; a hundred years later they were not much more intricate, as shown by the fairly simple shapes of the forty-two pieces of this puzzle. The fine illustration on the box lid shows four figures symbolizing the world's continents: the Indian mutiny puzzle was just one of a series published by Passmore covering the whole world.

This puzzle has recently come to the Library as part of a large collection of board games dating from the eighteenth to the twentieth centuries presented by Richard Ballam.

John Johnson Collection. Ballam Games:
Dissected puzzles (32)

CRUCHLEY'S
New Map of
INDIA
THE SEAT OF THE
MUTINIES.

English Miles.
0   50   100   150   200

PRESIDENCIES.
Bengal   Madras.   Bombay.

1857.

CHAPTER 3

Pride and Ownership

MAPS CAN BE USED TO EXPRESS PRIDE IN OWNERSHIP OF THE place depicted, the map itself, or both. It is easier to show land ownership on a map than to try to describe it. This applies to all scales of map, from a detailed plan showing the division between neighbouring houses, through an estate map of a larger area, to a boundary between nations. International boundary surveys are occasionally consulted decades after being made, in cases of dispute.

Some of the earliest land-ownership surveys in European countries were written estate 'terriers', which described the boundaries of the estate; the surveyor's job included assessing the value of the land. From the sixteenth century onwards these gave way increasingly to cartographic surveys, and surveyors became more focused on precise measurement of the land. With the publication of Ortelius's *Theatrum* and Saxton's atlas of England and Wales in the 1570s (both featuring in the previous chapter), there was a very significant increase in awareness of maps and geographical knowledge, at least amongst those who could afford such items as maps. Over the following centuries, the purchase of land became more common, in England partly as a result of the dissolution of the monasteries, and also as societies shifted from a feudal to a capitalist system, with previously common fields enclosed and subjected to individual ownership.

By the late eighteenth century surveying was a more populous, more scientific and higher-status profession, employing hundreds of people in England and Wales alone, and estate maps were increasingly used

FACING

This illumination shows Marco Polo departing on a sea-journey; the backdrop of the scene is Venice's St Mark's Square and its surroundings.

This plan of the manor of Pilemore in Devon, by Richard Cartwright, dates from 1805.

for land management. A map of an estate has one particular advantage over a text description: it is much more attractive to look at. Estate plans became increasingly decorative and were often made for display as well as use. It was unlikely that a large number of copies would be needed of an estate map, so many were produced in manuscript through the eighteenth and nineteenth centuries. Some of them were very elaborate, with individual trees and buildings beautifully rendered; there is a lovely early nineteenth-century example illustrated above. The map itself could be a treasured possession – pride in the land represented alongside pride in the object. Ownership of a beautiful and valuable map became a status symbol, showing that the owner was discerning and educated as well as wealthy.

Some of the maps featured in this chapter are complicated expressions of local and national pride rather than purely related to ownership. The lovely fifteenth-century Venetian portolan chart atlas was intended to be a thing of beauty as well as use. A contemporary illustration, reproduced at the start of this chapter, shows Marco Polo setting off on his travels; in this city of many seafarers there was pride in its most famous explorer even decades after his death, and Venetian landmarks such as St Mark's Basilica and the Doge's Palace can be identified in the background. This portrayal comes from an English illuminated manuscript produced around 1400. Similarly, admiration and promotion of Florence and Bruges can be seen in early city views and illuminations included respectively in this chapter and in the chapter on city maps.

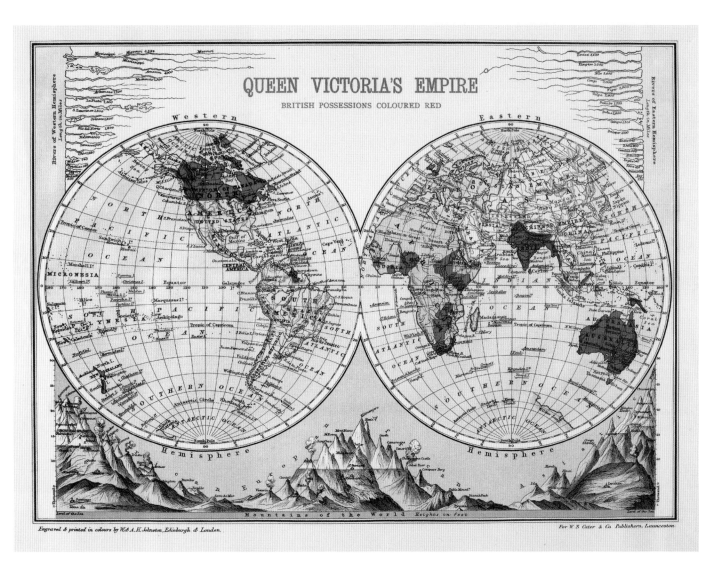

An information sheet on imports and exports, and another on educating the working man about the empire's geography, accompany this map of the British Empire.

Pride of possession also extended beyond the individual to pride in national territory and dominion. A map of the newly acquired English possessions in New England from the 1670s is featured in this chapter, but it was in the nineteenth century that some of the most memorable maps expressing pride in British command over the globe were made. The example on the preceding page, from around 1891, refers to 'Queen Victoria's Empire', suggesting pride in the Queen's person as well as in the national possessions. As was frequently the case, British possessions are coloured in red.

This map is one of a large number of similar Victorian world maps produced for the home market, but the role of local mapping in imposing control over such a large area was of much greater practical significance throughout colonial history. The appeal of access to 'empty' land in the New World was a powerful inducement to colonizers, and it was only by surveying the land and recording ownership of plots that individual rights could be formalized. Colonies did not all take the same approach to mapping; in some cases plots were surveyed and allocated in advance, in others people could claim land and legalize their claims after the event. The 1878 map of New Zealand (facing) shows which land was available to settlers and which had already been allocated or claimed by the Crown; there is no mention of the indigenous population. Similarly, the revenue surveys of India under British administration recorded field and settlement boundaries for tax purposes, disregarding the fact that India had a completely different system of land rights, including inherited rights to a share in the produce of land, which were not represented; millions of people were affected. There is a long history of those who control the land using mapping to legitimize their claims. It extends from the English peasants whose common fields were enclosed to the Native Americans and Australian Aboriginals whose land was parcelled up by European settlers.

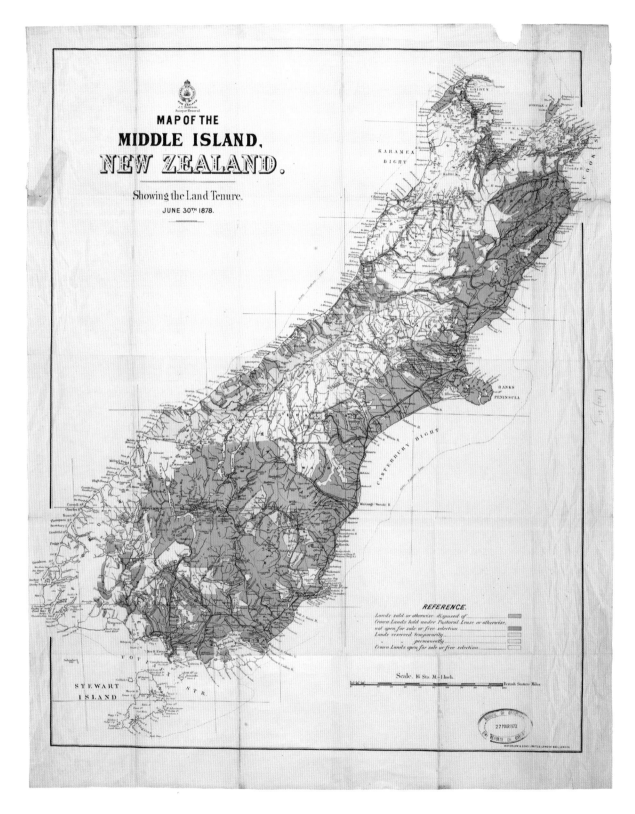

Looking at this 1878 map of land ownership in New Zealand gives the viewer no clue that the country has an indigenous population, much less that its members might have any claim to the land.

A Venetian set of portolan charts

Charts of this type, called portolans, were first produced in the thirteenth century, when Europeans began to use the magnetic compass, and continued to be made for over 400 years (see also pages 15 and 33). Colourful compass roses, the place names written closely along the coast-lines and the lack of inland information are typical of the portolan style. This volume covers the Black Sea, the Mediterranean and the west coast of Europe as far north as the British Isles in seven charts; all are oriented with south at the top. Further north the accuracy diminishes somewhat. The chart illustrated shows the east coast of Italy and the Adriatic Sea and is the most detailed in the book; 'Venezia' can be seen marked in red and the place names appear to be in the Venetian dialect.

The set of seven portolans to which this chart belongs was probably produced in Venice in the late fourteenth or early fifteenth century. The charts were pasted on to wooden boards, which were bound to form a book. Its first and last openings are decorated with religious miniatures. The style of the illuminations has been linked to the artist Niccolò di Pietro. At the beginning of the volume there is an Annunciation to the Virgin Mary and at the end portraits of St Mark (patron saint of Venice) accompanied by St Paul (possibly the patron saint of an owner of the set of charts), who was believed to have survived a shipwreck. Annunciation scenes and images of saints were standard devotional imagery produced for contemporary churches and for domestic interiors. Venetian portolans, which opened like diptychs, also contained such pictures. They could be used for daily prayer and were thought to give protection at sea. It is remarkable that in this case the late medieval book cover (shown below) and the custom-made container still survive. Both objects were not only functional and sturdy but also very decorative. The book cover is made of multi-coloured inlaid wood and ivory. The container is made of *cuir bouilli*, moulded leather ornamented with floral patterns and inscriptions. It also has suspension loops for a – now missing – string or shoulder strap. The techniques employed to make the binding and the case were typical for production of contemporary European furniture or domestic objects. Inlaid wood was often used to decorate chests, tables, chairs or beds. Snugly fitting and protective *cuir bouilli* cases were made for a variety of valuable and fragile artefacts, such as glass vessels, cutlery, writing implements, scientific and medical instruments or other prized possessions. This set of portolan charts would have been appreciated for its practical and decorative qualities and is likely to have been made for a wealthy Venetian merchant-sailor. However, apart from his first name possibly being indicated by the inclusion of a picture of St Paul in the manuscript, we now know nothing about this man.

MS. Douce 390, fol. 5v-6

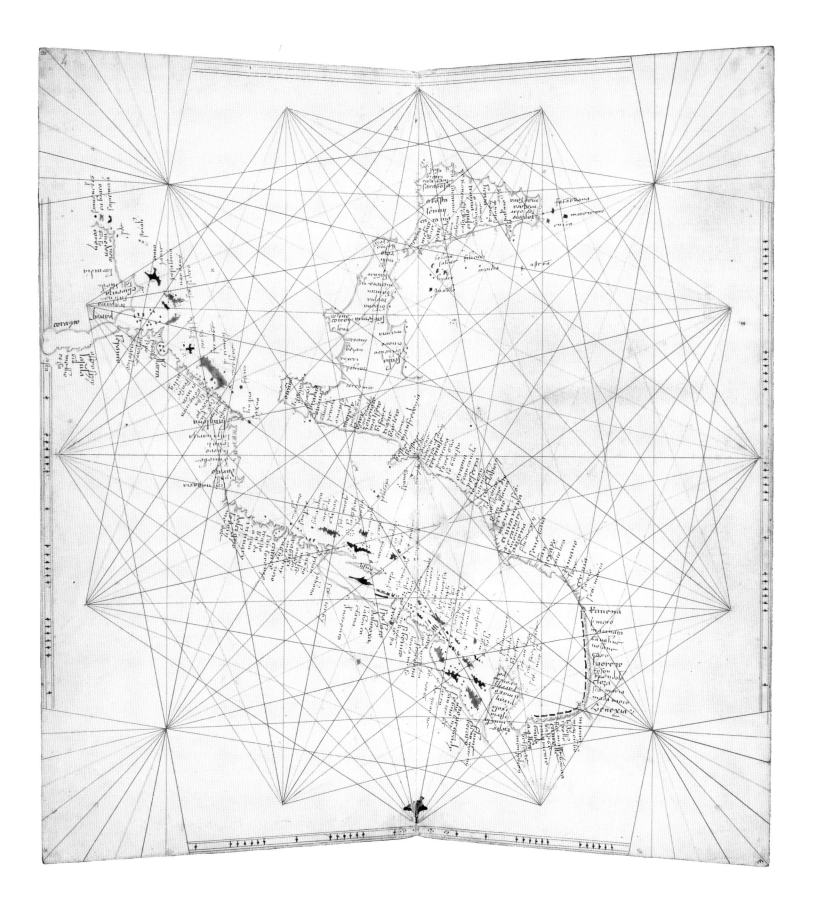

Florence

Fiorenza dentro da la cerchia antica,
ond'ella toglie ancora e terza e nona,
si stava in pace, sobria e pudica.
Dante, *La Divina Commedia*, 'Paradiso', Canto XV

Dante Alighieri (1265–1321), the Florentine poet known primarily for his *Divine Comedy*, wrote the above verses while exiled at a time of political unrest and living in Ravenna. Dante misses Florence and, longing to see it restored to prosperity, evokes an idealized vision of a city he imagines his ancestors to have experienced. The poet describes a 'peaceful, sober and pure' Florence, protected by its 'ancient city walls' and filled with a sound of church bells.

The city walls and many build-ings familiar to Dante can still be seen in the late fifteenth-century bird's-eye view of Florence from the Nuremberg Chronicle, an incu-nable printed in 1493. Being derived from a Florentine source, Francesco Rosselli's engraving executed *c.* 1482–90, the woodcut is tolerably reliable and depicts quite accurately numerous Florentine landmarks, admired not only by the locals but also famous abroad. Many of the old and still-surviving buildings, such as the Badia with its bell tower, were virtually on Dante's doorstep. Another, more imposing cathedral bell tower was designed by Dante's contemporary, the painter and architect Giotto. In the woodcut it partially overshadows the cathedral's dome, an iconic symbol of Florence con-structed by Filippo Brunelleschi between 1420 and 1436. The German text, written by Hartmann Schedel and printed above the woodcut, tells the history of Florence,

describes its achievements and lists its great men – among them Dante, Giotto and other brilliant scholars, writers, artists and their patrons.

Giotto's bell tower and Brunelleschi's dome, a masterpiece of Renaissance architecture and a source of Florentine civic pride, can also be seen in a late fifteenth-century illumination from another incunable – a Tuscan translation of Pliny's *Natural History*. The miniature shows the landmarks and the translator of the text, the humanist Cristoforo Landino. The illuminations in this book were com-missioned by a banker and patron of art and architecture, Filippo Strozzi (1428–1491), and celebrate his polit ical connections and service to the de facto rulers of Florence, the Medici. The book was printed by Nicolaus Jenson in Venice in 1476 and illumi-nated in Florence by Gherardo or Monte di Giovanni di Miniato (del Fora) *c.* 1479–83. Every detail of the form, decoration and contents of this volume reminds us that Florence was the cradle of the Renaissance. Much of what Florentine citizens achieved over the centuries can be attributed to the sense of pride in their civic and family heritage and to their eagerness to contribute to the greatness of both. Filippo Strozzi was one of those men: his commissions still add to the splen-dour of Florence, such as Palazzo Strozzi or Cappella di Filippo Strozzi in the church of Santa Maria Novella.

Auct. Q sub. fen. 1.7a

Florencia die edel vnd fürnamste statt vnder den stetten Etrurie wirdt irs vrspzungs halbe auff die zukunfft der Sillamschen ritterschaft den dieselb gegen von Silla dem römischen tathern zugeaignet wardt/ gezogen. vnd nachdem sie sich ersstlich daselbst bey dem fluss Arni nder gesetzt haben. So maynen ettlich das dise statt vō de fluss ersstlich Fluencia genant sey. Dann plinius/ dz ersstlich vō demselb end meldūg tūt/ heißt dieselben lewt Fluentiner. als bey dem fürstfliessenden Arno wonende. Nw sind dieselben ritterschaften daselb hin komen. nach erpawung der statt Rom. vi. lxvij. iar. Auß dem erscheint das dise stat bey lxxij. iarn voz zukunfft cristi vnsers gottes eine anfang gehabt hat. Dise statt Floicia ist vō de Fesulanen an die gestad des fluss Arni gepawē. vn die alten habe sie Fluenciam gehaissen. nach dem sie aber zu glückfaligem wesen vnd zugefalligen dingen wunderpeflichen weißzeerpaiten begunde so ist dise statt vil billicher Florencia. als ein plüende. daņ Fluē cia het sie verheret vnd verwüstet. die doch der groß Karolus widerauffricht vnd mit ein grössern vmbkrais vnd zinnen einsienge vnd mit loblichen freiheiten vnd burgerlichen regimenten gelaytet. Als aber Florencia mit gewalt vnd sunst die Fesulaner an sich bracht. nach der gepurt Cristi tausent vn iij. dem. xxiiij. iar hat sie an reich thümern vnd eren fast zugenomen. Desselben iars hat kaiser Henrich der erst sancti Miniatis kirchen bey dz mawz zu Florencz gepawen. Von derselben her ist die statt durch die vorderen der kunst vn panzertragen der gerechtigkeit. die man zu latein priores arcium et verisliferos iusticie nennt. als ietzo bischst geregt wozden. In diser statt sind außerhalb andere vngelewplicher zierden ein berümbte thumbkirch. mit ein wunderwirdigen schwin bogen oder gewelb gezieret. vnd in der ere der hochgelobten gloswirdige iunckfraw Marie geweyhet. darnach im vierden iar wardt ein hoher pallast. darin die voidern des regiments wonen zepawen angefangen vnd nach

folgend im fünfften iar. das ist das im lxxi. iar nach cristi gepurt ein pawmgart zepflanzt. die statt an zinne erweytert vnd vber sand Lorenzen kirchen an dem gestad des fluss mit ewigem vmbgang gelaytet. vnnd darnach im lxxi. iar ein köstlicher marmorstaininer glocken thurn auffgerichtet. alda dann der zaiger finger des voilawffers cristi in grosser ererbietung. gehalten wirdt. in des ere ein köstlicher tempel. den sie baptisterium nennen. an ein gelegnern ende der statt geweihet ist. daran die thoze von fester glocken speiß oder erze gemacht. vnnd die historien des neven vnd alten testaments mit vnaußsprechlichem werck darein ergraben sind. vnd nachdem aber Florencia ein plüm aller welschen stett genant wirdt. so hat sie außerhalb irer hübscher vnnd irer burger holdseligkait. auch man in allem gesiecht der tugent fürtreffenlich gehabt. nemlich zwen poeten Dantem aldegerium vnd Franciscum petrarcham. Item vnlang darnach Jothum den hohberümsten maler in kunst Appelli dem preißwirdige maler wol zegleichen. Item Accursium den fürsten der rechtgeleiten. vnd einen fürpündigen außleger der werltlichen recht. Item Tadeum einen hohberümbten arzt. Item Cosinum medicum. der an zustliffigkeit dz reichthümer holdseligkait vnd miltigkeit alle burgere in Europa vbertroffen hat. sein sun vnd engtlein samelin auch nochmaln sein glückseligkeit. die auch dz stat Floręz vil zierde zugelegt habe. vn sunderlich ein löblich closter sancti Marci darinn schöne gepew vnd ein libravey die andern all vbertreffende. Das feld darinn Florencia ligt treegt fast güete wein. die fürsichtigkeit der Florentiner ist in vil dingen loblich vnd preßlich. vnnd sunderlich in außlesung irer canzler vnd schreiber. dañ die sind hochgefliffen allweg zeerwelen vnd bey ine zehaben die besten vnd in der erfarung weißhait vnd kunst des gedichtes vnd wolredes voz andern hohberümbt. gelert. gebt vnd fürtreffenlich sind. darnach haben sie etwan Leonhardum vmb Karolum die Aretiner. auch Poggium. vnnd vor denselben Collucium bey ine gehabt die von art des schreibens vnd dichtens außpündig gewesen sind.

Florentz

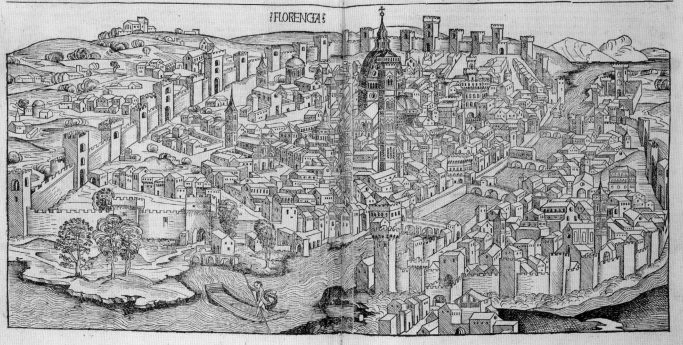

FLORENCIA

The warp and weft of Worcestershire

Almost all the details which enlivened the four tapestry-woven maps commissioned by the Catholic Ralph Sheldon around 1590 are visible on the section opposite, illustrating part of Worcestershire. Each was approximately 15 × 20 ft; each focussed on a single county – Gloucestershire, Worcestershire, Warwickshire and Oxfordshire – shown with a light background and bordered in red. Also included were areas of adjacent counties, brightly coloured in yellows and greens.

The placing of the county's settlements and natural features was plotted from topographical information contained in Christopher Saxton's county surveys (see page 64). Because the tapestry would be at least ten times the size of the prints, approximately an A3 sheet, the tapestry designer had space to depict both the physical and the man-made landscape in some detail. Rivers, some with red banks, might be named ('Avon Flvd'). They were bridged sometimes in stone – at Worcester, Tewkesbury and 'Parshore' (Pershore) – and sometimes in timber – at Defford, 'Poike' (Powicke) and Upton on Severn. Trees in forested areas like 'Wadborow' (Wadborough) might be larger than villages; occasionally dead timber appears, for example at Newland. They contrast with the less wooded areas round Broadway. Nearby the steep Cotswold hills rise in triangular bulk as do the named Malvern Hills on the other side of the county. All were outlined in a darker green on their right-hand side to emphasize height. Some small features were depicted – fire beacons, as at Broadway, and windmills, usually Sheldon property, at 'Spechley' (Spetchley).

The parks surrounding gentry houses were enclosed by gated wooden palings – Strensham, Wadborow and 'Batnol' (Battenhall). Villages, connected by yellow strips of road, were merely a cluster of houses dominated by the church, its tower, sometimes with a spire, placed centrally and not always accurate. Bird's-eye views of towns attempted to render architectural features: Worcester's defences, its apparently fortified bridge and the suburb of 'St Iones' (St John's) stand out more clearly than its cathedral; at Tewkesbury, Evesham and Pershore bridges and churches are prominent.

Outside the area illustrated many of the larger houses drawn in some detail had connections to the Sheldon family; comparison with later drawings suggests some were an attempt at factual rather than fanciful depiction –Weston, Compton Wynyates, Coughton and 'Sudley' (Sudeley). Antiquarian interest came to the fore with the depiction of the prehistoric Rollright Stones on the Oxfordshire border and the labelling of the 'Fowre Sheer Ston' (Four Shire Stone) at the meeting point of the four tapestry counties; a more recent event, the earthquake of 1575 at Marclay Hill near Kynaston, Herefordshire, was celebrated by Saxton's inscription.

Each tapestry showed the queen's arms (upper left corner), a scale and dividers (lower left); now missing here were the family arms, each showing a different generation (lower right) and a long text passage based on William Camden's *Britannia* (upper right). The map was enclosed within a broad border, where arcades might overflow with flowers or shelter allegorical and mythological figures. Doggerel verses described the nature of the land in English, but the points of the compass were indicated in Latin, '*Meridies*' (south), '*Occidens*' (west).

Woven to decorate Sheldon's new house at Weston in Long Compton, the tapestries conveyed a great deal of information in a form not yet familiar. Use of maps on this scale for interior decoration was relatively rare and therefore likely to have made a forceful impact on the viewer. Executed in an expensive medium and innovative though not unique, the scheme made a Warwickshire house one of the best decorated in England.

(R) Gough Maps 262

A fine prospect

This map of New England appears in a late edition of John Speed's world atlas, *A prospect of the most famous parts of the world*. It was published by London booksellers Thomas Bassett and Richard Chiswell in 1676.

The *Prospect*, the first world atlas published by an Englishman, was initially produced in 1627 as an adjunct to the *Theatre of the Empire of Great Britaine* (see page 68). After the success of Speed's *Theatre* in 1612, his publisher George Humble was keen to profit further from his success. The *Prospect* is presented as the work of Speed; his name appears on the title page and all but three of the twenty-two maps in the original 1627 edition were attributed to him – generally described as being 'augmented' or 'newly revised' by John Speed. However, he was reportedly losing his sight from the mid-1620s and it seems likely that his practical contribution was small; his connection to the atlas may have been largely commercial.

The maps in the original *Prospect* were mainly anglicized copies of maps in circulation in the Netherlands at the time. Many have decorative borders with town plans and costumed figures; it has been suggested that this similarity with the decorative maps produced for the *Theatre* motivated their use. The coverage is somewhat patchy, and may reflect the use of such maps as were available in suitable style rather than a coherent editorial policy. The map of the Americas is one of the first to show California as an island, beginning a misconception that would take more than a hundred years to die out completely. Several editions of the *Theatre* and the *Prospect* were prepared and sold together.

Speed died in 1629, but his atlas lived on in successive incarnations. The plates were passed to George Humble's son William on his death. They passed through other hands before the 1670s, when they reached Bassett and Chiswell, who issued a slightly revised version of the *Theatre* and an expanded edition of the *Prospect*. In the case of the latter, they took the opportunity to improve the coverage of areas of British interest in the New World, at a time of British colonial expansion. Both title pages mention the addition of 'the descriptions of His Majesty's Dominions abroad; with a Map fairly engraven to each description'. This map of New England and New York was engraved by the London map engraver Francis Lamb, and is one of many maps of New England and the surrounding region derived from Jan Jansson's *Belgii Novi* of c.1651. Lamb's copy naturally has place names in English. Settlements with English names cluster along the coast and rivers (Boston, unfortunately, in not quite the right place), while the names of Native American tribes appear across the map. 'New Iarsey' is described as 'Inhabited by Indians'.

The extensive text on the verso describes the land, natural resources, hazards, fish, animals and native people, and gives a history of European exploration and settlement in the area. The map lacks the formal decorative borders of some plates in the atlas, but makes up for this with pictures of local fauna; a stag, bears, beavers and storks all appear, possibly filling up inland areas for which geographical knowledge was limited. The hills and trees are shown pictorially and the general picture is of an attractive and resource-filled landscape. Even if the viewer were not inspired to set off for New England, the map would provoke a patriotic pride that others had done so.

Map Res. 112

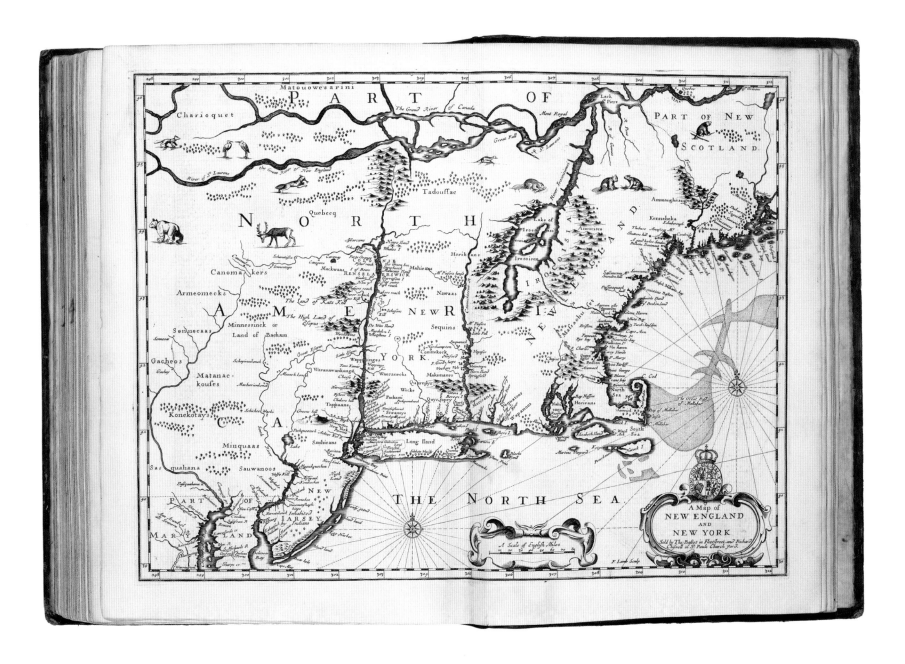

An extension to the Bodleian Library

In 1612–13 Magdalen College, Oxford, owned two houses on the west side of Catte Street in the city. The houses stood in the way of a major new university development which was to begin in 1613 – the building of a quadrangle to contain teaching schools and an extension to the Bodleian Library, now known as the Old Schools Quadrangle. The college agreed to lease the university the land on which the houses stood so that they could be demolished and the grand scheme could go ahead. The lease, dated on 13 September 1613, was for a period of forty years at a fixed rent of £2 3s. 4d. per annum, and to accompany the transaction William Webb, a mapmaker then working for Magdalen College, produced this small plan.

Little is known of William Webb, who, between 1612 and 1614, made detailed maps for the President and Scholars of Magdalen College of four of their Estates: at Golden Farm, Pyrton, Oxfordshire, in 1612 (MP/1/77); at Thornborough, Buckinghamshire, in 1613 (MP/1/5); at Romney Marsh, Kent, in 1614 (MP/1/24); and at East Bridgford, Nottinghamshire, also in 1614 (now in the Nottinghamshire Record Office). He was paid £6 1s. 0d. for his work (Magd. Coll. Liber Computi 1606-1620, fol. 63v) and in a cartouche on each he wrote that the maps were made 'by perambulation, mensuration, and observation' and that they had been 'delineated, measured & beautified' by himself. They are, indeed, fine examples of the art of an early-seventeenth-century estate mapmaker. The same cannot really be said of this small plan,

which measures 48 × 27 cm and, like the others, is on parchment attached to a roller. The accounts of neither the college bursars nor the university's vice-chancellor record any payment to him for this document. It is, however, very important since it provides for us the earliest surviving drawing of the projected shape of what is now one of Oxford's most famous buildings.

The inscription in an early seventeenth-century hand (not Webb's) on a paper label stuck on the plan explains that the plot of land in question lies within the periphery of the 'scholles wch are now erecting' and measures 83 feet and 6 inches from north to south and from east to west 81 feet and 9 inches 'by ye standard' – in area of 758 ⁴/₉ square yards. The lease of 30 September 1613 contained a clause that the college was to renew it on the same terms every time that it expired. This duly happened (with the rent rising only to £3) for the next 280 years until 1892, when Magdalen refused to renew and the university was obliged in 1893 to buy the land (by then said to measure only 658 ¾ square yards) for £7000. This little plan, then superseded by a larger one incorporated into the deed of sale (O.U. Archives WPα/46/5) became redundant as a working tool and was handed over to the Bodleian Library by the Curators of the University Chest in 1913, exactly three centuries after both its creation and the death of Sir Thomas Bodley, the Library's founder. The twentieth-century hand outlining the property's history after 1613 is that of Falconer Madan, Bodley's Librarian 1912–19.

(R) MS C17:70 Oxford (95)

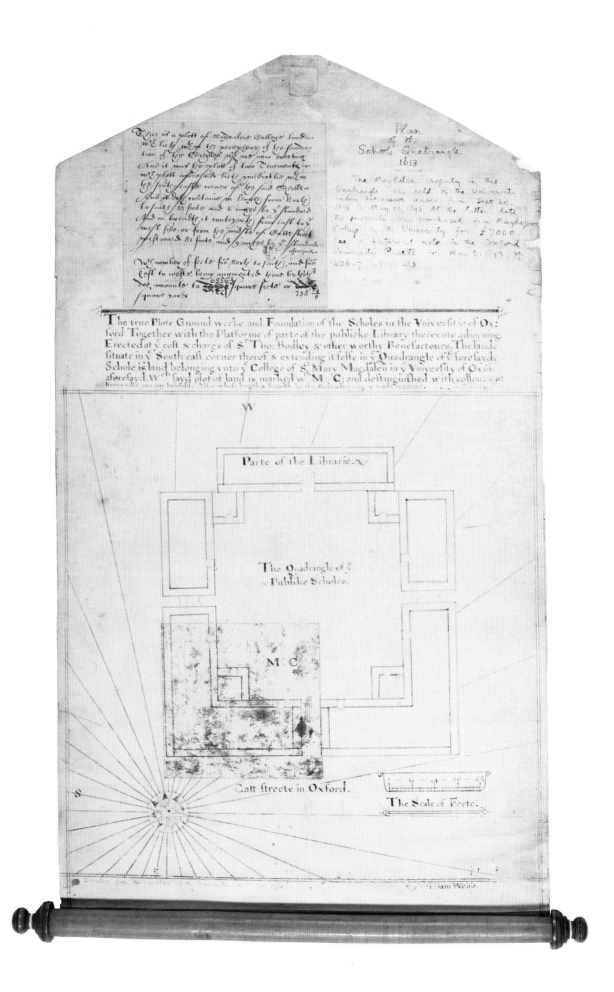

Plan of the Scholes Quadrangle 1613

The true Plote, Ground worke, and Foundation of the Scholes in the Vniversitie of Oxford. Together with the Platforme of parte of the publicke Library thereunto adioyning. Erected at ye cost & charge of Sr Tho: Bodley & other worthy Benefactours. The lande situate in ye South east corner therof & extending it selfe in ye Quadrangle of ye foresayde Schole is land belonging vnto ye College of St Mary Magdalen in y Vniversity of Oxon aforesayd. Wch sayd plot of land is marked with M C; and distinguished with colours as

W

Parte of the Librarie.

The Quadrangle of ye Publike Scholes.

M C

Catt streete in Oxford.

The Scale of Feete.

Feudal Laxton

This manuscript map, made in 1635 by Mark Pierce, tells us that Laxton's pattern of agricultural land use remains virtually unchanged since feudal times. It shows the layout of the open-field system surrounding the village and is accompanied by a ter-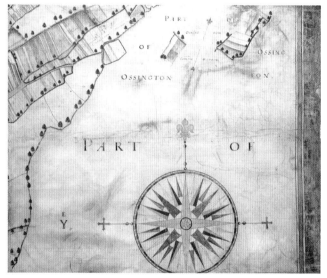rier describing each of over five thousand strips of land, measuring each strip's area, and identifying their occupying tenants.

The map is fully coloured in nine pieces, each measuring 76 × 59 cm at a scale of roughly 1:3,950. The accompanying terrier, measuring 35.5 × 48.5 cm, consists of 228 openings. Each strip of land has a unique numerical reference, which can be found in the terrier, revealing that strip's status at the time of the survey. The significance of the map can best be illustrated by tracing individual inhabitants. Robert Rosse, for example, is listed as being 'in question for freehold', occupying just over twenty-six acres in total, twenty-four of these being 'pasture and arable' the remaining two being 'meddow land'. He is shown to be occupying a cottage and yard in the tenement of Edward Alicock (plot 60 just northeast of the church), and is paying two shillings per annum to the Parsonage of Laxton. Elsewhere in the village itself Rosse occupies a further seven acres to the east (plot 68), and another small plot just south of the village green. In addition, he is shown to be working five strips in West Field, one in East Field, ten in South Field, seven in Mill Field, a plot in Shitterpoole Meadows, five more in Long Meadows, another in South Pound Meadows, and finally a strip in East Kirke Inge. None of these thirty-one pieces of land were adjoining.

Buildings are represented three-dimensionally, and very few are to be found beyond the two villages of Laxton and Kneesall. There is a splendid windmill in the centre of the map, but, in terms of human dwellings, all the buildings are by the roadside in both villages. There are no smaller lanes leading off the principal thoroughfares, and this facet of the landscape remains unchanged today.

In artistic terms, Pierce was ambitious, as the map also includes two tiny world maps – one at the centre of the compass rose and a second at the bottom centre of the title cartouche, an extravagant addition to the colourful depiction of seventeenth-century agrarian life in the English Midlands.

MS C17:48 (9)

A grand atlas

The seventeenth century in the Netherlands is sometimes described as the golden age of cartography. Many people's idea of what a decorative old map should look like is informed by this period, when beautiful maps were produced, often hand-coloured, with elaborate borders and decoration and illustrations of ships and monsters in the seas. Joan Blaeu's masterpiece, this vast, multi-volume atlas of the world, published from 1662, is arguably the finest example of mapping from this Dutch golden age. The *Atlas maior sive cosmographia Blaviana* ('Large atlas or Blaeu's cosmography'; also often referred to as 'the Grand Atlas') was the largest and most expensive printed book of the seventeenth century. It was years in preparation, following on from ever expanded editions of his *Atlas novus* through the 1640s and 1650s. It contained around 600 maps and was published in between nine and twelve volumes in the different language editions. The Latin edition, for the scholarly market, came first and was quickly followed by versions in German, French, Spanish and Dutch. Blaeu's vast print works at Bloemgracht in Amsterdam worked on all the language editions at the same time; the maps themselves were printed in Latin, from copper-plates as was standard practice at the time, with the letterpress text on the back in different languages. The atlas was produced partly as a result of his trade rivalry with Jan Jansson, the two competing to produce ever more impressive publications. Copies were sold to the wealthy and influential across Europe, and beautifully bound examples were presented by the Dutch authorities to foreign dignitaries.

Joan Blaeu's father Willem was a map publisher and scientific instrument maker. Joan had been publishing maps with his father from 1631, when he was in his early thirties. On Willem's death in 1638, Joan was appointed to the role of cartographer to the Vereenighde Oostindische Compagnie (VOC), which provided him with a valuable income as payment for the maps he produced. It was also a source of useful geographical information, as the records and discoveries of the company's ships were naturally shared with the cartographer.

Despite this, the maps in the *Atlas maior* are not particularly new; many of them are old plates that were re-used, sometimes without being updated. This beautiful map of Asia was first issued by Willem Blaeu in 1617 – the latinized version of his name, Guiljemo Blaeuw, appears in the title cartouche – and is reproduced here from the *Atlas maior* published nearly fifty years later. Korea is shown here incorrectly as an island rather than a peninsula, although a more detailed map in the same volume shows it correctly. The atlas covers the whole world in varying degrees of detail, with each volume covering a different region. The maps of the continents are particularly elaborate, with views of cities and illustrations of the inhabitants in the margins. Arguably the purpose of the *Atlas maior* was never to provide the latest geographical information. It was and remains a status symbol, by reason of its size, beauty and value.

Map Res. 51

A map for a book that never was?

This map of the Roanoake River, showing the boundary between Virginia and North Carolina, has an intriguing history. It has survived at all only thanks to a quirk of fate and the dedication of the antiquary and book collector Richard Rawlinson (1690–1755).

Rawlinson collected an enormous number of copperplates as a means of preserving and disseminating the information they held; this was especially valuable in an age before images could be easily reproduced. The value of copper was such that most copperplates no longer in use were re-used or sold for scrap, and their information

lost. In time, Rawlinson began to collect copperplates for their own sake, buying whatever was available, and amassing an eclectic collection. He was a widely travelled scholar and passionate collector, who aimed to preserve for future generations the resources that he felt were unappreciated by his contemporaries. He bequeathed almost all his vast collection of books and manuscripts, including the 754 copperplates, to the Bodleian. Restrikes were produced in the late twentieth century from some of the plates, enabling us to see this map as it was originally conceived.

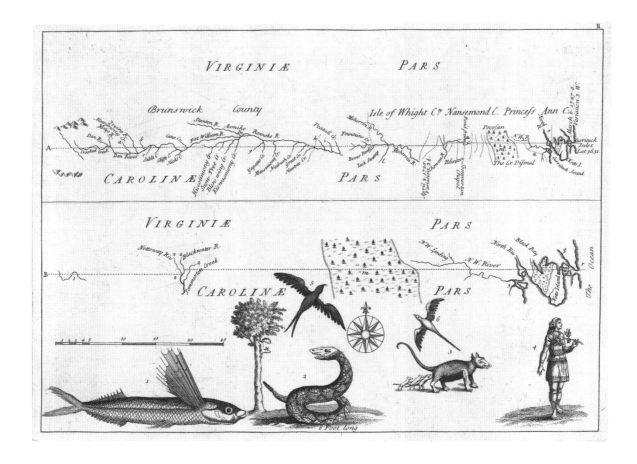

The map is thought to have been prepared around 1738 for William Byrd's 'History of the dividing line', which survives in an unpublished manuscript dating from 1737. Byrd was the heir to a large estate in Virginia and was the head of the Virginia commission to determine the state boundary with North Carolina in 1728. The top part of the map shows the border between the two states in relation to rivers flowing from west to east into the Roanoake on its path to the sea, locating it precisely. The larger lower section shows part of the same map, but with far less detail and more illustration – beautiful pictures of a tree, birds, other wildlife and, lastly, a Native American of the area in traditional costume. His inclusion is striking; he appears to be regarded as part of the natural environment in much the same category as the birds and animals. Although the map shows a boundary, it presents a peaceful scene and is an illustration and celebration of the region rather than a territorial claim.

There are many mysteries about the map. It appears to be part of a set of twelve related plates, including maps and depictions of flora and fauna, numbered in Roman numerals, of which eight are in the Rawlinson collection (this is number II). It is not known, despite years of research and speculation, for what purpose the set was assembled, what the missing plates were, or whether they were ever published. The pictures have been tentatively attributed to one of the English naturalists Peter Collinson or Mark Catesby. An edited version of Byrd's manuscript, with a different version of this map, was finally published over a hundred years later.

Rawl. Copperplate C.29
& (E) B5 (129)

Richard Davis of Lewknor

This large plan is a superb example of a late eighteenth-century estate plan by a brilliant local surveyor at the height of his powers. Measuring 243 × 134 cm, it is drawn at a scale of 20 inches to the mile (1:3,168).

At the beginning of the sixteenth century there had been virtually no surveyors in the country capable of producing such plans, but the creation of a land-owning class, as Henry VIII sold off the land he took from the monasteries, along with an ever greater enclosure of open fields in the country, led to a great demand for estate plans and for people capable of making them. By the time of the production of this plan of Benson, a sophisticated profession had developed, with three or four thousand surveyors at work in Britain.

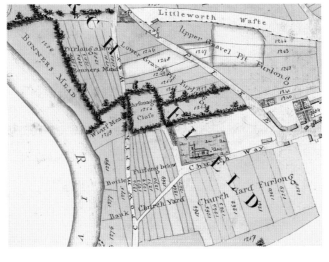

Richard Davis of Lewknor was a farmer and agricultural writer, an enclosure commissioner in Oxfordshire and Berkshire and, above all, a surveyor; he was Topographer to George III. He produced many estate plans, particularly in Berkshire, Buckinghamshire, Northamptonshire and Oxfordshire. Perhaps his *magnum opus* was a printed county map, his two-inch-to-the-mile *A New Map of the County of Oxfordshire* published on sixteen printed sheets in 1797 in response to the Society for Arts (now the RSA) prize of £100 for an original survey for each county to a scale of one inch to the mile or more.

The manuscript plan shown here was commissioned from Davis in 1787 by Christ Church, Oxford, to help those managing the college's estates work out the value of the tithes owing to it. This was a task made very difficult to complete because of the complex mixture of the large number of small parcels of land belonging to the different contiguous parishes around Benson. An accompanying three-volume written survey describes and indexes the 2,390 separate and numbered parcels of land shown on the map, along with their proprietors, occupiers, tenants and acreages. Davis employs a very clear colour scheme to distinguish the beneficiaries of the various parcels of land which he describes on the plan: 'The Arable Inclosures are Brown striped. The Pasture and Meadow coloured Green, and are titheable to Benson accept [sic] such as are tinged with yellow, which are titheable to Ewelme'.

Besides indicating the parcels of land, the plan shows roads, lanes, buildings, orchards, meadows, commons, hedges, large trees, copses, a picture of Benson Church, locks, a mill and a brick kiln. The western boundary is the Thames; at the north is a short stretch of the River Thame. The map and written survey of Benson successfully combine cartography with the traditional method of a detailed written record.

(R) MS C17:49 (141)

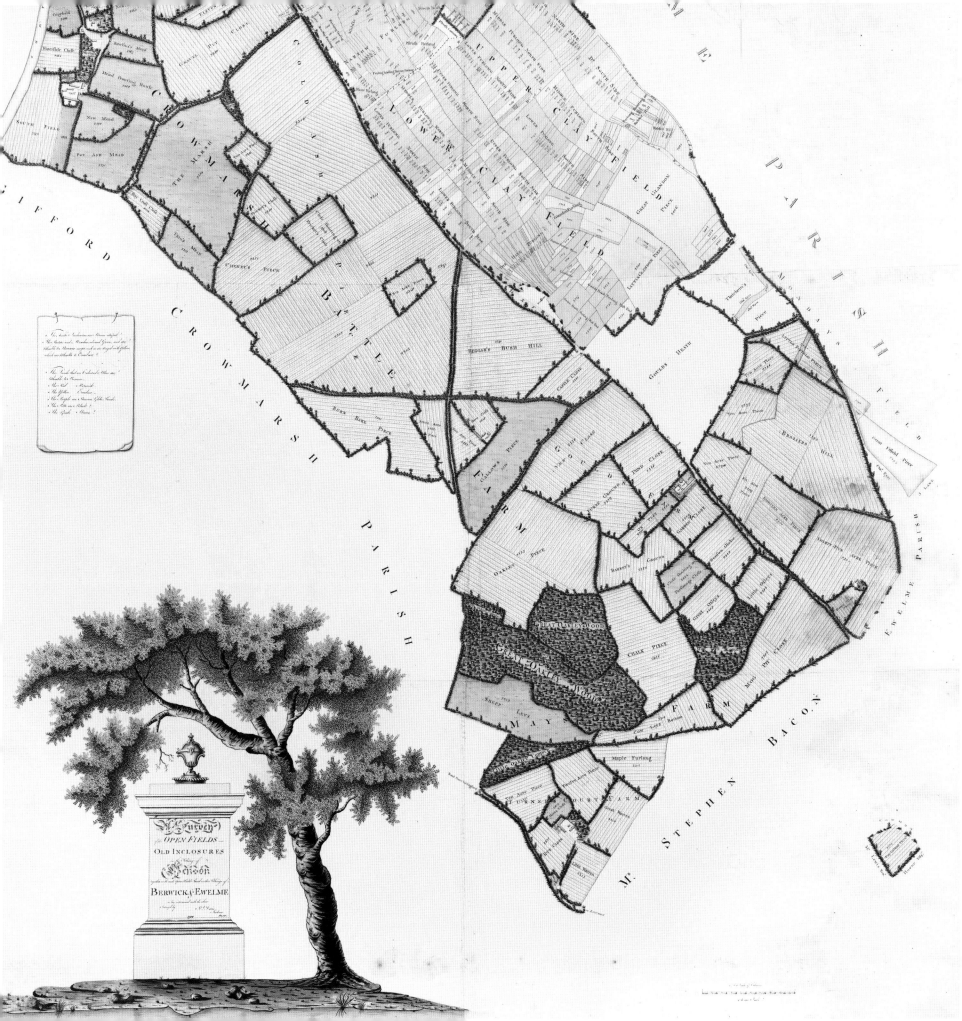

America's manifest destiny

By 1845 the national and state boundaries of the eastern United States had been established and, with a few exceptions, they have hardly changed since. In the west, however, the US remained in strategic competition with British North America (BNA) and Mexico for vast tracts of unsettled, sparsely explored territory – a state of affairs originating at the beginning of the century.

In the early 1800s, as the US worked to extend its borders westward from the Mississippi, it was not a foregone conclusion that the southern half of the country would be permitted to expand beyond the Great Plains. Spain had been extensively missionizing California and New Mexico for several decades. By the 1820s it appeared that Mexico might bar the path of America's continental spread, diverting it into the Pacific Northwest.

There, an 1818 Anglo-American treaty provided for joint land claims and settlements in Oregon. In 1824 the US and Russia bilaterally fixed Oregon's northern boundary at 54° 40' N. Britain hurriedly made a similar agreement with Russia in 1825. The US-BNA border through the Northern Plains lay at 49° N, but west of the Rockies there was no border. American sovereignty up to 54° 40' N would effectively deny BNA access to the sea, a position unlikely to be tenable.

America's eyes soon turned to Upper California and, in 1835, the US offered Mexico a large sum to adjust its northern border to approximately 37° 20' N. The proposal, carefully calibrated to assign San Francisco to the US but leave Taos and Santa Fe to Mexico, was declined. American support for annexing Texas steadily grew – an idea welcomed by the Lone Star Republic but regarded by Mexico as a *casus belli*. It seems that the prospect of 'renegotiating' the Mexican cession of territory

at the peace table made the probability of triggering a war more palatable to Washington. Territorial interests aside, America had a clear strategic requirement for a large port on the Pacific, either off the Strait of Juan de Fuca or in San Francisco Bay. Concerns over expanding slavery into southwestern states muddied the issue, but war with the fledgling Mexican nation was far preferable to taking on Britain. Furthermore, defeating Mexico militarily would signal American willingness to fight for the sovereignty of its expanding territory.

The Oregon dispute was, in comparison, fairly straightforward. By 1846 both parties agreed to a convenient solution: the border along 49° N was simply extended westward to the Pacific, doglegging south at the Strait of Juan de Fuca to award Vancouver Island to the British but leave Puget Sound to the US. It has been drawn by hand on to this copy of Wyld's map (see inset). For some Americans perhaps, willingness to abandon 54° 40' N was predicated on the assumption that the US would soon acquire some part of northern Mexico.

The link between the annexation of Texas (with the Mexican-American War resulting) and the Oregon Question was no great secret. In 1842 Secretary of State Daniel Webster attempted a trilateral negotiation, offering Britain Oregon as far south as the Columbia in exchange for Britain convincing Mexico to sell northern California to the US. The very title of the 1845 edition of Wyld's map, '*The United States and the Relative Position of The Oregon & Texas*', reflects this basic interrelationship. In December 1845, Texas was admitted as the twenty-eighth state of the Union and the phrase 'manifest destiny' entered the American vocabulary. By the following summer the Oregon Treaty was signed and the US and Mexico were at war.

(E) F6 (199)

THE
UNITED STATES
& The Relative Position
OF
THE OREGON & TEXAS
BY
JAMES WYLD, CHARING CROSS EAST.

Gosp

CHAPTER 4

Maps of War

GEOGRAPHY IS FUNDAMENTAL TO UNDERSTANDING WARS, BOTH their causes and outcomes. Many maps have been produced for military purposes, both for practical use and as propaganda.

Sometimes the practical uses of military maps are obvious. They are required for strategic planning and communications. Reconnaissance of an area before a planned attack or invasion helps reduce the disadvantage to invading troops, who are unfamiliar with it. Such maps can be historically interesting, giving a retrospective insight into the knowledge and tactics of those who prepared them. Examples in this chapter include the map used in plans to raise the siege of Dumbarton Castle in the 1640s and those in the invasion packs made by the Nazis three hundred years later. Similarly, the story of the maps used at Gallipoli hints at the difficulties of piecing together geographical information in the midst of war. The Bodleian also holds maps produced for training purposes and military exercises from the early nineteenth century onwards.

Detailed maps of the fortifications of the enemy, from the stone buttresses of old to the trenches or artillery positions of more recent conflicts, could be crucial to a successful attack. Early maps to show military fortifications were produced both for official and military use and as studies. Both the French and the English monarchs employed Italian surveyors to map and improve their fortifications in the sixteenth century. By the eighteenth century, Enlightenment principles of science and reason were beginning to be applied to the arts of war,

FACING

This plan of Portsmouth emphasizes its defences and military facilities such as the magazine.

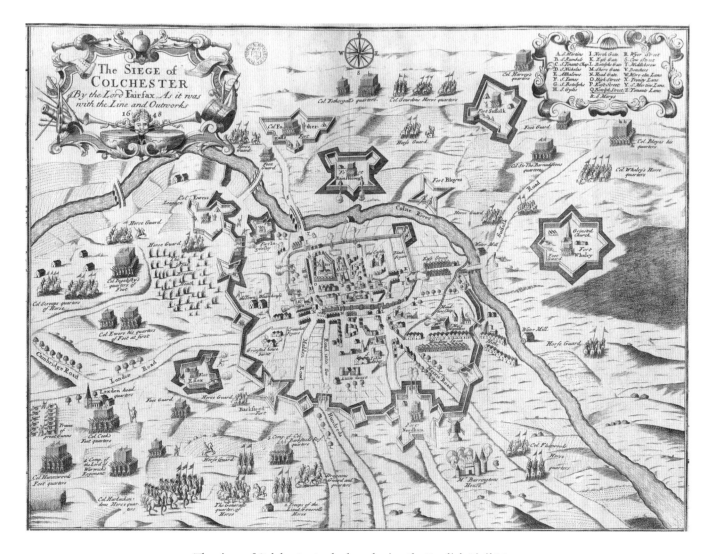

The siege of Colchester took place during the English Civil War;
the town was held by Royalist forces and besieged for many weeks by Parliamentarians
under the command of Lord Fairfax.

and large-scale military maps and exact surveys of battles and fortifications were produced both so as to train officers and for carrying out
operations. The 1716 manuscript plan of Portsmouth highlighting its
fortifications, shown on the previous page, is anonymous and came to
the Bodleian as part of the Gough collection. It is common for maps
of this type to be hand drawn, as having a large number of copies was
undesirable; the map would be a danger if it fell into enemy hands.

Maps of military engagements are also made to communicate about
the war to those at home. In the case of an unpopular war, anything that
can glorify victory (or, if desperate, defeat) is useful. Early broadsheet

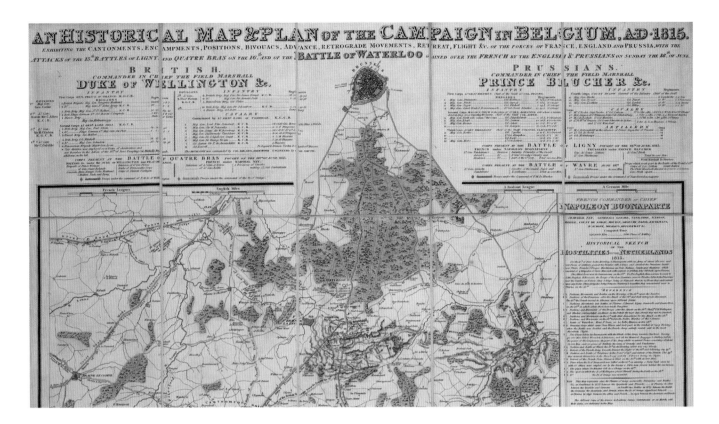

This map of the 'campaign in Belgium, AD 1815', including the Battle of Waterloo, was marketed to those who wanted to visit the scene of the action the succeeding year.

publications (separately published individual sheets) from the seventeenth and eighteenth centuries sometimes included topical maps of battles and sieges. The map of the siege of Colchester in 1648, shown opposite, is surrounded by text giving a detailed account of events. From the early eighteenth century, small-scale maps showing the 'theatre of war' – often an entire country or continent – were published in increasing numbers. During the American War of Independence, maps of military engagements (albeit not very good ones) were sometimes available in London within days of the news arriving, to inform a public agog for up-to-date information. The extract here from a map of the fields of battle in Belgium, including Waterloo, was published in London in March 1816, a few months after the victory; it is described as an 'historical map'. Maps of a battle or siege were often made on the spot by military officers. The Waterloo map claims to have been made by a 'near observer'. This can be compared with the extract from the map of the 1863 Battle of Gettysburg.

The latter was made in 1876 and 'reduced from one … deposited in the Archives of the office of the Chief of Engineers' (below).

The Crimean War of the 1850s is regarded as a milestone in terms of communication between the front lines and the civilian population. Innovations such as the electric telegraph kept the general public more up to date than had previously been possible. The Bodleian holds contemporary maps of the siege of Sevastopol published in the United States; interest in the war was not confined to those countries directly involved. The example opposite, showing the city's defences, has a handwritten note addressing it to the *Boston Post*, although its place of publication is unknown. A contemporary map and drawing of the siege of Kars also feature in this chapter.

Reasonably detailed accurate mapping now exists for most of the world's land. Technological advances since the early twentieth century

In this extract from a map depicting the second day of the Battle of Gettysburg, Little Round Top (successfully held by Union forces) can be seen. Union troop positions are shown in blue, Confederate in red.

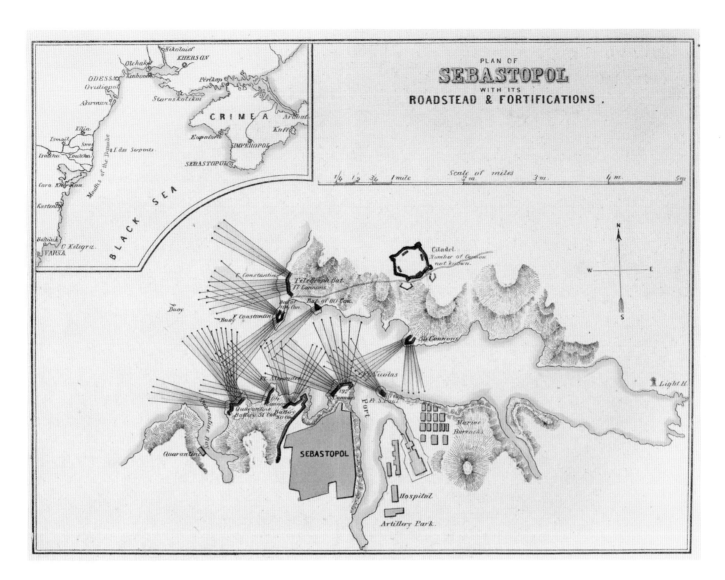

Sea approaches to the port of Sevastopol were heavily defended during the Crimean War.

have helped enable this. Aerial photography has long been crucial for military reconnaissance, as detailed in this chapter in relation to the maps produced to show the defences of Cherbourg in 1944. Techniques developed for military purposes are often used subsequently for civilian mapping. In many countries, national surveys were initially carried out by military organizations, and for some this is still the case. The situation in the United Kingdom and the United States, where separate civilian and military mapping organizations exist, is common but not universal. Detailed maps, especially of disputed border areas, may still be restricted from public sale even in the era of satellite imagery.

The siege of Dumbarton Castle

The map is among the papers of James Butler (1610–1688), 1st Duke of Ormond. In 1640 he was Earl of Ormond and second in command of the Irish army under Thomas Wentworth, Earl of Strafford. The Presbyterian Covenanters had rebelled against Charles I's religious policies, and from 1639 to 1640 fought the 'Bishops' Wars' against the king. A plan was hatched to bring an army over from Ireland to attack the Covenanters. Dumbarton would have been an ideal landing point, and so in the summer of 1640 the Covenanters laid siege to the royal castle. Strafford wished to land a force to raise the siege, and this map must have been used at a discussion about strategy. A carefully drawn chart forms the basis of the map, with shoals and soundings plotted, and a number of places marked, including the 'Moll of Cantire', 'Aren' and Bute, 'Grinock' and 'Dunburton' and its castle. On this Ormond scribbled numerous notes to highlight military, political and geographical factors which might help or obstruct the proposed expedition. Glasgow was not included in the original chart, but Ormond extended the Clyde and added 'Glaskoe. Hold this Towne from Trade and hinder them from fishinge'.

The power in the region was Archibald Campbell (1607–1661), 8th Earl of Argyll and chief of Clan Campbell, a leading Covenanter. His strongpoints are noted on the map, including his 'shipp of 16 piece of ordenance, 160 tunn built of one decke for saylinge', which lies in the mouth of the Clyde opposite Arran. Fresh intelligence has been added to the map, such as the fact that Argyll 'hath carried 5 faucons [falcons, a kind of cannon] to his house th[a]t stands in a laught [loch] which is his safety uppon a retreate'. This presumably refers to Inverary Castle on Loch Fyne, a sea loch extending north from the Sound of Bute. 'Magrigories Hilanders' appear in various places. The MacGregors, as outlaws dispossessed of their lands, and as Catholics, would be natural allies against the Campbells. In the channel between Arran and Kintyre, Ormond has noted the presence of MacGregors with '100 small boates which lie uppon the passages … armed with small shotts, pistols, bowes and arroes'. The lands of the royalist peers Hamilton and Lennox are also marked. On the far left-hand side of the map appears the name 'Knokfargis', the ancient name for Carrickfergus in the north of Ireland, the point of departure for the expedition.

Further documents in MS. Carte 1 provide details of how the expedition was to be undertaken. A memorandum from Captain John Taverner of around 1 July 1640 demands 'three or fowre boates … with twelve men a peece and oares to rowe, if the wind should not serve them to sayle'. He also wishes to have 'one of his Majestie's shipps to guard him as farr as the Isle of Bute, and farther if occasion require'. He then states that 'he makes noe question (notwithstanding any impediment the Covenanters have made in the River of Clyd to hinder this designe) to releive the Castle of Donbarton within 48 howers after he setts out of Knockfergus with a faire winde'.

The expedition never set out; Argyll's preparations, and military defeat elsewhere, made the attempt at first too difficult, and then pointless. Dumbarton Castle held out until shortly after Royalist forces had been defeated by the Covenanters at Newburn Ford in Northumberland, 28 August 1640.

MS. Carte 1, fols. 333v-334r

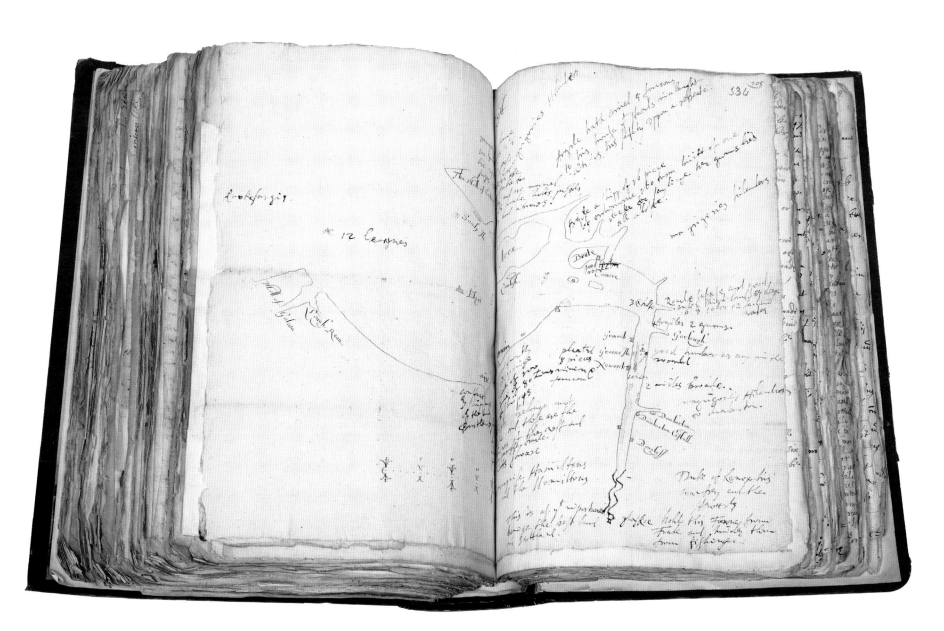

Conflict and trade on the Gold Coast

Europeans had long known that the gold circulating in North Africa had been transported across the Sahara from West Africa. In the 1480s the Portuguese became the first Europeans to establish forts on the coast of Guinea. A century later, other European nations followed. Eventually the Dutch, Swedes, Danes, French, English (in 1662) and Prussians acquired trading settlements along what became known as the Gold Coast.

These forts changed hands frequently. Sometimes they were exchanged but most often they fell into the possession of another nation (occasionally African) as a result of direct conflict. The English were relative late-comers, but by 1872 they had gained control of all the forts along the Gold Coast. This was finally achieved through a series of complex treaties that put an end to the Anglo-Dutch wars in Europe and defined spheres of British and Dutch influence in Asia, South America and the Caribbean.

The Gold Coast Survey Department's map shows the location of many of these trading settlements and the approximate tribal divisions existing in 1700. There is no mention of any commodities that were traded. The record of the occupying nation and the date each fort changed hands is a simple and unadorned document of the history of European struggles in foreign lands.

It is interesting to compare this historical summary to an eighteenth-century map – Boulton's *Chart of the Gold Coast*. This first appears as an inset on d'Anville's map of Africa, published by Robert Sayer in 1772, and then inset on Boulton's 1787 wall map of Africa (an updating of the d'Anville map). This wall map was later adapted to appear in Sayer and Kitchin's *Universal Atlas* of 1792. The same copious notes accompany all the maps. This publishing history illustrates the astuteness of Robert Sayer. The updating of maps, using the name of the highly respected d'Anville in all the titles, and re-use of material all helped cover the initial high cost of engraving.

The inset map itself gives some historical context but is more of a snapshot of the Gold Coast in the 1760s. The elaborate notes discuss the types of gold produced, its value to the Dutch and English, and the European's view of the indigenous peoples:

The land of Awine produces a great quantity of Gold and its Inhabitants are reputed the Civilest and fairest Dealers .... The Soil of the Gold Coast is very fertile and abounds with all sorts of Fruit; The European Inhabitants never the less Complain very much of ye unwholesomeness of the air, and give the worst character to the Natives.

Is this a criticism of the European trader, or a veiled criticism of a commerce that everybody knew about but did not want to mention?

The notes accompanying the main map of Africa give more information: 'English Traders export abundance of Slaves from Angola' as they cost less than in Guinea.

These poor creatures are packed as close as Herrings 7 or 800 in a Ship ... kept with no better food than Horse beans, tho' their profit should induce the merchant to use them well. For a Slave purchased for three or four pounds a head is worth 20 or 25 pounds in America.

It is worth remembering that these notes were first published in 1772 – a decade before the Quakers presented the first slave trade petition to Parliament. Some mapmakers may have been early Abolitionists.

E34 (195) & Allen LRO 14

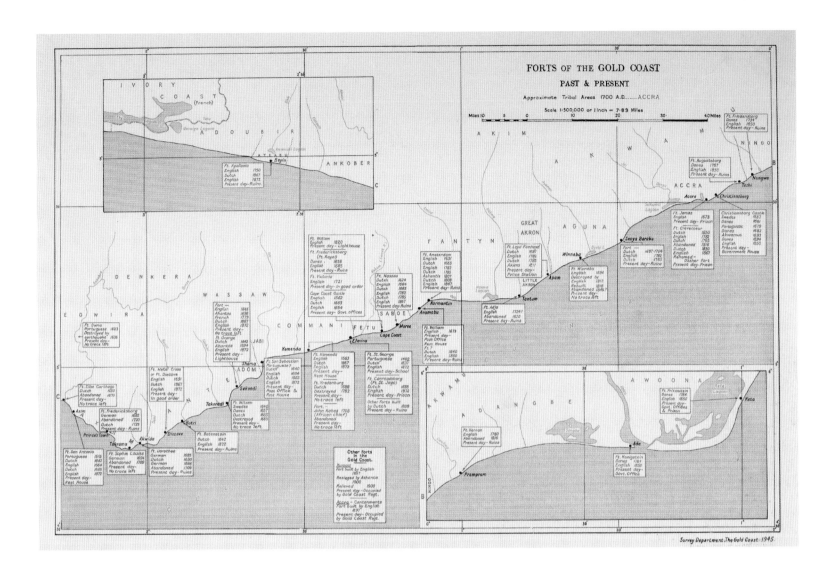

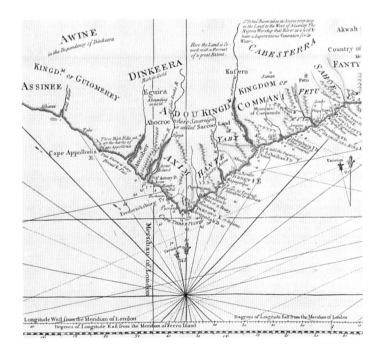

Headline news: San Fernando de Omoa

In late 1779, as the outcome of the war in the American colonies grew less and less certain, reports of the British capture of a Spanish fort in the Caribbean and with it 2 million silver dollars were received in Whitehall with great jubilation. The fact that San Fernando de Omoa was abandoned a mere five weeks later was of no great interest to London propagandists. The story of a daring British night-time escalade up the walls of a mighty fortress was celebrated for months. The apocryphal tale of a Jack Tar gallantly offering his cutlass to an unarmed Spanish defender began as a satire but years later featured in popular English histories. At Quantrell's Gardens in Norwich, on the king's birthday, the battle was lavishly re-enacted in a firework display involving 'fireships' – there were no fireships at Omoa.

Such was the enthusiasm for the news that, the very day after the British commander's report arrived, the *London Gazette* printed all six pages of it as the lead story of their 18 December edition. Within a month, the exhaustive account was republished in at least two gentlemen's magazines as well as *The Annual Register*. It was only natural that a plan of the battle should be commissioned, and Robert Sayer and John Bennett (successors to the famous Thomas Jefferys) instantly met the demand.

In their haste to illustrate a breaking story, they committed two major cartographic errors.

Their base map copies Joseph Smith Speer's hydrographic chart from *The West-India Pilot* (1766). Unfortunately, his north arrow in fact points west! Sayer and Bennett unwittingly transferred this blunder into their own work – their north arrow should point 'up'.

The more unfortunate error is in the map's subject-matter. Sayer and Bennett evidently worked without the benefit even of an eyewitness's sketch. The fortifications at Omoa actually comprised two structures – an earlier rectangular fort (El Reale) and a later fort with an unusual triangular form, one curtain wall parallel to the seafront and three landward bastions. The seaward wall was dramatically curved outwards, supposedly to brace it against storm surges. The fortress's unconventional design intrigued the occupying British officers, who produced a detailed drawing (B).

Sayer and Bennett did not show any of this in their plan. Instead, their fort is a stereotypical square-shaped bastioned fortress, with three landward ravelins. Interestingly, this is not pure fiction. Their seaward wall is not recessed behind the bastions but is instead bowed slightly outwards. This is virtually identical to an early design concept for the fort, indicated on a 1757 manuscript map (tracing A) drawn by its architect, Francisco Alvarez, and subsequently abandoned. Sayer and Bennett even show a detail of the fort as an inset – all of it completely wrong! However, the fact that they drew the seaward wall in the curved configuration strongly suggests that they had access to Alvarez's early design for the fort, which would probably have constituted a Spanish state secret. The concurrence of the two errors proves that they consulted (and ignored) the accurate as-built depiction of the fort on Speer's 1766 map.

---

536 t.1 (1)

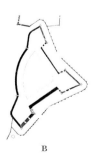

A   B

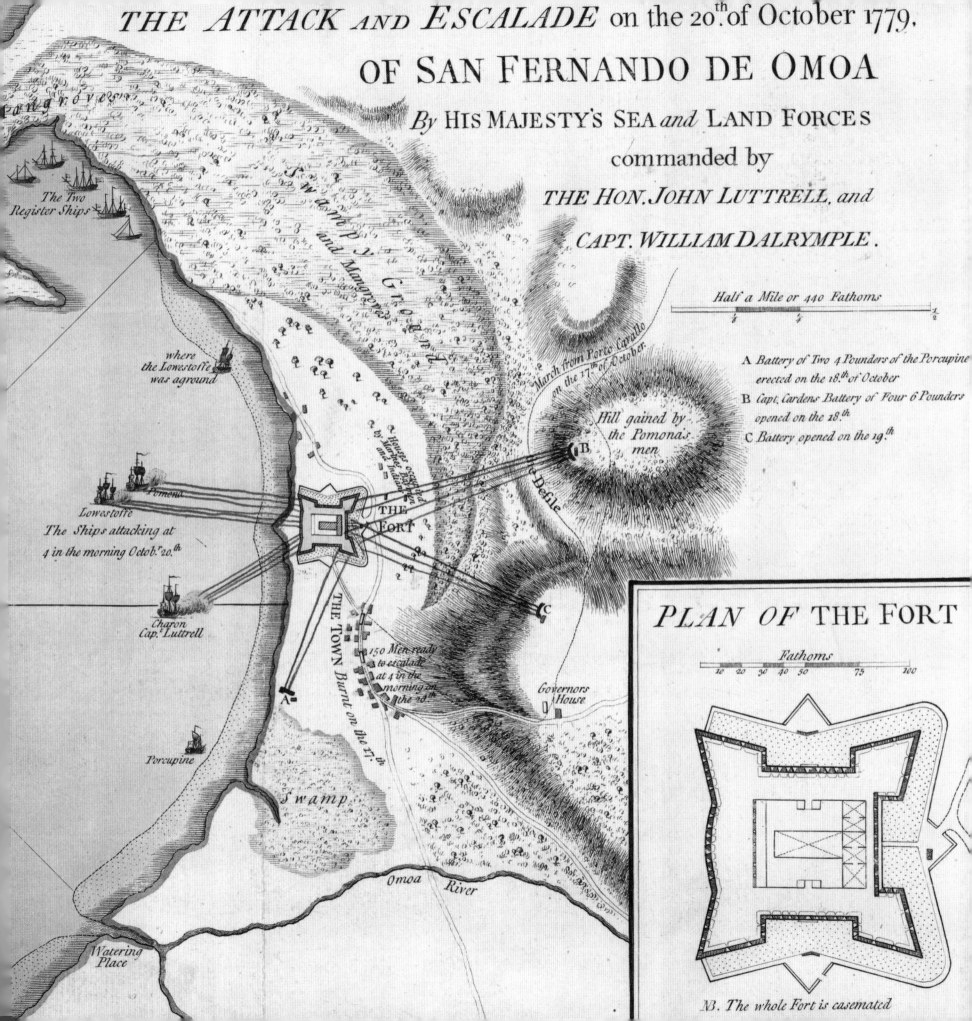

THE ATTACK AND ESCALADE on the 20th of October 1779,

OF SAN FERNANDO DE OMOA

By HIS MAJESTY'S SEA and LAND FORCES

commanded by

THE HON. JOHN LUTTRELL, and

CAPT. WILLIAM DALRYMPLE.

Pangrove

The Two Register Ships

Swampy Ground and Mangrove

where the Lowestoffe was aground

Half a Mile or 440 Fathoms

March from Porto Cavallo on the 17th of October

Hill gained by the Pomona's men

A Battery of Two 4 Pounders of the Porcupine erected on the 18th of October

B Capt. Cardens Battery of Four 6 Pounders opened on the 18th

C Battery opened on the 19th

Pomona

Lowestoffe

The Ships attacking at 4 in the morning Octobr. 20th

Houses occupied by Marine Piquet and Indians

Defile

THE Fort

Charon Capt. Luttrell

THE TOWN Burnt on the 17th

150 Men ready to escalade at 4 in the morning on the 20th

Governors House

A

Porcupine

Swamp

PLAN OF THE FORT

Fathoms

10 20 30 40 50 75 100

Omoa River

Watering Place

NB. The whole Fort is casemated

The last invasion of Britain

This map illustrates the Battle of Fishguard, the last invasion of Great Britain by foreign troops. The event was something of a damp squib, beginning on 22 February 1797 and ending with the surrender of the invading troops two days later.

The action took place on the coast of Pembrokeshire in Wales. A French invasion force of up to 1,400 troops landed at Carregwastad Head ('Cerrig Gwastad Point' on the map). This is just around the headland from the small town and port of Fishguard, which was defended by a fort. The aim was to invade Great Britain as part of an attack in support of Republican forces in Ireland, during the War of the First Coalition. About 800 of the invading troops were 'irregulars', including convicts; these were undisciplined and many soon deserted, looting surrounding properties and getting drunk. A hastily assembled force of local militias and volunteers under Lord Cawdor set out to repel the invaders the following day, but were forced to retreat by gathering dusk. That evening, however, Cawdor managed to negotiate a French surrender, exaggerating the size of his own outnumbered forces. The French troops surrendered and laid down their arms on the beach at Fishguard the next morning, 24 February. It was said that, as locals gathered to watch, the French troops mistook the Welsh women in their traditional red cloaks and tall hats for soldiers, and were further led to believe that they were outnumbered. This may also serve partly to explain how local women, led by Jemima Nichols, who remains a local heroine, managed to round up twelve drunken French soldiers and imprison them in the church. There was a small number of deaths and injuries resulting from minor skirmishes between French soldiers and locals, but overall there were few casualties.

The map does a good job of illuminating the rather chaotic situation. A letter key refers to the landing point, the routes taken by both sets of forces, and the point of surrender in chronological order, giving a clearer sense of the progress of the invasion than can be acquired from written accounts alone. The map has a large scale (around 5 inches to the mile) and shows in detail the landscape that the troops had to cross between their landing point and Fishguard itself. This consisted of narrow lanes, isolated farms and settlements, small fields (their boundaries lightly indicated), steep hills and marshland. Individual buildings are shown within the farmsteads and towns, a few of the more important ones pictorially. The locations of skirmishes are shown, with numbers of those killed or injured; sadly there is no mention of Jemima Nichols's exploits. The map is dedicated to Lord Cawdor. The list of troops below the dedication includes 'His Lordship's Troop of Yeomen Cavalry, a detachment of the Cardigan Militia' and goes on to list two troops of Fencible Infantry, two companies of seamen, 'besides several hundred Gentlemen Volunteers and others'. Certainly anyone available in the area was pressed into service and many volunteered willingly.

The map was drawn by Thomas Propert, a local mapmaker who is otherwise known only for a few local surveys. It was published by him in Llanryan near Haverfordwest, and also in London by four major London publishers (Bowyer, Faden, Cary and Wilkinson). The date of publication on the map, 24 February 1798, was clearly chosen to commemorate the anniversary of the victory.

(E) C17:50 (13)

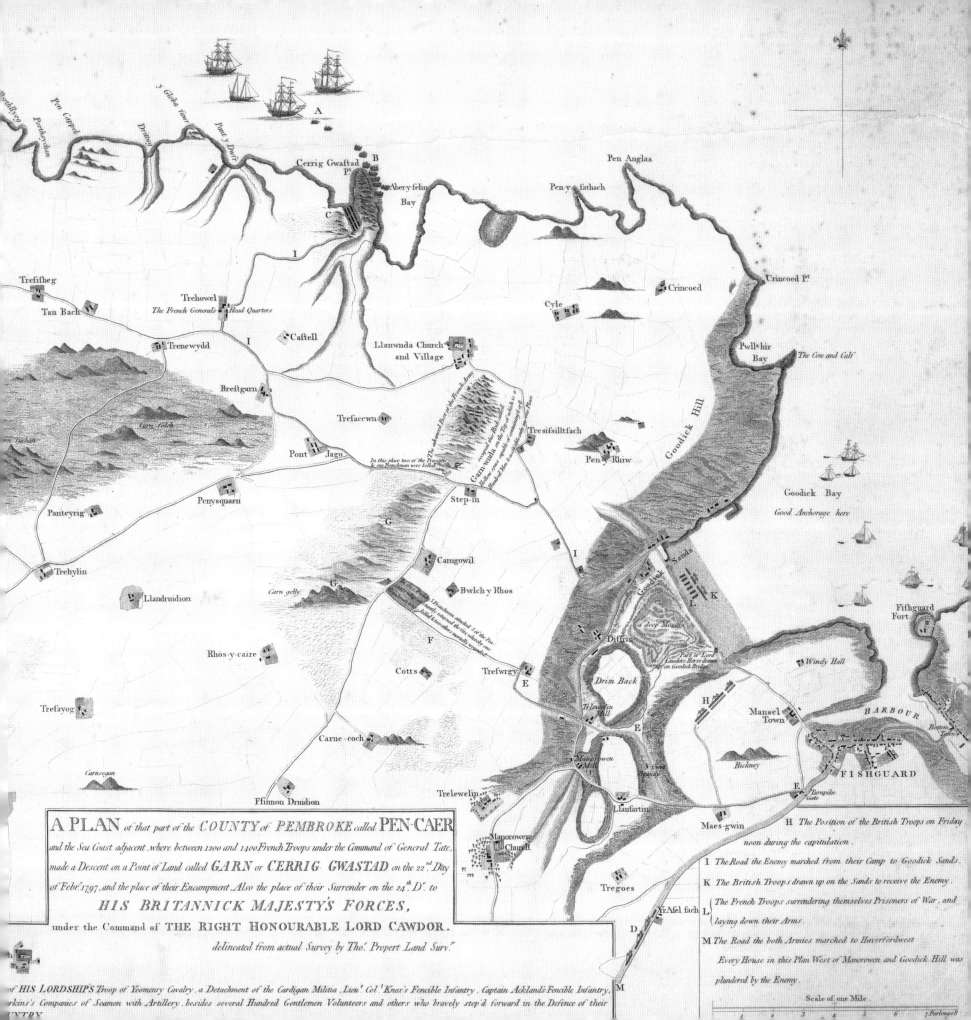

A
y Globe fawr
Porthbychan
Pen Cappel
Drering
Pont y Dwfr
Bardilltog

Cerrig Gwastad Pt
B
Abery felin Bay
C
I

Pen Anglas
Pen-y-fathach
Crincoed Pt

Trefisheg
Tau Bach
Trehowel
The French Generals Head Quarters
I
Castell
Trenewydd
Bresgarn
Trefaccwn
Llanwnda Church and Village

Crincoed
Cyle

Pwll-hir Bay
The Cow and Calf

Carn folch
Pont Jago
In this place two of the Peasants & one Frenchman were killed
The advanced Post of the French Army
Garnwnda *on the Top of which is a Hollow space capable of containing 6 or 800 Men & secure from every thing but Bombs*
Step-in

Tresifsilltfach
Pen-y-Rhiw

Goodick Hill

Goodick Bay
Good Anchorage here

Panteyrig
Penysquarn
G

Carn gelly
G
Carngowil
Bwlch y Rhos
3 Frenchmen attacked 5 of the Peasants, who instantly returned the fire whereby one was killed & another mortally wounded

Goodick Sands
K
L

Fishguard Fort

Trehylin
Llandruidion

Rhos-y-caire
F
Cotts
Trefwrgy
E

Diffrin
a deep Marsh
Part of Lord Cawdors Horse drawn up on Goodick Bridge

Windy Hall

Trefayog
Carne-coch

Drim Back
Trelewelin Mill
E
H
Mansel Town
HARBOUR

Manorowen Mill
Bickney
Bottom Town

Carnsegan
Ffinnon Druidion
Trelewelin
Llanfartin
Manorowen Church
E
Turnpike Gate
FISHGUARD

Maes-gwin
Tregoes
Yr Afel fach
D
M

A PLAN *of that part of the* COUNTY *of* PEMBROKE *called* PEN-CAER
*and the Sea Coast adjacent, where between 1200 and 1400 French Troops under the Command of General Tate,
made a Descent on a Point of Land called* GARN *or* CERRIG GWASTAD *on the 22nd Day
of Febr. 1797, and the place of their Encampment. Also the place of their Surrender on the 24th Do. to*
HIS BRITANNICK MAJESTY'S FORCES,
under the Command of THE RIGHT HONOURABLE LORD CAWDOR.
delineated from actual Survey by Thos. Propert Land Survr.

H *The Position of the British Troops on Friday
noon during the capitulation.*

I *The Road the Enemy marched from their Camp to Goodick Sands.*

K *The British Troops drawn up on the Sands to receive the Enemy.*

L *The French Troops surrendering themselves Prisoners of War, and
laying down their Arms.*

M *The Road the both Armies marched to Haverfordwest
Every House in this Plan West of Manorowen and Goodick Hill was
plundered by the Enemy.*

of HIS LORDSHIP'S *Troop of Yeomenry Cavalry, a Detachment of the Cardigan Militia, Lieut. Col. Knox's Fencible Infantry, Captain Ackland's Fencible Infantry,
..rkins's Companies of Seamen with Artillery, besides several Hundred Gentlemen Volunteers and others who bravely step'd forward in the Defence of their
..NTRY.*

Scale of one Mile.

A city under siege

Mention the Crimean War and thoughts automatically turn to the Crimea itself, to the charge of the Light Brigade and the siege of Sevastopol. Tension between the Russian and Ottoman Empires had been steadily increasing in the years leading up to the war, and fears of Russian control in the Black Sea drew an alliance of British, French, Ottoman and Sardinian forces to launch a combined attack against the Russian naval base in Sevastopol in 1854. In an attempt to alleviate the pressure building against Sevastopol, Russian troops moved against Ottoman troops in Anatolia the following year, in the process laying siege to the strategically important city of Kars.

Kars has had a turbulent history, fought over by Russians, Turks and Armenians. Now in the northeast corner of Turkey, at one time it was the capital of the Armenian state, after which control of the city was held by the Byzantine Empire, the Georgians, the Mongol Empire under the leadership of Tamerlane, until it was captured by the Ottomans in 1534.

This map, *Plan of the Fortress of Kars shewing the detached works ...*, is dated 1855 and shows the defences and layout of the city at the time of the siege. It also shows, with a clever use of shading, the topography of the area. A gazetteer from 1856 describes Kars thus: 'Its citadel is built of unhewn stone, and lines the face of a steep hill, at the foot of which the straggling town commences but is commanded by heights within musket range, on the opposite side of the deep ravine in which the Arpachai runs. Two stone bridges unite the two portions of the city divided by the river'.

On 29 September 1855 Russian troops attacked from the west. In a battle lasting seven hours and starting before first light Russian losses greatly exceeded those of the defenders and, despite capturing a number of the defensive positions shown on the map to the north and northwest of the city, Russian troops were unable to hold them. After prolonged and heavy fighting they were forced into general retreat. Artillery from numerous batteries (shown on the map as '*Tabias*', the Turkish word for entrenchments or batteries) played a part, as the Anglo-Turkish forces were able to use the high ground to their advantage. The Russians were compelled to fire their artillery up the slope they were attacking, often at targets out of sight, and a large number of their shells fell amongst their own troops.

Included below is a pictorial map of the attack on 29 September ((E) D30:80 Kars (3)). The battery in the foreground is seemingly a safe distance away from enemy action but actually one of the few sites where the defenders suffered casualties that day.

(E) D30:80 Kars (1)

ARMAMENT.

Nº	Names of Forts.										
1	Hafiz Pasha Tabia			1			1				6
2	Koltuk					1					
3	Karadagh				4				1		2
4	Arab				4						
5	Teesdale			1	1						
6	Thompson				1						
7	Zohrab			1	1						
8	Churchill										2
9	Williams Pasha										
10	Fort Lake	1	1	1			2		1		1
11	Laz Tabia										
12	Tetek										3
13	Rennison Lines										
14	Shabanadja			2			2				
15	Yuksek Tabia										
16	Yarimti			1			2				
17	Tachmash				2						
18	Tachmash Lines							2			
19	Vasuf Pasha Tabia	1	2	2		1					6
20	Tek										2
21	Suwarri										
22	Kanli	1	1				2				6
23	Feyzi Bey			2							
24	Yeni			2							
25	Lelek										
26	Yussuf Pasha										
27	Chichek										
28	Chatlak										
29	Teli										
30	Citadel										
A	Forts constructed										
B	since the Battle										
C											
	Reserve										5
	TOTAL	2	8	5	20	23	1	7	2	2	54

Mapping the Dardanelles campaign

Maps are an essential tool used by those who fight campaigns. When that tool is found wanting the finger of blame is quick to point, and when commanders fail the map is a convenient scapegoat.

In the Second Boer War, Cape Colony – let alone the Boer Republics of Orange Free State and Transvaal – was largely unmapped, and the inadequacies of the skeleton quarter-inch maps of South Africa, and others made by the War Office Intelligence Department, were subject to deep enquiries by the Boer War Commission

The Dardanelles Commission, appointed to investigate the disastrous failure of the invasion of Gallipoli in 1916 during World War I, also addressed map inadequacies and its *Official History* labours the point of poor maps. Without doubt, the three-sheet 1:40,000 scale map provided for the landings, based on a French reconnaissance map made en route to the Crimean War, was inaccurate and lacking in detail.

Soon afterwards, however, Turkish 1:25,000 maps were found on captured or dead Turkish soldiers. These were sent to the Survey of Egypt in Cairo, where they were copied and reproduced at 1:20,000 scale. The Ottoman script was removed. English place and feature names were added and map squares included for position referencing. A series of seven sheets, named 'Gallipoli 1:20,000', covering the whole of the area of operations, with the military series designation GSGS 4000, was introduced for operational use on the peninsula just in time for the early August offensives at Anzac Cove and Suvla Bay.

The new series was a decided improvement on the empty and inaccurate 1:40,000 scale series and was well received. In his September *Report on Operations between 6 July and 5 August*, General Godley, commanding the New Zealand and Australia Division stated: 'A new map of portions of the Gallipoli Peninsula was issued and brought into use on the 1 August. It is a great improvement on the old one and has proved to be very accurate.'

For the demanding night march and dawn assault on the dominant hill-features of Chunuk Bair and Sari Bair in the ANZAC sector, an enlargement of part of the 1:20,000 scale map to 1:10,000 scale was made and printed by the Printing Section RE based at GHQ on Imbros Island. The 'Gallipoli' series was later superseded by an extended 'Dardanelles' series of eighteen sheets, which included a geographical graticule (a network of lines representing latitude and longitude).

That these series were found reasonably accurate is not surprising because they were direct copies of a Turkish defensive survey made in the years immediately preceding the war and thus were probably the most up-to-date maps used in World War I. A Mapping Section of the Turkish General Staff, headed by Colonel Shevki Pasha, had been established in 1895 with the responsibility of observing a triangulation (the accurately surveyed control point that provided the base for the survey) and producing topographic maps of the whole of the Ottoman Empire with priority given to the strategic defence areas.

Ayia Sophia Mosque in Istanbul was the geodetic datum for the triangulation, but an independent triangulation, each with its own base line, was established for each of the key areas of Rumelia, the Dardanelles, Erzerum, and the Chatalja Lines and eastern approaches to Istanbul. At the same time, a rapid reconnaissance survey for 1:200,000 scale maps was also started in order to achieve country-wide medium-scale cover while the more detailed 1:25,000 surveys were in progress.

This wholly Turkish mapping programme was a very considerable achievement. In comparison with similar British series of the period, the specification and content of both the 1:25,000 and 1:200,000 series were extremely detailed.

At the end of the war copies of all available Turkish military maps were procured by the British Geographical Section, General Staff, and both the 1:25,000 series and the 1:200,000 reconnaissance series remained the basis for British military maps of Turkey until beyond the end of World War II.

D30:3 (20) 385

Trench maps

Trench maps are an important source of information regarding topography, defences and changes in the position of front lines in World War I. They are also, for those looking back at the war from the distance that a century brings, a stark representation of how close enemy forces were to each other. Detailed maps such as the one shown here reveal a no-man's land often less than 100 metres across. At first maps were based on existing French and Belgian pre-war sheets, but problems with marrying up scales and grids used on these sheets meant that by late 1914 the War Office and the Ordnance Survey took over production of trench maps, and from then until the end of the war a large number of sheets of different scales and designs were published to meet the varying demands of the British Army.

The development of trench warfare in late 1914 meant a fairly static front-line position. This, along with increasing importance in the use of artillery, led to both a need for accurate mapping of enemy positions and the time in which to produce the maps. Trenches that did not move and positions that stayed stable for months at a time meant that surveying, mainly by aerial observation and photography, produced maps that were often available before any changes in territory held made them obsolete, though this was not always the case during the major offensives launched later in the war. For instance,

a map produced by the War Office for the Passchendaele area went through nine different editions during the Third Battle of Ypres between July and December 1917.

Detailed trench maps such as the one featured here were crucial in the role that artillery played in the conflict. Important enemy positions were marked on maps with red circles and positions were given by using, first, the number in the square and then the lines along the edge of the square, called 'tick lines', in the text along the right-hand side of the map, to break the square up into ten imaginary areas, and finally the red circled number. This may seem a confusing system but it allowed for coordination between different groups within the army, infantry and artillery or high command for instance, to plot manoeuvres or to focus on important targets in enemy territory.

The map featured here is one sheet in a large series covering the Western Front in great detail, at a scale of 1:10,000 (the map is reproduced here at a reduced size). For security reasons only the front lines of the British trenches are shown while the full range of the German trenches is clearly defined in red. As well as British-produced maps, the Bodleian's map collection includes maps by the French and German armies of the Western Front and Allied and Turkish trench maps from the Gallipoli campaign in 1916.

C1 (3) [1449] Sheet 57D N.E. parts 1 & 2

Planning for invasion

During World War II, before German forces advanced into enemy territory officers in the army would use pamphlets such as the one shown here to help plan the occupation of invaded countries and to provide information on the local population and its dialect, customs and language. The pamphlets were created by the Generalstab des Heeres, the General Staff of the German army, and published in Berlin. They covered all the countries in Europe, as well as those in the Middle East and North Africa. Neutral countries such as Spain and German allies such as Italy and Romania were included. In most cases there were one or two packs per country but for some key areas there were numerous parts. Fourteen volumes covered England and Wales, while it took twenty-three to cover the Soviet Union.

The packs include a book of photographs of key strategic points – railway stations, bridges, docks and industrial areas – and information on the economic, social and transport conditions of the country, as well as gazetteers, translations of key phrases and maps. These books were usually compiled by academics familiar with the country in question and often used existing maps, which were then overprinted with additional information highlighting important points – bridges, stations, hospitals and civic buildings, for example.

The pamphlet shown here is the pack covering Poland issued in July 1939 and was one of the first of these invasion plans produced. Early packs were housed in a strong red case, but soon production switched to a cheaper card version, possibly as a result of the increased production of the packs required to cover the growing territorial ambitions of the German army and its leaders.

Despite there being a large number of maps of Germany and German cities and towns made by the Allies, there is no equivalent booklet published by Allied forces in the Bodleian collection. There is, though, something similar for British troops fighting on the Italian front in 1917. *Notes on the Italian Theatre of War and short vocabulary* includes, as well as a map of the area, a brief history of the war, a short piece on Italian customs, money, army dress and wine ('Italian wines are more potent than might be imagined'). There is also an English-Italian dictionary, including important phrases such as 'I want stabling for 16 horses', 'Tell all the people not to be afraid' and 'Undress yourself'.

As with many of the items featured in this book there is a heavy weight of history attached to these packs. Many feature one or more of the official stamps used by the different military organizations, while a few have written additions in pen or pencil by officers and soldiers of the Third Reich. When viewing them you cannot help wondering at their path through the conflict and their fate.

At the end of the war a large number of German maps, books and packs were captured by Allied forces, and have since been donated to academic institutions.

C31 e.1

KRAKAU

World War II silk escape maps

This map dates from 1943 and is part of a set of military escape maps printed on silk. This might seem a surprising material with which to make a military map but it had many practical advantages.

The very earliest known military silk map is from China and dates from the second century BCE, and there are a few examples of silk maps from the intervening centuries, but it was with the outbreak of World War II that silk military maps were produced in large numbers. The December 1939 formation of MI9, a ministry within the British War Office for escape and evasion, marked a sea change in the attitude to prisoners of war. Previously it had been considered somewhat shameful to be taken prisoner, but after World War I the authorities came to the view that captured servicemen should be helped and encouraged to escape; they could bring back valuable information as well as returning to help the war effort.

The World War II military maps were initially the inspiration of Christopher Clayton Hutton at MI9, a creative though eccentric individual. He realised that if air crew carried silk (rather than paper) maps they could be concealed easily on the body, would still be serviceable when wet and could help pilots landing behind enemy lines to find a way to safety. Hutton faced various challenges in putting the plan into practice: even though the mapmaker John Bartholomew generously donated all the necessary small-scale mapping, there was some difficulty in printing a clear image on silk. He enlisted the help of John Waddington Ltd, the games manufacturer, which had had experience of printing silk theatre programmes; their involvement in the serious endeavour

of military map printing remained secret for decades afterwards. Hutton also devised a number of other ingenious escape aids that air crew could carry, including buttons that concealed a miniature compass, small kits of emergency rations and hollow-heeled flying boots in which a map could be hidden.

The first series of small-scale maps of parts of Europe was augmented with a set covering the border areas of Norway and Sweden at the larger scale of 1:100,000. Waddingtons also assisted in the printing of 1:1,000,000 scale maps of the European theatre of war in 1943, one of which is shown here, and of East Asia in 1944. After the supply of silk ran short (most of it was needed for parachutes) other materials such as rayon and mulberry leaf paper were used. The United States began printing its own escape maps on rayon from 1942 after a contingent of American intelligence officers visited the UK.

One of the aims of MI9 was to maintain the morale of those taken prisoner. As well as items that could be carried by those on active service, great efforts were made to smuggle silk maps to inmates of prisoner-of-war camps. The maps and other escape aids such as local currency were often disguised as parcels from fictitious charitable organizations. Some prisoners of war made copies of their maps for other prisoners, in one or two cases even managing to construct a basic printing press for this purpose. An estimated 35,000 Allied service personnel managed to escape and return home from behind enemy lines; many more must have been encouraged by the hope of escape and the possibility of constructive action while held in the most discouraging and tedious of circumstances.

(F) C1 (597)

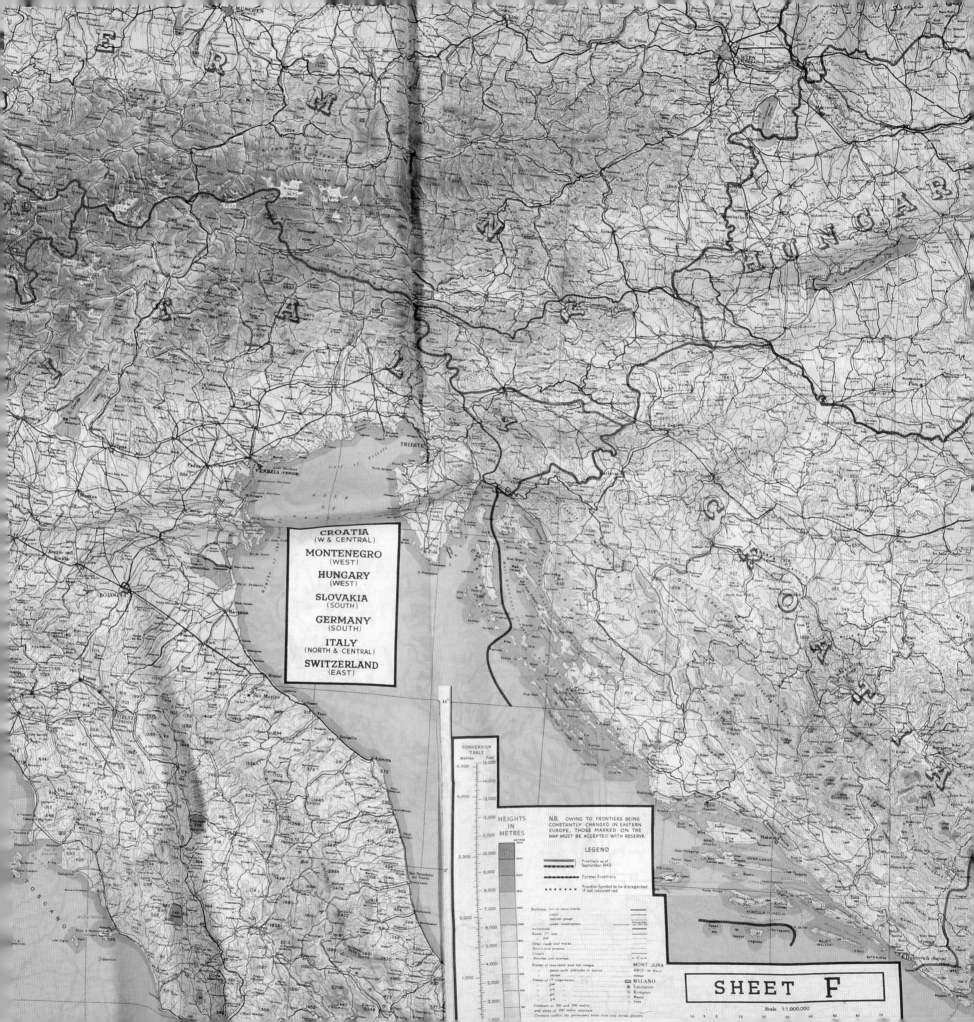

CROATIA
(W & CENTRAL)

MONTENEGRO
(WEST)

HUNGARY
(WEST)

SLOVAKIA
(SOUTH)

GERMANY
(SOUTH)

ITALY
(NORTH & CENTRAL)

SWITZERLAND
(EAST)

CONVERSION
TABLE
Metres   Feet
4,500 —— 15,000

4,000 —— 13,000
       —— 12,000

HEIGHTS
IN
METRES

N.B.   OWING TO FRONTIERS BEING
CONSTANTLY CHANGED IN EASTERN
EUROPE, THOSE MARKED ON THE
MAP MUST BE ACCEPTED WITH RESERVE.

LEGEND

Frontiers as at
September 1943

Former Frontiers

Frontier Symbol to be disregarded
if not coloured red

SHEET F

Scale 1:1,000,000

Maps for D-Day

Following the successful use of aerial photographs for revision of maps of the Western Front in World War I, the War Office set up an Air Survey Committee to devise methods by which military maps could be made from aerial photographs. Published in 1927, *Flying for Air Survey Photography* recommended a method that required parallel strips of overlapping vertical photographs to be taken with a Survey camera in order that large-scale maps for the artillery and infantry could be made by RE Survey units.

The RAF was naturally reluctant to commit to flying such cover over an enemy territory in Western Europe but agreed it might be acceptable in such countries as Afghanistan, and in the 1930s several such aerial surveys were carried out in the Middle East and Africa.

The wartime task was allocated to Army Co-operation Command, which was equipped with inadequate aircraft and, during the 'Phoney War' period, little survey quality photography of northwest France and Belgium was obtained. After Dunkirk the high-altitude Spitfire, and later the Mosquito, were used for the task

In 1942 planning commenced for 'Operation Overlord', the invasion of Normandy, and the Geographical Section of the General Staff, under Colonel Hotine, planned a new survey of Normandy and Brittany, later extended northeastwards beyond Paris, to provide accurate new maps at 1:25,000 scale.

The programme of aerial photography and map production which followed was named the 'Benson Project' after the RAF airfield where 140 Squadron RAF was based. The requirement for Survey-standard area cover was relaxed and any photography flown in strips, using the 12-inch focal length Fairchild K-8A.B. camera, taken at altitudes of 25–30,000 feet, was accepted.

The production was based on the 'Arundel Method', conceived by Hotine while in the Air Survey Committee, based on radial line plotting of detail along strips of photos. Mirror stereoscopes and parallax bars were used for contouring ground shown on the overlaps of pairs of photographs.

With the arrival of the American and Canadian survey units, slotted template equipment was used to densify plan control and Multiplex stereo-plotters were used for plotting detail and contouring.

An Air Survey Group was formed to produce the adjusted planimetric control for the mapping and from 1942 to June 1944 the American, British and Canadian Field Survey units compiled the maps.

Sheets of the Benson series, designated Series GSGS 4347, were constructed on the French Lambert Nord de Guerre grid, each sheet covering 15 × 10 km of ground. This size sheet could be printed on the lorry-mounted printing presses used in the field by Field Survey Companies, though bulk stocks were also printed by civilian print firms just in time for D-Day.

The series design met tactical operational requirements while keeping the production process simple and the number of colours minimal – black for detail and names, blue for water and brown for contours. The design included field boundaries, which proved invaluable during the close fighting in the *bocage* country.

It was essential that details of enemy defences should be depicted on the coastal sheets. The Army Photographic Interpretation Section, working in the Theatre Intelligence Section, interpreted the enemy defences which were depicted on the maps by the Field Survey Companies RE. Purple and orange Defences overprints on the topographic bases were in accordance with the Theatre Intelligence Section's 'Martian Legend', which was designed to provide standard military symbols easy for troops of the five Allied nations to understand. Top Secret 'BIGOT' Defences overprints were produced from the very latest photographic interpretation right up to the invasion date.

The accompanying map extract of the heavily defended port of Cherbourg shows that the Benson programme extended well beyond the Calvados coast.

C21(19B), sheet 31/22 S.W.

Querqueville

Fort de l'Ouest

Fort de Chavaignac

BELIEVED TO BE 138 m.m.
NAVAL GUNS OF WHICH
ONLY MOUNTINGS ARE
VISIBLE.

Fort Central

Fort de l'Est

Ile Pelee

Fort
de l'Ile Pelee

BUILT
CONCRETE

8 GUN MED BTY PRESENTLY IN
COURSE OF RECONSTRUCTION-
4 CONCRETE CASEMATES ARE U/C
N°5 GUN IS MASKED BY NEW CASEMATE

COMPLETED

DRY MOAT ROUND PORT MILITAIRE
FORMS ANTI-TANK DITCH

21 WEAPON PITS
ALONG RAMPARTS

EXCAVATIONS (DEMOLITIONS?)

Digue du Homet

Fort du Homet

Digue des Flamands

UNSPECIFIED
UNDER WATER
OBSTACLES

Pointe des Greves
SEA WALL
HEDGEHOGS

2
IN THIS AREA

ROADS LEADING NORTH & SOUTH
FROM RUE VAL de SAUVE ARE BLOCKED

EQUEURDREVILLE

BRIDGE DESTROYED
NEW BRIDGE U/C
UNCONFIRMED

GUN CASEMATES
75 GUN IN EACH

CHERBOURG

Bourbourg

SOUND
DETECTOR

CASEMATE
NOW COMPLETED

ON
TOWER

TURNTABLE FOR N°1 GUN
OBSTRUCTED BY SPOIL

TANK TURRET
UNCONFIRMED

5 ROWS
NO GAP

Hau
du Tot

STAKES

TANK TURRET

WRECK

HEDGE
CLEARANCE

RLY. CUTTING FORMS
A/T DITCH

DELETE CABLE
NEW LENGTHS AS SHOWN

TUNNELLING
OPERATIONS

TUNNELLING
OPERATIONS IN
FACE OF QUARRY

POSSIBLE TUNNELLING
IN SMALL QUARRY

THERE HAVE BEEN NUMEROUS REPORTS
OF RAILWAY GUNS IN THE TUNNELS

CAM COVERING
FOR PARKED M.T.

TOURLAVILLE

OCTEVILLE

OVERHEAD CABLE CONVEYOR

ABANDONED

DELETE 3
SUBSTITUTE
4 M.T BAYS
AS SHOWN

ROAD BLOCKED BY SPOIL

M.T. BAYS

Hau
Digard

ROAD
MINED

Hau
Gringor

UNDERGROUND
DUMP

RAILWAY LINES ENTER
THESE TUNNEL ENTRANCES

Tank 'Goings' Map

This map is an example of the links between Oxford University and the military during World War II. Material of this nature arrived in Oxford to support the war work of academics. This colourful sheet, Basra Sheet Iran-Iraq 1: 500,000 No. H-38/NE Geographical Section General Staff no. 4359, was published by the War Office in 1942. It is a Tank 'Goings' map, to indicate the terrain across which tanks could be driven, and it shows the Iraqi Marshes, which would have presented something of a challenge. 'Goings' maps were produced for many countries in Europe, North Africa and the Middle East.

Kenneth Mason, the first holder of the Chair in Geography at the university, was promoted to Lieutenant-Colonel; he had formerly been with the Survey of India and was the General Staff Officer for Intelligence in Mesopotamia in World War I. Combining his academic duties with work for the Inter-Services Topographical Division (ISTD) he was able to coordinate the efforts of the Oxford sub-centre of the Naval Intelligence Division in the production of seventeen of the thirty-one titles of the Geographical Handbooks. Civilians then couriered material by motor-cycle between the ISTD, based in the New Bodleian, now Weston Library, and Harris Manchester College, and the Admiralty in London. This map was used in the preparation of the *Persian Gulf Handbook* (B.R. 524), published in September 1944 and prepared by the Oxford sub-centre.

These handbooks, 'produced by trained geographers' were 'designed to provide Commanding Officers with information in a convenient and comprehensive form about countries they may be required to visit'. This applied not just to naval personnel but all forces. They had to be produced quickly and accurately; lives might depend on the information included. It is impossible to know to what extent they were used on active service, as the books themselves were secret until 1955. After this they were declassified and provided a sound introduction for undergraduates across the UK to the various countries covered.

In order to aid the production of these volumes the ISTD assembled aerial photographs into continuous horizontal strip photographs of the beach landscape. To update obsolete maps, intelligence and up-to-date photographs were used, including magazine illustrations and holiday photographs collected from the public. New maps were then produced for the planning staffs and operations forces.

Other members of the School of Geography were seconded into the RAF to assist with aerial photographic interpretation – J.N.L. Baker, for example, who was commissioned as a Flight-Lieutenant in the Topographical Section of the Joint Intelligence Committee and promoted to Squadron Leader by October 1942. Amongst other duties he was involved in the production of 'Route Book Folders', mapping flight paths out of the UK down to Gibraltar (flying over the Atlantic) then on to either Cairo along the southern Mediterranean coast or Maiduguri, east of Kano in Northern Nigeria.

D19:13 (1)

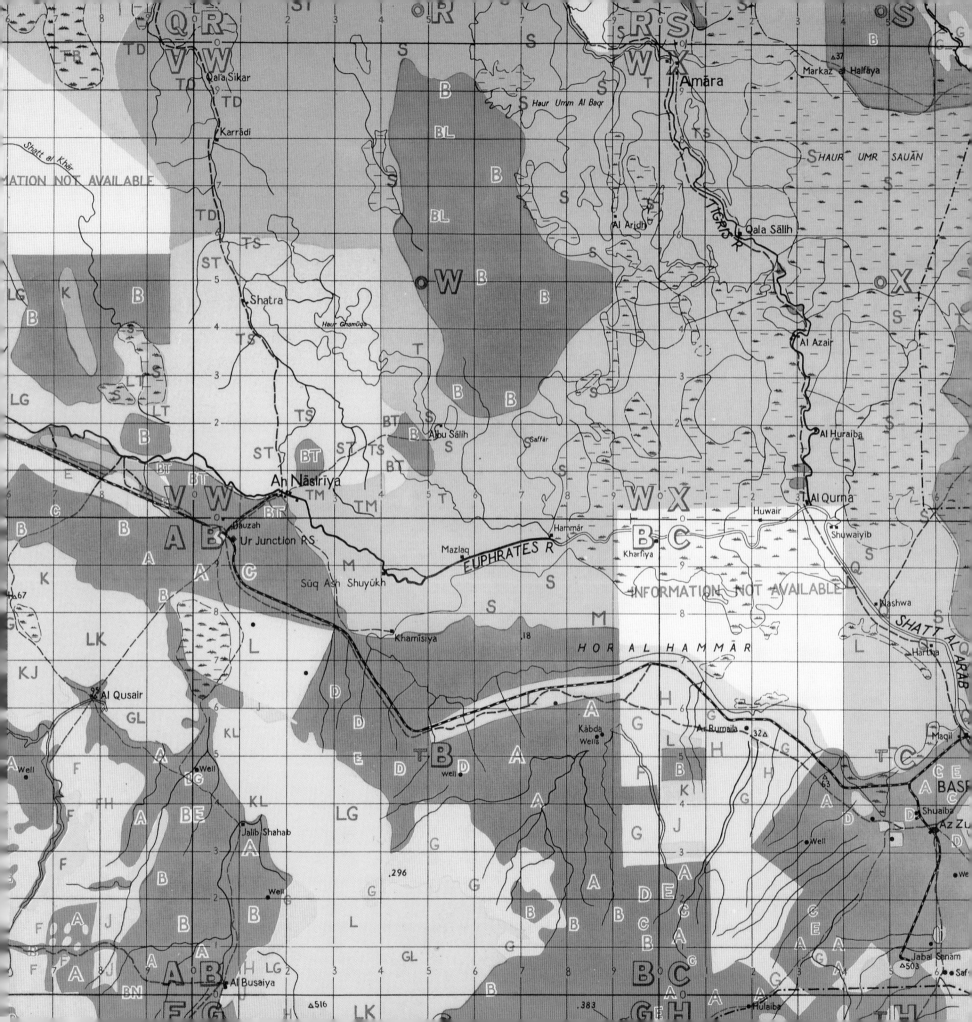

BABYLON, AEGYPTI MAXIMA VRBS

Pyramides hæ in Ægypto nihil aliud fuerunt, quam Regum otiosa ostentatio. Cupiebant enim reges, aut potius tyronatæ, hoc modo nomen suum in terram scribere, & longissime relinquere memoriam, cum tamen nullius rei fama sit in muliore. Nam aut quis Architectus, aut quis rex insanus aliquam pyramidem erexerit, non constat.

Turbæ

Montes Peripsematu.

Cerberum Insula

Hoc ponte transitur crescente Nilo

A Cahyra veteri ad pyramides, sunt passuum 12. milia.

Hoc caput constat vno Saxo, cuis fragmenta teget, facies decem hexapedes minores habet. Strabo ait, esse sepulturæ mulieris Rodopes nòie, monumentů. Quæ formosa Thraciæ meretrix, à rege in vxorem sumpta, post mortem eius hoc caput, et Pyramidem fieri curauit. Petrus Martyr ait, habere in ambitu 88. passus.

Arena

Arena

NILVS FLV.

Dactui.

16

1. Hic obeliscus vnico constat lapide viuo, longus passus XII. latus autem palmas VII.
2. In hoc loco balsamus colligitur. 3. Palatium Campsonij Campsoniæ, de quo lege Petrum Martyr. lib. de ipsius legatione.
4. In hoc loco abluuntur panni. Maghor, autem illorum effossorum modu nunc periit. Ceterum multæ admodum Berecit, piscinæ in vrbe sunt, ad publicas necessitates, et ad liquidi.
5. Montes peripsematum. 6. Moorestum, hoc est, hospitale, vbi pauperes excipiuntur, esui, ingenti prouentu.
7. Turbæ, seu Turbiæ, ædificia, vbi sepeliuntur magnates.
8. Arx Sultani, ex edito loco potest subigere tormentis igni vomis totam ciuitatem. 9. Promptuaria, vbi Principes reponut frumeta, vbi et ligna et carbones distribut.
10. Hæc rota facit, vt aqua in hos aquæductus exaltata, in arce decurrat.
11. Massæ hatur, id est, Ægyptus, seu Cahira vetus, quæ dicta est Babylonia.
12. columna hæc posita est, vt ex ea Nili incrementum noscatur, vn de certissimum petitur aut visitatur, aut caritatis ànonæ indicii.
13. Cum his rotis, seu tympanis, adaquantur horti.
14. In hoc loco fiunt festa hippodromica, seu equestres cursus, in agilitatis lanceis, et quouis modo exercitandis equis, & alijs plerisq, ludis, Turchis et Mamlucis vsitatis. In illis ea asinum docent, quæ ne credas vllam simiam facere. 15. Sic vehuntur nobiles fœminæ, cum aureo ornamento in capite, Ex lossino panno ornatæ, facie cooperta, quæ videre, sed videri non possut.
16. Sic asinos faleratos equitant domini, quos tanti faciunt, quàm ti nos mulos nostros aut equos.
17. Arbores cassiæ producetes, vbi et palmæ, earudq, fructus, dactuli.

CHAPTER 5

The City in Maps

THERE IS SOMETHING PARTICULARLY APPEALING ABOUT CITY MAPS. Perhaps a city is small enough to be encompassed in the imagination in a way that a larger region or country is not. The area of a city can be mapped relatively easily, and the map may be a demonstration of civic pride as well as being of practical use.

City maps have a long history; there are Ancient Greek depictions of towns as perspective views from the second or third century BCE. Some early printed city maps are fairly inaccurate, showing a generic group of buildings that may bear little resemblance to the original. This is a notable feature of some of the city views in the famous 1493 Nuremberg Chronicle, in which the same image was used for more than one city (although the image of Florence included in this chapter is identifiable). From the late fifteenth century, plan views (showing cities in perspective) became increasingly popular and accurate, although most British towns were not mapped at all until the sixteenth or seventeenth century. John Speed's 1612 county atlas (see page 68) included a town plan for almost every county and original surveys were required for many of these. The city maps in this chapter date from the sixteenth to the nineteenth centuries.

Perhaps the greatest landmark of urban mapmaking was Georg Braun and Franz Hogenberg's *Civitates orbis terrarum* (usually translated as *Cities of the world*), published in six volumes between 1572 and 1617, depicting over 500 cities, mainly European but including some from Asia, Africa and the Americas. The idea originated with Hogenberg,

FACING

Cairo is one of the hundreds of cities depicted in the *Civitates orbis terrarum*, and one of a small number outside Europe; the artist may never have actually seen a pyramid.

who engraved the plates, while Braun carried out the work of collating the source material. The title clearly echoes Ortelius's *Theatrum orbis terrarum*, and there is evidence that Braun corresponded with Ortelius and valued his opinion on the project. Images of cities were contributed by many European mapmakers and even by merchants, who brought maps and pictures of cities from further afield. The newly engraved maps and city views were supplemented with descriptive commentary and illustrations of local dress and customs, creating a vivid picture of the major centres of Europe in the late sixteenth and early seventeenth centuries. The atlas was deservedly popular and successful, and copies and smaller extracts were published for some time afterwards, Jan Jansson issuing a reorganized version in the 1650s. The map of Cairo from the *Civitates* appears at the opening of this chapter and that of Bruges is featured further on.

From the late seventeenth century town surveys became more precise and mathematical, and were made for a wide variety of purposes. Town maps were made for military reasons – both for use, and to commemorate battles and sieges. Maps for visitors could also serve as advertisements for the gracious and rational urban schemes they depicted, as seen later in this chapter in Wood's plans for Bath in the 1730s. Here a map of Paris from around 1860, described as *Nouveau Paris*, shows the major boulevards following Haussmann's mid-nineteenth-century redesign and illustrates the main buildings pictorially.

From the mid-nineteenth century, the Ordnance Survey began to produce city maps at scales of up to 5 feet to the mile. These show an extraordinary level of detail, including not just buildings but curbs, walls and even individual lamp posts. They are drawn as plans, so they show buildings, roads and so on exactly to scale, rather than represented symbolically. These were valuable at the time for practical purposes of planning and sanitation, and now form a useful historical record. The extract overleaf showing part of Edinburgh Castle dates from 1894; it is reproduced at around half the size of the original.

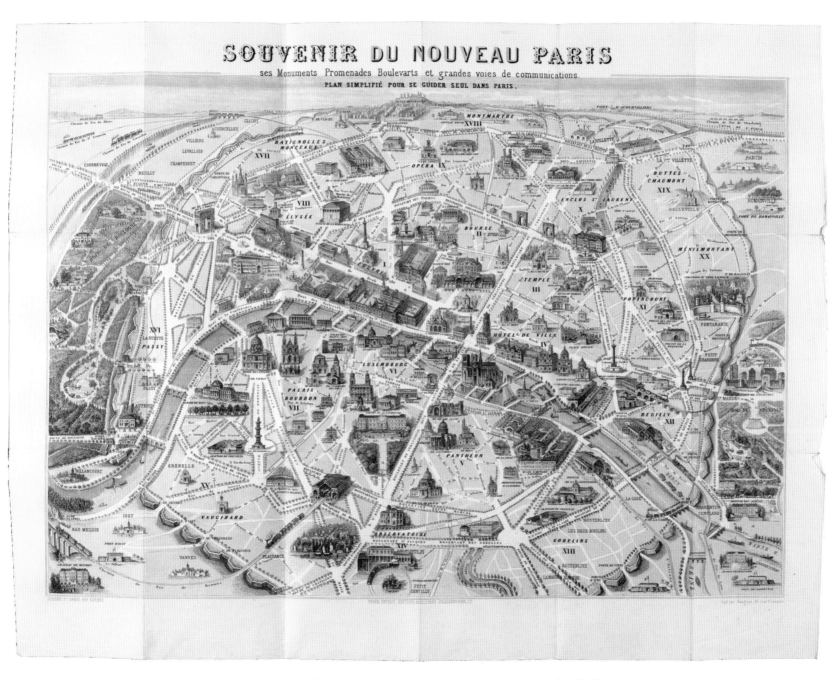

This map of Paris combines a clear plan of the streets with detailed
illustrations of major buildings and monuments.

City maps continue to be widely produced and sold today, including local transport and tourist maps. Modern town maps marketed to tourists are sometimes produced as bird's-eye views; these may be easier for people to understand than conventional maps, especially an audience not much accustomed to looking at maps, as must have been the case when the *Civitates* was published. This form also had a resurgence in the mid to late nineteenth century following the invention of the hot air balloon, which for the first time made it possible to see a city in perspective from above.

The Bodleian continues to contribute to historical research on urban history, especially through Oxford University's involvement with the

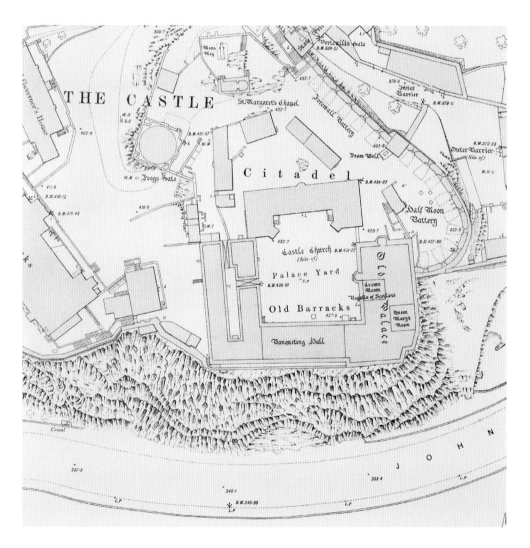

The wealth of detail in the OS large scale town plans at 1:500 can be seen in this sheet covering Edinburgh Castle, reproduced at about half the size of the original.

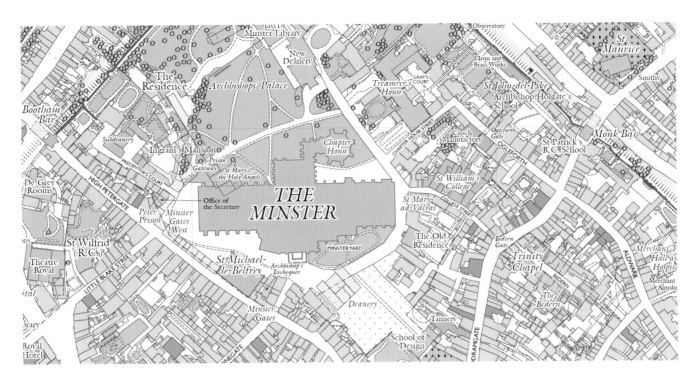

This historical map shows York around 1850. Significant ancient buildings, medieval and later, are highlighted in colour, and the sites of known medieval buildings which are no longer standing are indicated.

Historic Towns Atlas project. This has been producing historical maps – reconstructions of major British towns at different periods – for many years, as part of a Europe-wide programme, using cartographic and other sources to display what is known about the cities of the past. Tantalizingly, these maps give a glimpse of what the towns looked like in an earlier era, to modern cartographic standards, assembled from the evidence that survives. An extract from the volume covering York is illustrated here.

Views of Bruges

Bruges was one of the leading European cities of the Middle Ages and excelled mainly in trade, banking and art. Its access to the North Sea, a navigable canal system, frequent trade fairs, the first stock exchange and a large community of foreign bankers and merchants contributed to the prosperity of the town. Bruges was also a centre of Flemish cloth production and home to one of the seats of the Burgundian dukes. Arts, especially painting and book illumination, flourished here mainly in the fifteenth century and in the first half of the sixteenth century.

The fortunes of the town turned in the sixteenth century, when the city's access to the sea was silting up and Antwerp became its rival. The first detailed bird's-eye view of Bruges, produced in 1562, at the time of decline of the town, was to re-promote its assets. This *Map of Bruges,* famous for its wealth of detail, was designed and etched on ten copper-plates by Marcus Gheeraerts (*c.*1520–*c.*1590). The engraving shown here is based on Gheeraerts's plan and comes from one of the volumes of *Civitates orbis terrarum* printed in Cologne between 1572 and 1617. The text (in Latin) was edited by Georg Braun (1541–1622) and most of the engravings were produced by Frans Hogenberg (1535–1590). This city atlas was aimed at the general public and consisted of 546 views, plans and maps of cities from all over the world. The maps were accompanied by figures in regional costume and short notes on history and architecture. Bruges was described as a beautiful town with magnificent private and public buildings and a double moat. Its circular plan was considered to be ideal.

The appearance of Bruges's (and of neighbouring Ghent's) inner city, its outskirts and surrounding lands was also of considerable interest to earlier generations of local painters and illuminators, such as Jan and Hubert van Eyck, Hans Memling, Gerard David, Gerard Horenbout and Simon Bening. Townscapes and landscapes including scenes from daily life set in the open countryside, in the streets, in courtyards or in interiors of buildings are particularly frequent in fifteenth-century and early sixteenth-century European manuscript illumination. This general trend was especially well represented in the luxurious books of hours (personal prayer books) produced on commission or for the open market in Bruges and Ghent. Principal landmarks of those towns can sometimes be spotted, though many miniatures portray non-specific, but nevertheless characteristically Flemish, architecture, mostly Gothic in style. The realistic-looking depictions show timber, brick and stone houses built along canals, which were so vital for that region's success. The illumination of a man walking by a canal and carrying a hare comes from such a Flemish book of hours, illustrated with many other city views and produced *c.*1500 (MS. Douce 112, fol. 43).

Broxb. 67.8

BRVGÆ, FLANDRICARVM
VRBIVM ORNAMENTA.

BRVGÆ, vulgo Brugk Teuto-
niæ Flandriæ vrbs omnium
pulcherrima, nitidißimaque, publi-
carum siquidem, priuatarumque
ædium in hac orbe splendor et
magnificentia, omnem ratio-
nem, omnem dicendi faculta-
tem superat. Optimam vrbi:
uni formam, hoc est, orbicula:
rem, situ obtinet, aquis pro-
bè instructa, duplici fossa
ambitur; florentißimum quō
dam emporium fuit.

Oxford seen from the air

Oxford is particularly rich in town mapping, and any cartographic history tour commences with Ralph Agas's map – the oldest map of the city in the Bodleian's collections, and the only surviving copy. It was drawn in 1578 and engraved ten years later by Augustine Ryther on eight folio plates. The map's title very much sets the scene. It is grandly described as *Celeberrimæ Oxoniensis academiæ avlarvm et collegiorvm ædificiis totivs Evropæ magnificentissimis cvm antiquissima civitate conivnctæ elegans simvl et accvrata descriptio* (an elegant and at the same time accurate description of the most celebrated university, with the buildings of its halls and colleges, the most magnificent in all Europe, along with the most ancient city) – a clear example of town and gown in the form of a map produced to highlight the significance of both sectors of the community.

Agas (*c.*1540–1621) was a land surveyor who rose to eminence in the reign of Elizabeth I by making estate maps in the east of England from the 1560s onwards, before working on his Oxford map, and also surveying many of the estates owned by Corpus Christi College. Agas recommended use of the theodolite, an instrument for exact measurement of angles, to measure the land using geometrical techniques, thus positioning himself amongst the vanguard of surveyors.

The plan of Oxford now assumes a rather dark and faded presence. It was deemed to be sufficiently important that back in 1728 it was re-engraved by Robert Whittlesey on behalf of the University, resulting in a much 'cleaner', clearer image, frequently reproduced in publications over the intervening centuries (an extract appears below).

Agas's original map is clear enough to reveal the city, with south at the top, presented as if seen by a bird flying over it. Numerous sections of the map demonstrate damage, but the castle is still seen to the right of the map's centre, and both Broad Street and St Giles are prominent in the lower half, the city wall visible running along the southern side of Holywell Street and Broad Street. The street plan remains familiar to the twenty-first-century map reader, the courses of the sweeping curve of High Street and the gentle descent of St Aldate's to the Thames apparently unaltered. The earlier colleges are prominent. Perhaps most striking, however, is the abundance of vegetation in the city centre, trees filling many of the undeveloped central plots within Oxford's walls.

Agas's lead in placing south at the top of his map did not go unnoticed. This pattern was replicated by the likes of Hollar (1650), Loggan (1675), Tielenburg (*c.*1730), Williams (1733) and others. It was not until the late eighteenth century that Oxford was seen to rotate, and the conventional interpretation of the city oriented to the north became the cartographic norm.

Map Room

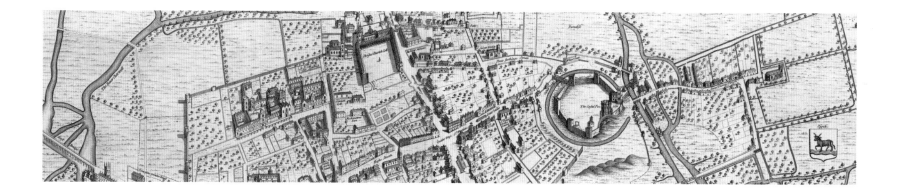

London before the Great Fire

London in the early years of the seventeenth century was a place of change from Elizabethan to Jacobean. It was also a time when John Speed published his ground-breaking atlas *The Theatre of the Empire of Great Britaine* (see page 68), and it was against this backdrop that a Dutch cartographer, Claes Visscher, produced his grandiose panorama. Drawn and engraved by Visscher from sketches and existing map views, it was published by Jodocus Hondius in Amsterdam in 1616. What makes it more remarkable is that there is no evidence that Visscher came to London at all. At over 2 metres in length the map was an ambitious and confident undertaking. From Whitehall in the west to St Katherine's-by-the-Tower in the east, Visscher's panorama provides a magnificent representation of the city in the early modern period. The level of detail is extraordinary and several street scenes can be seen if one looks closely, but it is the impression of wealth and power that is immediately obvious.

Amid the many houses, churches and public buildings several sites stand out. The most commanding feature is the old London Bridge, which shows the southern gate-house displaying London's most notorious and gruesome sight – that of the severed heads of traitors on spikes. The bridge at this time had become very overcrowded so at busy times it could take an hour to cross it. The buildings, which look sturdy, were in reality ramshackle and a major fire hazard, with fires consuming parts of the bridge at different times. Some buildings stood seven stories high and overhung the bridge.

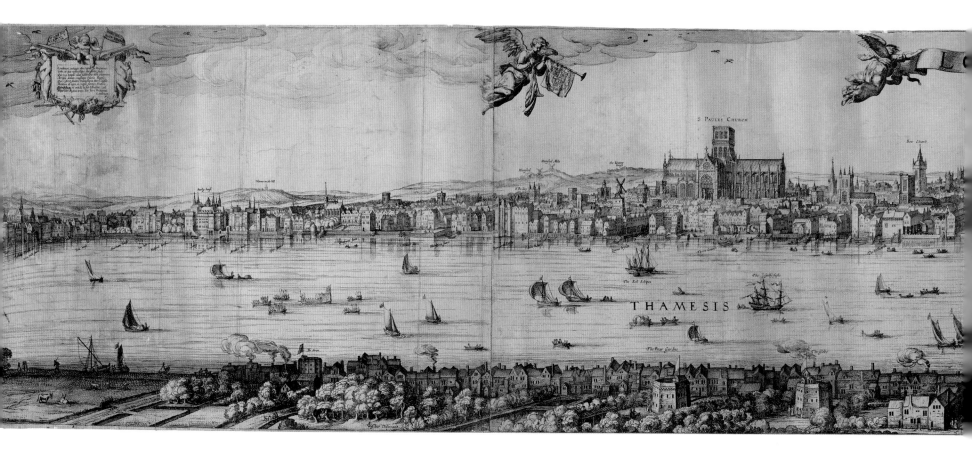

The River Thames, being a hive of activity and a major transport artery, shows shipping of all shapes and sizes, from small boats for hire to cross the river to large ocean-going galleons. London was prospering with a thriving shipbuilding industry and a vibrant port, a departure point for exploration to all corners of the world.

St Paul's Church, now cathedral, dominant on the skyline at this time, was one of the greatest churches in Christendom and the most recognizable landmark to Londoners and visitors alike. Shown here in its Gothic form, it was rebuilt less than a century later in the Baroque style by Sir Christopher Wren. The original spire had been destroyed by lightening in 1561 and never replaced, giving the tower a rather truncated look. The distortion of perspective by Visscher over the whole view only serves to emphasize its importance.

The Globe Theatre and the nearby Bear Garden are clearly shown on the south bank. Further to the east is the larger Swan Theatre. All of these were hugely popular places of public entertainment. Shakespeare and Ben Jonson's plays were being performed as people of all classes enjoyed the playhouses. It was said that Queen Elizabeth's favourite sport was bear-baiting.

This view of London, while appearing so solid and permanent, was merely transitory. Exactly fifty years after publication it was changed forever by the Great Fire.

Douce Prints a.53 (2)

An unreliable map of Oxford

This map of Oxford seems at first glance to be an interesting, if less than detailed, record of an important time in the city's history. By 1644 the English Civil War had been going on for two years, and Oxford had been the military headquarters of the Royalist forces for much of that time.

This copper-engraved map shows the fortifications round the city and other important fortified towns on the course of the River Thames on the way to London. The other towns are shown at a much reduced scale compared to Oxford, an interesting and unusual way, for the time, of showing locations in relation to each other. The map, though, suffers from a variation of the regular cartographic curse of the age, that of copying from earlier examples and leaving in any original mistakes.

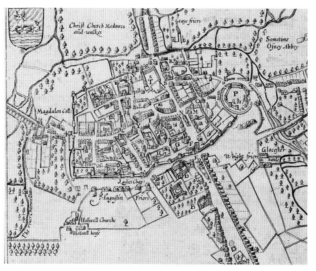

The convention that we now take for granted of north being always at the top of a map has not always been the rule, and contemporary sixteenth-century maps of Oxford almost all show south at the top (see above, page 142). With this map an unknown cartographer has set north at the top, putting the castle (the round building at the left of the city) to the west and the crossing of the Cherwell by Magdalen Bridge to the east. So far so good, but in depicting the buildings and streets between the two the cartographer seems to have copied directly from an earlier map, most likely Speed's map of Oxford from his 1611 *Theatre of the Empire of Great Britaine* (inset, below). Speed's map is oriented with south at the top. The layout of the buildings in Speed's map and the map here are the same – even the same letters are used in the index – the only difference being that Speed has deliberately made his map with this orientation and our cartographer has done this mistakenly, and only partly so at that, resulting in a map that has numerous errors.

This map is part of a collection of well over a thousand books, pamphlets and writings gathered together by Anthony Wood, an Oxford historian who died in 1695. Wood published a number of books about the city, one of which included his own plan of the city during the war, but also managed to fall out with most of those he came in contact with, one of whom described Wood as 'a conceited, impudent coxcomb'. His contempt for the map shown here can be seen in a note added at the very bottom of the page, 'This map is made very false'.

Wood 276b (30)

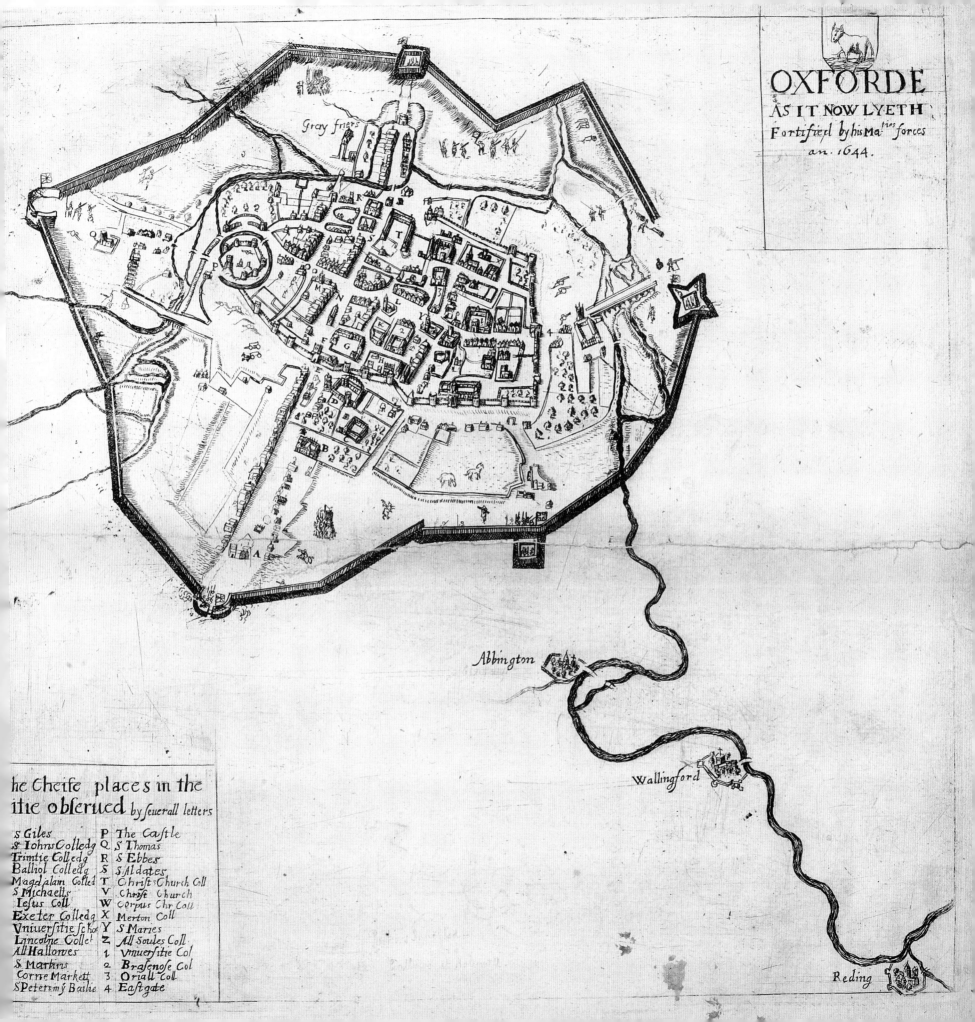

OXFORDE
AS IT NOW LYETH
Fortified by his Ma:ties forces
an. 1644.

Gray friers

Abbington

Wallingford

Reding

he Cheife places in the
itie obserued by seuerall letters

s Giles	P	The Castle
S Iohns Colledg	Q	S Thomas
Trinitie Colledg	R	S Ebbes
Balliol Colledg	S	S Aldates
Magdalain Colled	T	Christ Church Coll
S Michaells	V	Chryst Church
Iesus Coll	W	Corpus Chr Coll
Exeter Colledg	X	Merton Coll
Vniuersitie scho	Y	S Maries
Lincolne Collet	Z	All Soules Coll
All Hallowes	1	Vniuersitie Col
S Martins	2	Brasenose Col
Corne Markett	3	Oriall Coll
S Peters mÿ Bailie	4	Eastgate

Demilitarized Devonport

John Milton's six plans and elevations of England's Royal Dockyards unequivocally assert her global naval supremacy on the eve of the Seven Years' War. His 1754 plan of Portsmouth – the historic epicentre of the Royal Navy's power – is festooned with vignettes of eight of the twelve French capital ships captured in 1747 at First and Second Finisterre, now all flying the White Ensign. Milton's elevation of Plymouth is similarly charged with evocative imagery – a fleet of British men-o'-war ready to sail and a 70-gun third-rate firing a salute as she enters harbour, a large French prize in tow.

The visually stunning Dockyard series was Milton's tribute to British shipbuilding, seamanship and naval power. It is intriguing that, when he produced his Plymouth piece in 1756, he simultaneously published a second, extended version of it with a rather demilitarized look. He inscribed this to Sir John St Aubyn, owner of a large tract of land encompassing the dockyard, wharf and surrounding areas.

His Plymouth 'naval plan' is confined precisely to the area of the naval facilities, bounded to the east by Artillery Ground, Queen Street and Dock Wall. The only civilian areas shown are the few streets separating the dockyard and the wharf, operated by the Admiralty and the Board of Ordnance respectively. The 'St Aubyn plan', on the other hand, extends twice as far inland, to the fully built-up area of Devonport, then known as Morice Town and Stoke Town. Several of the streets bear the names of St Aubyn and his relations.

The token few, lacklustre ships shown in the harbour are mostly 'in ordinary'. The military escutcheons above the legends are downsized. The only improvement in the St Aubyn plan is that it more accurately shows the operation of Edmund Dummer's double wet/dry dock, the first stepped stone dock in Europe.

Milton clearly extended this second edition to include lands that St Aubyn owned, but why the sharply contrasting theme? At least part of the reason is likely to be political. St Aubyn's father (the third baronet) was a Tory extremist, sympathetic to the Jacobites and privy to secret French plans to invade England and help restore the Stuarts. Although the third baronet died in 1744, his son witnessed the Government's crushing defeat of the Jacobites in the following year. The fourth baronet might easily have regarded a map of his own lands that celebrated British military might as rubbing salt into the wounds of his father's lost cause.

The cartouche is a cornucopia of standard masonic symbols and emblems – the twin pillars, the three lights, the first line of the Gospel of John, the mosaic pavement, the book, the square, the compass, the level and the plumb. The prominent crossed leeks at top centre are unusual, possibly indicating a Welsh connection. The small scroll on the right shows a masonic representation of the 47th Problem of Euclid, an obvious choice for a lover of geometry and surveying. The counterpart on the left, however, is not a masonic symbol and may simply be Milton's own invention to fill in the space. It incorporates figures of zero, one, two and three dimensions – a point, a line, a rectangle and a cube. A masonic connection between Milton and St Aubyn seems likely and may well explain the genesis of the map. 'Bro[the]r Milton invt' appears below the cartouche, and St Aubyn's son (fifth baronet) was provincial Grandmaster of the Freemasons for fifty-four years.

Gough Maps Devonshire 8

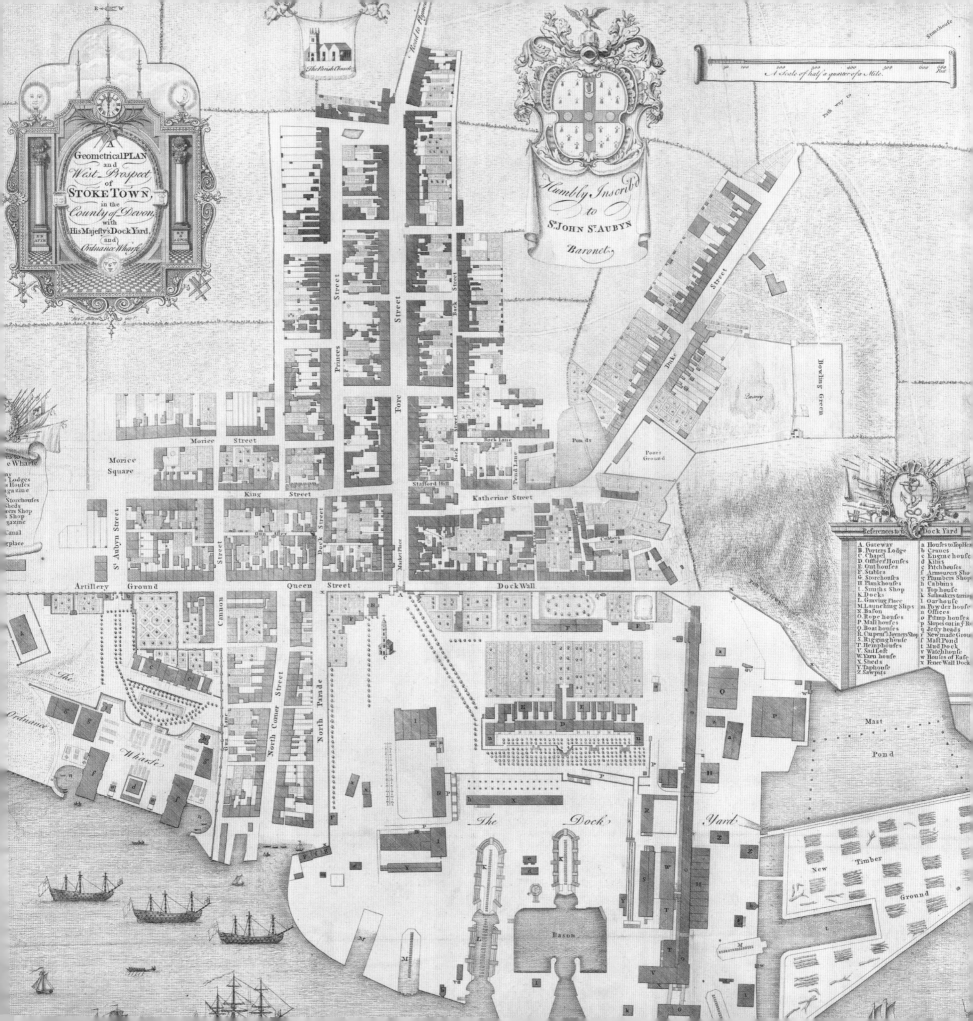

A Geometrical PLAN and West Prospect of STOKE TOWN in the County of Devon, with His Majesty's Dock Yard, and Ordnance Wharfe.

The Parish Church

Humbly Inscrib'd to Sr JOHN St AUBYN Baronet

A Scale of half a quarter of a Mile.

Road to Plymouth

Stonehouse

Bowling Green

Quarry

Poors Ground

Ponds

Drake Street

Back Street

Prince's Street

Fore Street

Back Lane

Pond Lane

Stafford Hill

Katherine Street

Morice Street

Morice Square

King Street

St Aubyn Street

Gun Alley

Dock Street

Market Place

Queen Street

Dock Wall

Artillery Ground

Cannon Street

North Corner Street

North Parade

Gun Lane

The Wharfe

Ordnance

Cribbers

The Dock Yard

Mast Pond

Bason

New Timber Ground

References to ye Dock Yard
A. Gateway
B. Porters Lodge
C. Chapel
D. Officer Houses
E. Out houses
F. Stables
G. Storehouses
H. Plankhouses
I. Smiths Shop
K. Docks
L. Graving Place
M. Launching Ships
N. Bason
O. Rope houses
P. Mast houses
Q. Boat houses
R. Carpenters & Joyners Shop
S. Rigging house
T. Hemp houses
V. Sail Loft
W. Yarn house
X. Sheds
Y. Taphouse
Z. Sawpits

a. Houses to Top Hers
b. Cranes
c. Engine house
d. Kilns
e. Pitchouses
f. Armourers Shop
g. Plumbers Shop
h. Cabbins
i. Top house
k. Sailmakers taning
l. Oar house
m. Powder house
n. Offices
o. Pump house
p. Slopes eating Room
q. Jeddy heads
r. New made Ground
s. Mast Pond
t. Mud Dock
u. Watch house
w. Houses of Ease
x. Fence Wall Dock

Building Georgian Bath

In the early eighteenth century John Wood returned to his native Bath with a mission, signalled in this map, to make his name as the architect who remodelled the city as a Palladian theatre for the polite society then flocking there to enjoy the spa waters and social scene.

Wood is 'Mr John Wood, Architect' – no mere master mason like those responsible for most building in Bath at this point, but a trained professional with pretensions to gentlemanliness. The instruments of his profession adorn the cartouche and suggest that his 'Original Survey' for the map is based on scientific principles. Disdaining the bird's-eye view and pictorial representations of many earlier maps, Wood's plan view set the style for later maps, just as his architecture set the pace for later building.

Wood's map sits within an oval frame with west at the top. Within the city walls he delineates public buildings such as churches and baths, but also gardens and orchards, which show how little developed the city was. In the west John Strahan's new building on King's Mead had moved tentatively away from the vernacular, but was completely eclipsed after 1735 by the projects of John Wood and his son and namesake – Queen's Square, the Royal Forum, the King's Circus and the Royal Crescent. Of these, only Queen Square to the northwest of the city wall was begun when the map was printed. It is shown prominently, as well it might be, since it incorporated the first palatial façade in England (a row of terraced houses built to look like one palace, with a single central pediment and terminal pavilions). It was the catalyst to the construction of the new Upper Town north of the city wall, and it established Neoclassicism, if not strict Palladianism, as Bath's architectural language of choice. In the map's bottom right corner, superimposed on the printed orchards and gardens, manuscript addenda show Wood's North and South Parades, Pierrepoint Street and Duke Street – his Royal Forum, which recreated the city's Roman glory. Nearby on the river Avon 'Mr Allen's stone wharf' marks where the oölitic limestone for building arrived from the quarry of Wood's patron, Ralph Allen. The elegant stone and Neoclassical style gave visual coherence to Bath's Georgian developments.

The map's oval border is surrounded by text, which is a typically eighteenth-century mix of puffs, deference and naked advertising. Wood puffs up Bath's 'pleasant and healthy' situation, its buildings, 'erected in a Magnificent manner', and the 'Familys of Distinction' among its visitors. He defers to actual patrons (Ralph Allen and the 'Masterpiece of Mechanism' which unloads his stone at Bath) and potential ones (the mayor and aldermen who take 'great Care to preserve the Peace and good Order', and 'Mr Nash', or Beau Nash, arbiter of manners). The arms of the city and the see of Bath and Wells in the map's frame ensure that no influential body is left unflattered. Finally Wood includes advertisements for the bookseller who printed the map and for his own yard, where fine deal (pinewood from the Baltic) may be had cheap.

The map shows a liminal moment in Bath's history as the city became prominent in British architectural and social developments, and in its cartography, since it was drawn by a trained architect. It set the style for subsequent maps, and, with its manuscript alterations, shows that even maps from 'original survey' could not keep up with the heady pace of Bath's development. New buildings rapidly changed the Bath scene which Wood showed on his map, while some developments which his map confidently delineated were realized in different form, as with the hospital identified as '30' on the key, or only many years later, as with the lock for circumnavigating the town weir at '40'.

Gough Maps 28, fol. 46

WEST

SOUTH

NORTH

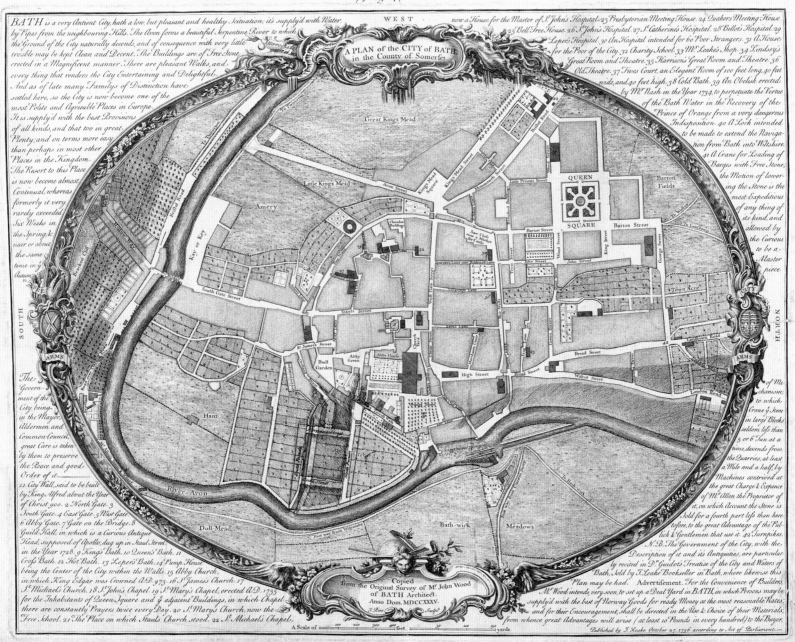

A PLAN of the CITY of BATH in the County of Somerset.

BATH is a very Antient City, hath a low but pleasant and healthy Scituation; it's supply'd with Water by Pipes from the neighbouring Hills. The Avon forms a beautiful Serpentine River to which the Ground of the City naturally decends, and of consequence with very little trouble may be kept Clean and Decent. The Buildings are of Free Stone, erected in a Magnificent manner. There are pleasant Walks, and every thing that renders the City Entertaining and Delightful. And as of late many Familys of Distinction have settled here, so the City is now become one of the most Polite and Agreeable Places in Europe. It is supply'd with the best Provisions of all kinds, and that too in great Plenty; and on terms more easy than perhaps in most other Places in the Kingdom. The Resort to this Place is now become almost Continual, whereas formerly it very rarely exceeded Six Weeks in the Spring, &c near or about the same time in y Autumn.

The Government of the City being in the Mayor, Aldermen and Common-Council, great Care is taken by them to preserve the Peace and good Order of it.

1. City Wall, said to be built by King Alfred about the Year of Christ 900. 2. North Gate. 3. South Gate. 4. East Gate. 5. West Gate. 6. Abby Gate. 7. Gate on the Bridge. 8. Guild Hall, in which is a Curious Antique Head, supposed of Apollo, dug up in Staul Street in the Year 1728. 9. Kings Bath. 10. Queen's Bath. 11. Cross Bath. 12. Hot Bath. 13. Leper's Bath. 14. Pump House being the Center of the City within the Walls. 15. Abby Church, in which King Edgar was Crowned A.D. 973. 16. St James's Church. 17. St Michael's Church. 18. St John's Chapel. 19. St Mary's Chapel, erected A.D. 1735 for the Inhabitants of Queen's Square and y adjacent Buildings, in which Chapel there are constantly Prayers twice every Day. 20. St Mary's Church, now the Free School. 21. The Place on which Staul's Church stood. 22. St Michael's Chapel,

now a House for the Master of St John's Hospital. 23. Presbyterian Meeting House. 24. Quakers Meeting House. 25. Bell Free House. 26. St John's Hospital. 27. St Catherine's Hospital. 28. Bellot's Hospital. 29. Leper's Hospital. 30. An Hospital intended for 60 Poor Strangers. 31. A House for the Poor of the City. 32. Charity School. 33. Mr Leake's Shop. 34. Lindsey's Great Room and Theatre. 35. Harrison's Great Room and Theatre. 36. Old Theatre. 37. Fives Court, an Elegant Room of 100 feet long, 40 feet wide, and 40 feet high. 38. Cold Bath. 39. An Obelisk erected by Mr Nash in the Year 1734, to perpetuate the Vertue of the Bath Water in the Recovery of the Prince of Orange from a very dangerous Indisposition. 40. A Lock intended to be made to extend the Navigation from Bath into Wiltshire. 41. A Crane for Loading of Barges with Free Stone, the Motion of lowering the Stone is the most Expeditious of any thing of its kind, and allowed by the Curious to be a Master piece of Mechanism; to which Crane y Stone in large Blocks seldom less than 5 or 6 Tun at a time, descends from the Quarries, at least a Mile and a half, by Machines contrived at the great Charge & Expence of Mr Allen the Proprietor of it, on which Account the Stone is sold for a fourth part less than heretofore, to the great Advantage of the Publick & Gentlemen that use it. 42. Turnpikes.

N.B. The Government of the City, with the Description of it and its Antiquities, are particularly recited in Dr Guidot's Treatise of the City and Waters of Bath, sold by J. Leake Bookseller in Bath, where likewise this Plan may be had. Advertisement. For the Convenience of Builders, Mr Wood intends very soon, to set up a Deal Yard in BATH, in which Persons may be supply'd with the best of Norway Goods for ready Money at the most reasonable Rates, and for their Encouragement, shall be directed in the Use & Choice of their Materials, from whence great Advantages will arise / at least 10 Pounds in every hundred / to the Buyer.

Copied from the Original Survey of Mr John Wood of BATH Architect Anno Dom. MDCCXXXV.

J. Pine Sculp.t

A Scale of ... feet ... yards

Published by J. Leake October 27, 1736 according to Act of Parliament.

Great Kings Mead

Little Kings Mead

Amery

Queen Square

Barton Fields

Barton Street

Ham

River Avon

Doll Mead

Bath-wick

Meadows

High Street

Bull Garden

Abby Green

Life in Revolutionary Boston

This map of Boston, Massachusetts, during the American War of Independence, or Revolutionary War, carefully depicts the strategically significant town at one of the most important conjunctions in its history, and tells us much about who was drawing, buying and using maps in the late eighteenth century, and how and why.

The cartographer was Richard Williams, a British lieutenant engineer, who is probably the 'Lieut. Richard Williams of the Royal Welsh [actually Welch] Fusilliers' identified by Walter W. Ristow in 'Cartography of the Battle of Bunker Hill' as the creator of a map of that battle, drawn after the event. In Williams's clear, workmanlike map of October 1775 there is no elaborate cartouche or florid lettering, and pictorial elements are confined to the Roxbury Meeting House and a few trees. Instead there are a clear legend, a simple scale bar, and a set of features shown in plan rather than elevation. Williams selects geographical features of strategic or tactical importance ('This Shoal and all the rest thus Shaded are Dry at Low Water'), and uses hachuring to show heights which command the terrain. He shows the human features which bear directly on the war – the street layout which would help a commander see the thoroughfares that needed to be controlled, and the many military installations around the city.

The map shows how important cartography had become to the pursuit of war by the late eighteenth century. Using maps, armies of outsiders – here 'his Majesty's Army' – could more effectively confront local people – here 'the Rebels' – who, armed with intimate personal knowledge of the city and word of mouth from sympathetic locals, relied far less on maps for information and planning. The map also shows the versatile engineer's training which lay behind the production of both the map and the geometric fortifications which it depicts. Finally, it shows the burgeoning middle-class market for maps, which would help an interested public follow the events of the war.

The text on the map makes the claim that the map shows 'the true SITUATION' and, in support of this claim, the publisher tells us that it has been surveyed on the spot by an officer and reached the publisher by the hand of 'a Nobleman'. It rests then, in typical eighteenth-century fashion, on a mix of empirical evidence observed at first hand and the touch of persons of quality and thus credit.

For the military and the buying public the engineer shows not just a snapshot of the situation, but a report on past events and a guide to future ones. Map and legend tell the antecedents to the present position ('Redoubt taken from ye Rebels by Gen. Howe'); the daily grind of the war ('A hill from whence the Enemy annoy ye Centries & Officers with small Arms, but seldom do any Execution'); and hint of trouble to come ('A Strong Post of the Enemy Fortified …. with great Judgment … from whence with a 24-Pounder they can just reach the Lines'). The chosen place names are a mix of royalist propaganda ('King Str.', Hanover St.'), the vernacular ('Noddles Island'), and the unrespectable ('Mount Whoredom', a name in common use by soldiers and locals but for which developers later substituted 'Mount Vernon', which was more seemly in this supposedly godly city).

(E) F6:60 Boston (1)

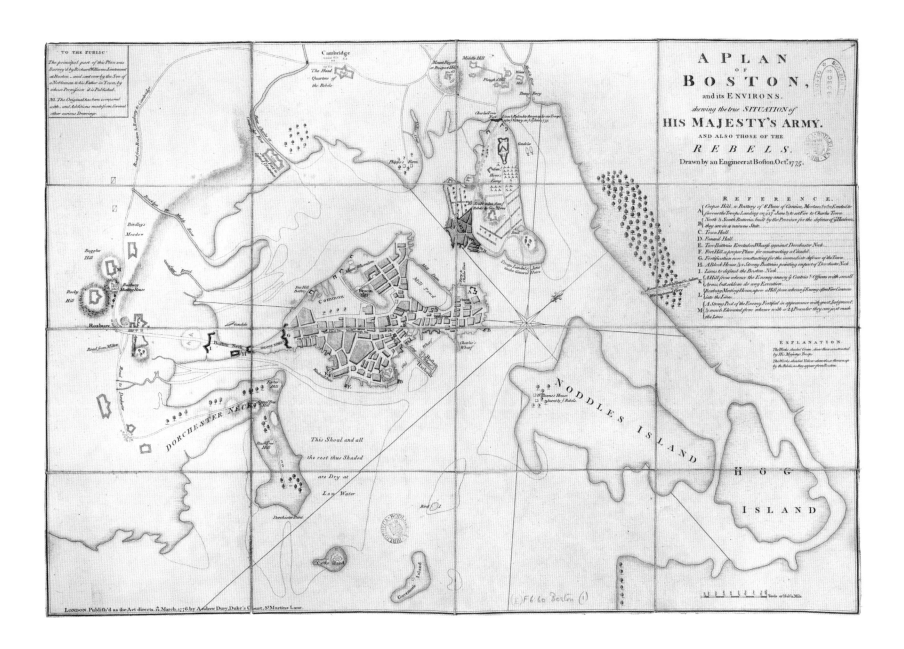

A PLAN
OF
BOSTON,
and its ENVIRONS.
shewing the true SITUATION of
HIS MAJESTY'S ARMY.
AND ALSO THOSE OF THE
REBELS.
Drawn by an Engineer at Boston, Oct.ʳ 1775.

LONDON. Publish'd as the Act directs, 25 March. 1776 by Andrew Dury, Duke's Court, St Martins Lane.

A glimpse of Calcutta

This map, a town plan of Calcutta, was issued from 1842 as part of the Family Atlas of the Society for the Diffusion of Useful Knowledge (SDUK). The SDUK, founded in 1826 with Henry Brougham as its chairman, aimed to provide instructive reading to the masses of Great Britain. Moreover, at a time of such political unrest, the SDUK offered a 'safe' alternative to those who fought for workers' rights and parliamentary reform – the radical press. The SDUK published works on a wide range of subjects from history and ornithology to optics and hydraulics, but their most successful publication was *The Penny Magazine,* which sold 200,000 copies weekly at its peak.

The SDUK formed a Map Committee in 1828, and, headed by the enthusiastic Captain Francis Beaufort, they produced their first sheets the following year – modern and ancient Greece. Releasing the maps two sheets at a time, the SDUK completed their atlas almost fifteen years later, arguably the first widely affordable atlas for use at home. Furthermore, despite its raising the production costs, the SDUK chose to engrave their maps on steel. Steel-engraved plates would not only survive more reprints than their copper counterparts, but would also offer a higher quality of image. Taking this into account, the Society settled on selling their maps for 1s., or 1s. 6d. for coloured editions. The SDUK's maps were very popular, and continued to be printed even after the Society ceased operations in 1845. Overall, the Society printed over 200 maps, including fifty-one town plans, a rail and canal map of Britain, and six star charts.

This plan offers the reader a glance into the streets of Calcutta, marking places familiar to those in the metropole such as the post office and hospital, but it also individually lists the city's churches and cathedral, while other sites of religious worship receive no attention. The map's most prominent feature is Fort William. Built by the British East India Company in 1696, the Fort stands as a symbol of British rule in India, reminding the reader of India's status as a colony. Similarly, the accompanying illustrations at the bottom of the map demonstrate Calcutta's beauty, and, more importantly, emphasize its colonial attributes. The third image depicts a fleet of ships at harbour marking India's connection with colonialism and commerce. Calcutta was a vital component in Britain's maritime trade and not only were valuable items such as textiles, salt and tobacco exported westwards to Britain, but Calcutta was also the heart of the opium trade to the East. Indeed, the names of merchants' and tradesmen's factories line the river.

This map, particularly when read in conjunction with the Society's other works on India, would allow the working-class readership vividly to picture Britain's empire, an empire that they were at the heart of as Britons.

2027 b.37

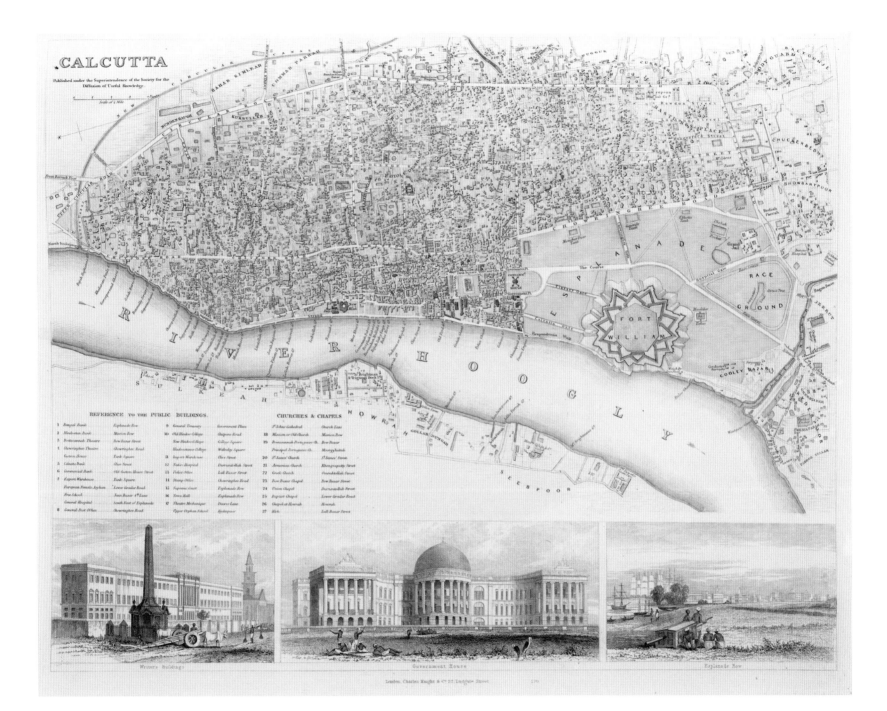

CALCUTTA

Published under the Superintendence of the Society for the
Diffusion of Useful Knowledge.

Scale of ¼ Mile

REFERENCE TO THE PUBLIC BUILDINGS.

1	Bengal Bank	Esplanade Row	9	General Treasury	Government Place
2	Hindostan Bank	Mission Row	10	Old Hindoo College	Chitpore Road
3	Brittanarnick Theatre	Bow Bazar Street		New Hindoo College	College Square
4	Chowringhee Theatre	Chowringhee Road		Hindoostanee College	Wellesly Square
5	Gorton House	York Square	11	Imp. or Warehouse	Clive Street
5	Calcutta Bank	Clive Street	12	Native Hospital	Durrum-tah Street
6	Commercial Bank	Old Custom House Street	13	Police Office	Lall Bazar Street
7	Export Warehouse	York Square	14	Stamp Office	Chowringhee Road
	European Female Asylum	Lower Circular Road	15	Supreme Court	Esplanade Row
	Free School	Jaun Bazar 4th Lane	16	Town Hall	Esplanade Row
	General Hospital	South East of Esplanade	17	Theatre Mechanique	Dacres Lane
8	General Post Office	Chowringhee Road		Upper Orphan School	Kidderpore

CHURCHES & CHAPELS

	St Johns Cathedral	Church Lane
18	Mission or Old Church	Mission Row
19	Brunswanah Portuguese Ch.	Bow Bazar
	Principal Portuguese Ch.	Mozzyhuttah
20	St James' Church	St James' Street
21	Armenian Church	Khengraputty Street
22	Greek Church	Oazukdollah Street
23	Bow Bazar Chapel	Bow Bazar Street
24	Union Chapel	Durramdollah Street
25	Baptist Chapel	Lower Circular Road
26	Chapel at Howrah	Howrah
27	Kirk	Lall Bazar Street

Writers Buildings

Government House

Esplanade Row

London, Charles Knight & Co. 22 Ludgate Street.

Huskisson Dock, Liverpool

Although not favoured by the Saxons, who dismissed it as 'a muddy creek', Liverpool and its docks have had an extraordinary career, seeing many changes over the centuries. At its height, Liverpool had become the second largest port in the British Empire and was bustling with a labour force of nearly 30,000. This coincided with the Ordnance Survey (OS) producing some of its most detailed mapping of the city and docks, beautifully represented in the image on the opposite page.

This map segment shows an extract from four 1:500-scale maps surveyed by the OS in 1890 and published in 1891. The section portrays some of Huskisson Dock, part of the northern dock system at Kirkdale. It was designed by Jesse Hartley and named after William Huskisson, a former Treasurer of the Navy and Member of Parliament. Opening in 1852, the dock consisted of a main basin and two branch docks. To the right of the two Huskisson Locks is Sandon Dock, which opened a year before, with two of the six graving docks showing. Some of the sheds used to store timber, the principal product for the dock at the time, can be seen. Also shown, on the side closest to the river Mersey, is the Cunard Engine Works. Huskisson Dock was used for Cunard's weekly turn-round of their ocean liners up until the 1960s and engine maintenance would have been carried out here.

Liverpool became an internationally significant port in the eighteenth century, mainly owing to trade in sugar and tobacco and its involvement in the Atlantic slave trade. The onset of the Industrial Revolution helped the port grow further as it became a key hub for the exporting of finished products from the mills of surrounding Lancashire and the import mainly of grain, sugar, cotton and timber.

The advent of war saw Liverpool docks play an important strategic role, but after World War II had ended an increase in trade with Europe meant that southern ports flourished whilst Liverpool declined. Liverpool is still the largest of England's west coast ports, however, and new industries are starting to thrive.

Though Albert Dock may be more famous now for its shops, museums and galleries, the northern dock system is finding its own way of regenerating. Currently, Huskisson Dock has a wood-pulp burner and generator, leading the way in alternative energy, and is also involved in handling general bulk cargoes. Sandon Dock, rather unceremoniously, has been filled in and is now the home to a sewage treatment plant and pumping station.

The OS started producing the 1:500 scale in 1855 and had completed surveying most towns with a population over 4,000 by 1895. Colour maps could be purchased at a cost of three shillings each and were originally printed by a process called photozincography. This allowed for the printing of images on to zinc from photographic negatives, a method developed by the OS. The various colours were then applied by hand, with each one depicting buildings types or topography. Masonry buildings are red, and grey was used for those built from iron or wood. Water is shown with a blue wash. The colour certainly adds an extra dimension to the surveyed detail.

These large-scale maps show the skill involved in surveying and mapping in such intricate detail, while also providing an accurate and colourful record of one of England's industrial heartlands.

C17:70 a.230

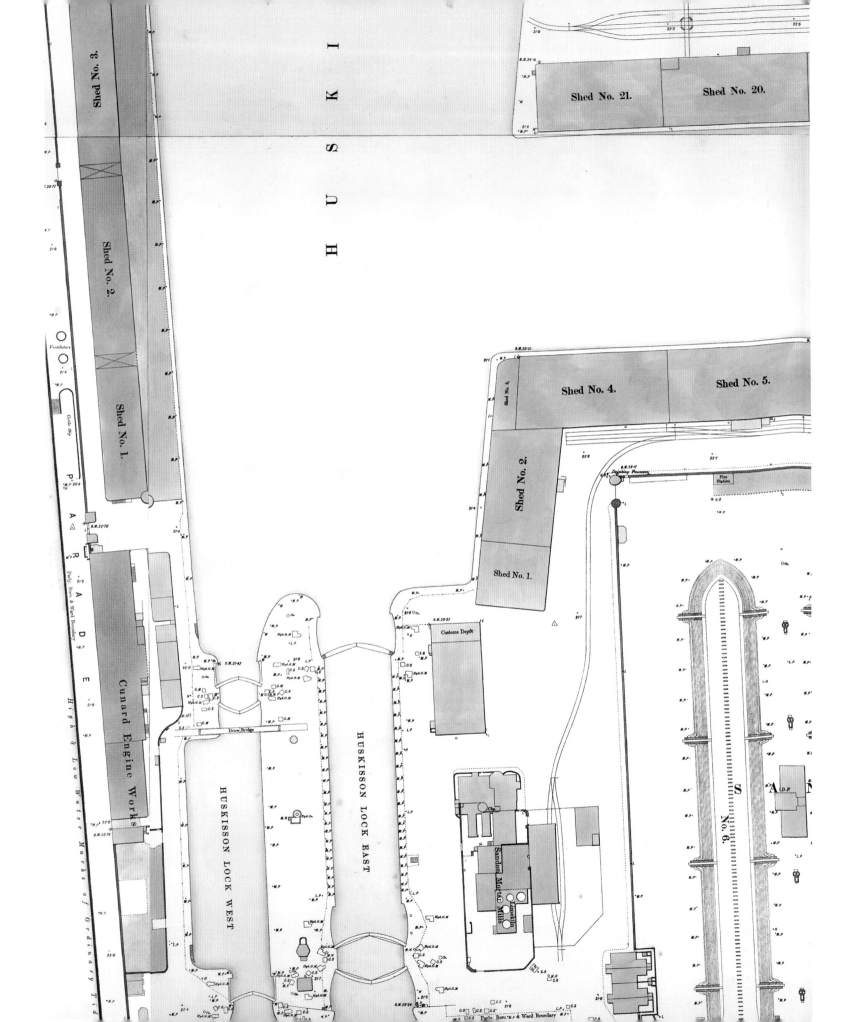

Shed No. 3.

Shed No. 21.

Shed No. 20.

Shed No. 2.

Shed No. 4.

Shed No. 5.

Shed No. 1.

Ventilators

Shed No. 3.

Shed No. 2.

Cable Ship

P⁴

Shed No. 1.

Fire
Station

Drinking Fountain

A

R

A

D

E

Cunard Engine Works

Customs Depôt

High & Low Water Marks of Ordinary Tide

Parly Town & Ward Boundary

Draw Bridge

HUSKISSON LOCK WEST

HUSKISSON LOCK EAST

Sandon Mort. & F. Mills

Sandon

S   A   N

No. 6.

S   A. D. F.

Parly. Boro' M.P. & Ward Boundary

Cholera in Oxford

Thematic cartography and public health have a number of early pioneers in common. John Snow (1813–1858) is celebrated by doctors for his research into anaesthetics and the establishment of the speciality of epidemiology, and by cartographers for the drafting of a seminal map of the incidence of cholera in Soho, London, during the outbreak of 1854 (an extract from which appears as an inset, right). Sir Henry Acland (1815–1900), Regius Professor of Medicine in the University of Oxford, is honoured for pioneering the systematic teaching of science and medicine, for work in public health and sanitation, and for detailed, coloured maps of the cholera epidemics in Oxford.

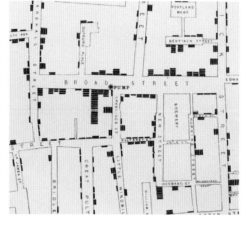

Acland was appointed Consulting Physician to the city's Board of Health and became closely involved with the management of the outbreak of cholera in Oxford between 6 August and 22 October 1854. He ensured that physicians attending the 317 victims of cholera (of whom 129 died) recorded details of the sex, age, occupation and place of residence of the victims. His analysis of the substantial body of statistics that resulted, along with observations on the epidemics of 1832 and 1849, was published in 1856 as *Memoir on the Cholera at Oxford in the year 1854, with considerations suggested by the epidemic*. The work was illustrated by a number of coloured maps of the outbreak, of which the largest and most important was the 'Map of Oxford ... showing the localities in which cholera & choleraic diarrhoea occurred in 1854, and cholera in 1832 & 1849'.

Acland's work was pioneering in that he was, like Snow, interested in the spatial component of the outbreak, and sought geographical as well as medical factors to explain the incidence of cholera. Acland's map marks in black the locations of confirmed cases of cholera and of choleraic diarrhoea (similar illnesses, but in the latter the symptoms are not entirely in keeping with cholera) and in blue the locations of the outbreaks of 1832 and 1849. Red numbers on the road refer to a table of yards and courts off the main streets. He records contours at intervals of five feet descending from the highest point of the city at Carfax (49.64 feet above the normal level of the River Thames at Folly Bridge); undrained districts of the city; and the polluted branches of the Rivers Thames and Cherwell. Whereas Snow charted only the locations of cholera outbreaks and public water pumps in Soho, Acland marked the main points of entry of polluted water into the river courses and, using red circles, the specific locations in the city which had been recommended for improved drainage and sanitation by a commission. The use of colour on the map for differentiating different themes is of considerable importance.

As well as the housing, social and moral conditions of the victims, Acland analysed a number of geographical factors in the spread of cholera, including density of population, elevation, weather conditions and the level of the rivers. He noted that the County Gaol (just south of the castle mound, and taking its water from a polluted mill-race) recorded thirty-one cases, but the City Gaol (which had a different water supply) none. However, although Acland was sure of the correlation between the epidemic and the quality of water and the standard of drainage of the most affected areas, unlike Snow he did not unequivocally assert the hypothesis that cholera was a water-borne disease. Nonetheless, the clarity of his mapped information, and the advantage that he demonstrated of mapping statistics with a spatial component, surely of themselves form a lasting legacy.

C17:70 Oxford (15)

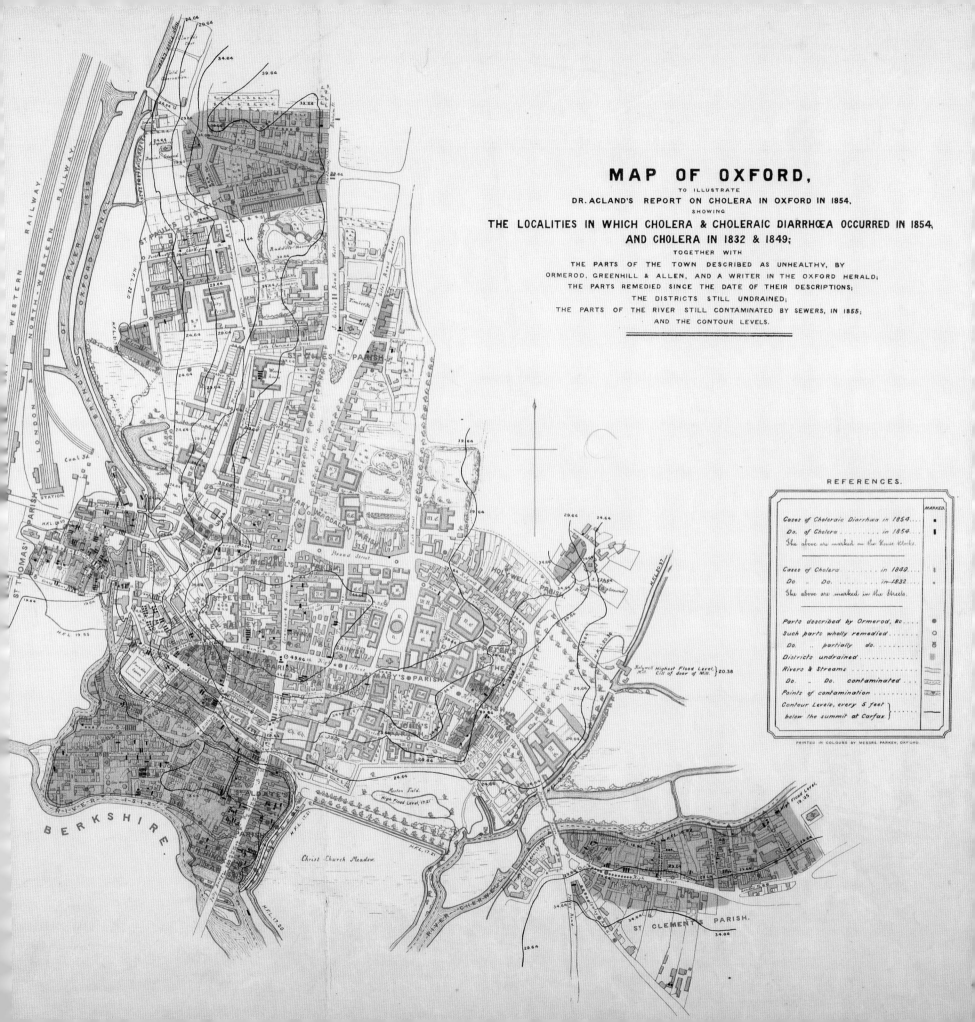

MAP OF OXFORD,

TO ILLUSTRATE

DR. ACLAND'S REPORT ON CHOLERA IN OXFORD IN 1854,

SHOWING

THE LOCALITIES IN WHICH CHOLERA & CHOLERAIC DIARRHŒA OCCURRED IN 1854,

AND CHOLERA IN 1832 & 1849;

TOGETHER WITH

THE PARTS OF THE TOWN DESCRIBED AS UNHEALTHY, BY
ORMEROD, GREENHILL & ALLEN, AND A WRITER IN THE OXFORD HERALD;
THE PARTS REMEDIED SINCE THE DATE OF THEIR DESCRIPTIONS;
THE DISTRICTS STILL UNDRAINED;
THE PARTS OF THE RIVER STILL CONTAMINATED BY SEWERS, IN 1855;
AND THE CONTOUR LEVELS.

REFERENCES.

	MARKED.
Cases of Choleraic Diarrhœa in 1854...	
Do. of Cholera .... in 1854...	
The above are marked on the House Blocks.	
Cases of Cholera ... in 1849...	
Do. Do. ... in 1832...	
The above are marked in the Streets.	
Parts described by Ormerod, &c....	
Such parts wholly remedied........	
Do. partially do.	
Districts undrained...........	
Rivers & Streams	
Do. Do. contaminated ...	
Points of contamination	
Contour Levels, every 5 feet below the summit at Carfax.	

PRINTED IN COLOURS BY MESSRS. PARKER, OXFORD.

A balloon view of London

This sheet is a view of London as seen from a hot air balloon. It was first published in 1851, the year of the Great Exhibition, on the same day that the exhibition opened. It is a panorama of London from the air, looking south towards the Thames and further afield.

Hot air balloon ascents were a popular form of entertainment from the 1820s, and map views purporting to be drawn from balloons had a corresponding surge in popularity, although it is not known how many really were drawn from up in the sky. Towards the top of the map the landscape has been distorted slightly to show areas that would actually be over the horizon.

The map shows in great detail many features of note in London which at the time were new, such as the early railways and stations. It shows nine of the city's bridges, not including of course Tower Bridge, which was of later construction. This is a view of early Victorian London, before the huge expansion of housing began in earnest. Some parts of south London have quite a rural feel. North of the river many of the railway stations are very new. They are identified only by the name of the line, for example Great Western Railway Station; the only named station is Euston.

The first edition showed the huge glass building, known as the Crystal Palace, for the Great Exhibition in Hyde Park (a more detailed map of the Crystal Palace itself appears on page 178). By the time this edition was published in 1859, the Crystal Palace had been moved to Sydenham, so it was expertly erased from the map plate and the area filled in with trees. Its new location, and the new railway for accessing it, appear rather unrealistically on the horizon.

As the viewer is looking south, from a viewpoint above Hampstead, the map appears 'upside down' compared to most maps of London with north at the top. This may have been to give prominence to more populated areas and important buildings north of the river. The map follows the usual convention, in maps that show three-dimensional buildings or hill-shading, of having the light source top left. In maps with north at the top, this is the northwest. The light source in this case is in the southeast, a more realistic direction.

The map was first published by J.H. Banks, who had produced an earlier view of London from the south. It ran to many editions, of which this 1859 version with hand colouring was one of at least two published by the major London mapmaker Edward Stanford; he added the hot air balloon. The full panorama measures 63 × 109 cm; an extract from the centre appears here. It was printed from a steel engraved plate, which would have facilitated the very fine engraving as well as being more durable than copper. The steel plate was last recorded being sold with the stock of G.F. Cruchley in 1877, although the map had one subsequent incarnation as a lithographic transfer published by G.W. Bacon in 1878.

This is a wonderful view of the capital, then the centre of a huge empire at its height, a celebration of London. The Thames is shown to be a busy working port, which at that time would have been filled with vessels from all parts of an empire that stretched across the world.

C17:70 London (327)

THE RIVER THAMES
CHELSEA REACH

RIVER THAMES

ST JAMES'S PARK

GREEN PARK

HYDE PARK

REGENTS PARK

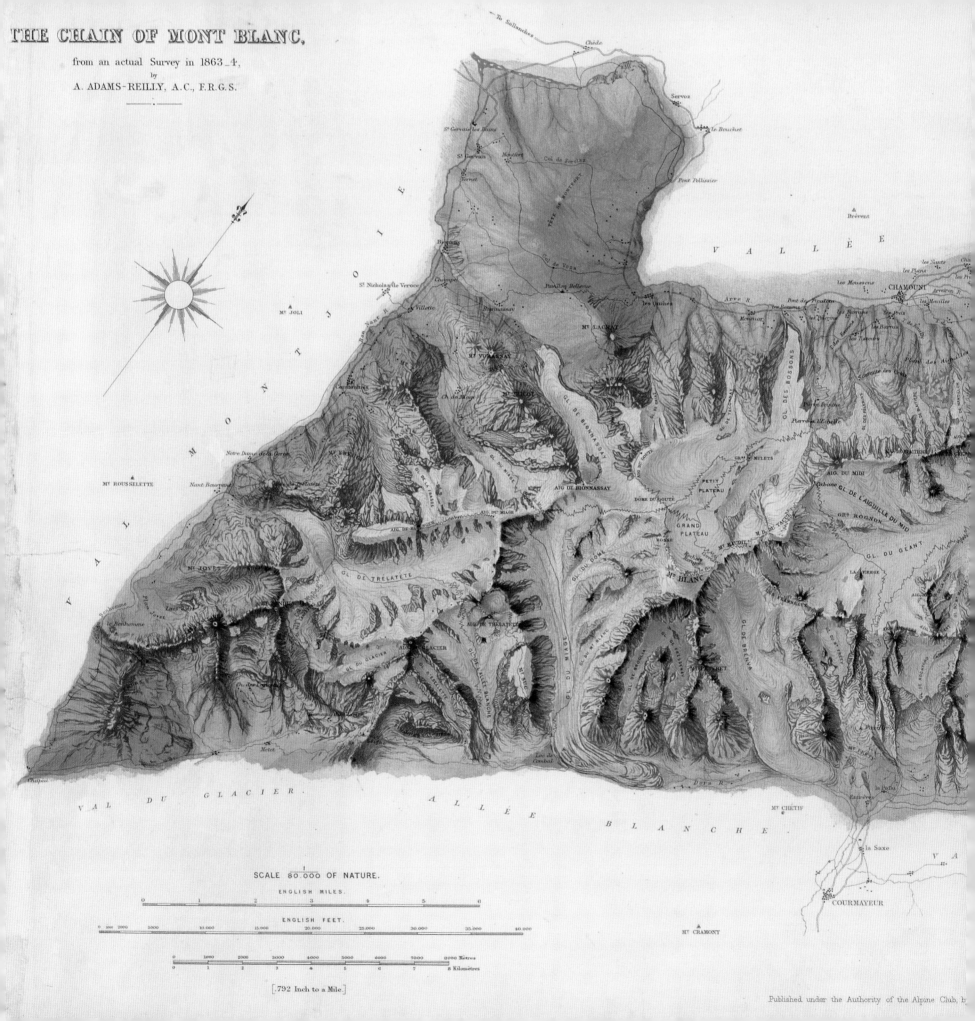

THE CHAIN OF MONT BLANC,

from an actual Survey in 1863_4,
by
A. ADAMS-REILLY, A.C., F.R.G.S.

SCALE $\frac{1}{80.000}$ OF NATURE.

ENGLISH MILES.

0   1   2   3   4   5   6

ENGLISH FEET.

0 1000 2000   5000   10.000   15.000   20.000   25.000   30.000   35.000   40.000

0   1000 2000 3000 4000 5000 6000 7000 8000 Mètres
0   1   2   3   4   5   6   7   8 Kilomètres

[.792 Inch to a Mile.]

Published under the Authority of the Alpine Club,

CHAPTER 6

Maps for Fun

ONLY A SOCIETY WITH A FAIRLY AFFLUENT AND LEISURED POPULATION can support a demand for maps for fun, whether this involves hiking, skiing, tourist attractions or simply admiring the scenery. It is notable that maps produced solely for the purpose of enjoying the landscape are a comparatively recent phenomenon, although this chapter does include one exceptional early example of a tourist guide.

The idea of admiring the landscape as a recreational activity probably dates back only as far as the eighteenth century. By the latter half of the nineteenth, however, a growing interest in sport and tourism developed simultaneously. The British Alpine Club was founded in 1857, and other countries followed suit; by the early twentieth century it was one of many local and national alpine clubs across Europe and North America. Outdoor activities such as sailing, canoeing, walking and climbing were often promoted by tourist organizations as the participants brought economic benefits; these activities required maps. The map of the Mont Blanc chain, of which an extract appears opposite, was published in London under the authority of the Alpine Club in 1865; the mapmaker was a member of the Club and also the Royal Geographical Society. Adventure as recreation was getting established, at least amongst the more affluent.

Meanwhile, the massive increase in railway provision in Britain from the mid-nineteenth century meant that travel for leisure purposes became available to an ever-growing number of people. Thomas Cook began organizing railway excursions as package tours in the

FACING

The first detailed map of the Mont Blanc massif was published by Anthony Adams-Reilly, an Irish-born and English-educated alpinist, cartographer and artist. It took him two seasons to survey, using a combination of trigonometrical surveying and panoramic drawing.

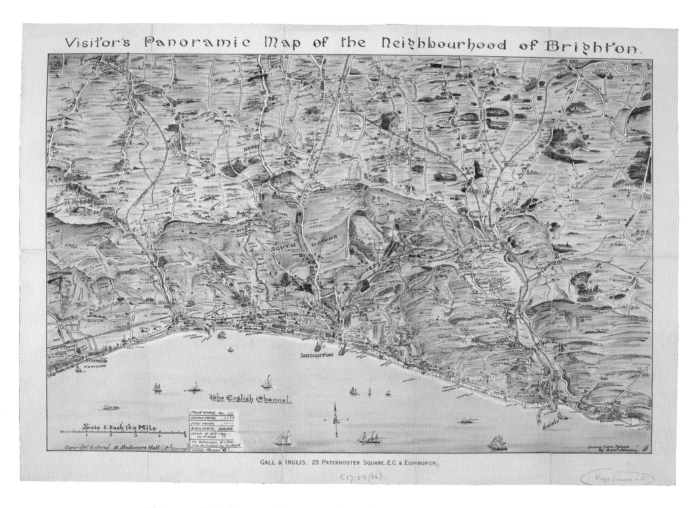

This map of Brighton and its surroundings shows the rolling green hills around the popular seaside town.

1840s. Seaside resorts such as Brighton, fashionable since the Regency period, became increasingly accessible to the masses. Railways are conspicuous in Samuel Johnson's *Visitor's panoramic map of the neighbourhood of Brighton,* illustrated here. Rail travel was also significant in the development of some US national parks as tourist destinations.

As well as sparking new demand for maps, tourism and leisure encouraged the development of different map forms and new marketing approaches. The cartographic tradition of displaying places in perspective view rather than from directly 'above' can be traced back for many hundreds of years, as can be seen in the previous chapter on city maps. This form is still used for maps produced for novelty value or as souvenirs, such as the map of Brighton here. Such an overview is enticing partly because it is impossible to achieve in reality from

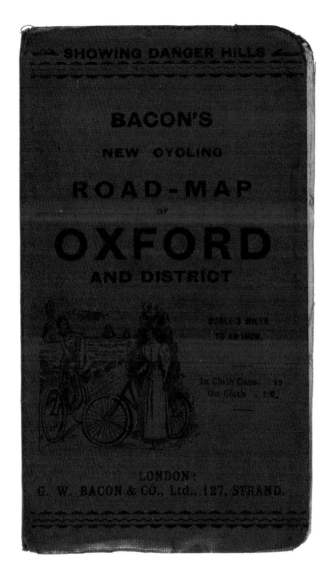

Bacon's map cover suggests that cycling offers exercise, scenery
and chance encounters with the opposite sex.

a single viewpoint – panoramas are of necessity a composite of different views. The art form, somewhere between a painting and a map,
gives a vivid sense of overlooking the landscape, bringing it to life in
a way that is more accessible to the viewer than a conventional map.
Panoramas were increasingly popular through the nineteenth century,
with some large panoramas on permanent public display as tourist
attractions (such as Thomas Hornor's enormous 360° view of London
from the top of St Paul's Cathedral, displayed for many years in the
Colosseum building in Regent's Park). The view of Yellowstone Park
and Tombleson's panoramic map of the Thames, both included in this

chapter, fall into this category. Modern ski maps often follow a similar style, perhaps to make it simpler for the map's users to look down from the top of their run and visualize their route to the bottom.

The Ordnance Survey's maps are familiar to many British users for their aid in planning outings and country walks. Marketing of maps for recreational purposes was to prove increasingly important to the organization in the twentieth century. Companies such as G.W. Bacon & Co. and G.F. Cruchley produced maps which often boasted attractive covers and claimed to be '... improved from the Ordnance Surveys'. For example the cover of Bacon's 1910 *Cycling road map of Oxford and district*, shown on the preceding page, hints at the possibilities of romance to be found on the road. These maps out-sold OS products to such an extent that, despite initial reluctance to take a more commercial approach, the organization sought to be more in line with its competitors. To achieve this, OS map covers were made more attractive, with illustrations by artists such as Ellis Martin and Arthur Palmer (facing page). Many of the map covers present aspirational images of people hiking, cycling, motoring or boating amid attractive landscape. The images evolved over time, a rather formally tweed-clad gentleman of the early twentieth century being succeeded in the 1930s by more casually dressed young men and women enjoying the scenery. There were also many covers that celebrated individual regions and places – a punting couple for Oxford, a landscape scene for the Lakes, or iconic landmarks, such as St Michael's Mount in Cornwall. The cover of the Loch Lomond map shown here was first used in 1920.

Happily, information first collected for scientific and military purposes could be re-purposed. The OS has its roots in the surveys of the south coast of Britain made during the Napoleonic wars; and the first surveys of Mount Kenya, for instance, were made in a spirit of geographical discovery. The information gathered is now more likely to be used by people setting off up hills seeking enjoyment, personal challenge and adventure.

OS map covers illustrated by Ellis Martin and Arthur Palmer in the 1920s and '30s celebrate the beauty of the landscape and the possibilities of roaming through it with a map.

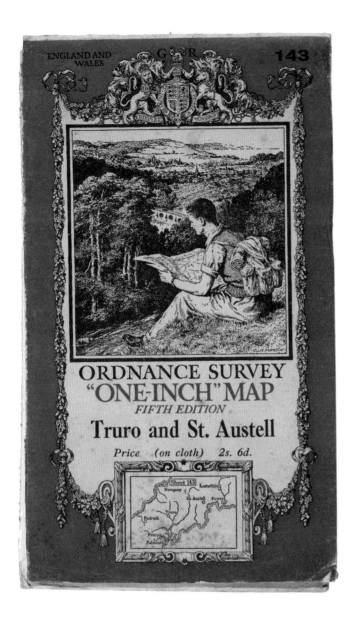

ORDNANCE SURVEY
"ONE-INCH" MAP
FIFTH EDITION
Truro and St. Austell

Price (on cloth) 2s. 6d.

Sheet 143

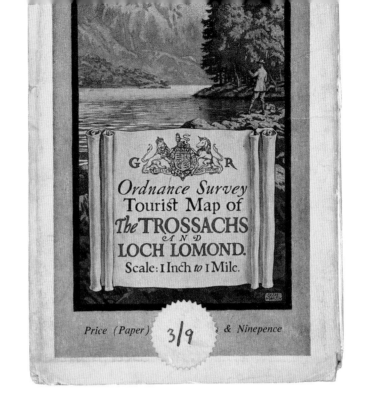

G R
Ordnance Survey
Tourist Map of
The TROSSACHS
AND
LOCH LOMOND.
Scale: 1 Inch *to* 1 Mile.

Price (Paper) 3/9 & Ninepence

ORDNANCE SURVEY
"ONE-INCH" MAP

Dorking & Leith Hill
Mounted in Sections
Price Four Shillings & Sixpence Net.

Published by the Ordnance Survey Office, Southampton

N4293

SPECIAL SHEET. POPULAR EDITION.

ORDNANCE
SURVEY

DISTRICT
MAP

Tourist or pilgrim?

The map of the Holy Land opposite comes from a book that has a fair claim to be the first tourist guide. Bernhard von Breydenbach (1440–1497) travelled in 1483 from his home in Mainz, where he was a canon at the cathedral, via Venice to the Holy Land and on to Cairo. Amongst his party was Erhard Reuwich, an artist from Utrecht, who drew views of the places they passed through. Reliable city maps were a rarity at this time, as mentioned in Chapter 5. The party stayed for three weeks in Venice, long enough for Reuwich to make detailed sketches, before embarking for the Holy Land. He drew views of five other Mediterranean towns and islands on the way, and this spectacular one centred on Jerusalem, of which a section is reproduced here. The views were as innovative in format as in content, with the first folding plates to appear in a printed book. The map of the Holy Land contains a detailed depiction of Jerusalem and the surrounding landscape, portraying towns, rivers, hills and holy sites. Reuwich has taken some liberties with scale, enlarging the city to dominate the area. To the south Alexandria, the Nile Delta and Cairo are included; the vista extends to the Red Sea with Arabia and Mecca on the other side.

The party returned home to Mainz (incidentally the birthplace of the printing press) the following year; the plates were published there by Reuwich in 1486, along with Latin text long attributed to Breydenbach but now thought to have been written by a Dominican, Martin Roth. The book, *Peregrinatio in Terram Sanctam*, includes many of the features of a tourist guide, giving information on the history of the area, illustrations of curiosities encountered on the way, and practical advice. This last includes medical advice for travellers, such as remedies for seasickness and against vermin,

and a phrasebook containing Arabic vocabulary translated into other languages. There are details of tourist attractions, mainly places where saints' relics were to be found, but there is, for example, a full description of the Church of the Holy Sepulchre in Jersusalem, along with details of the entrance fee (5 ducats).

Can this be seen as a tourist guide? The journey was certainly undertaken from religious rather than recreational motives. Breydenbach was on a pilgrimage to atone for the sins of his youth. However, this does not preclude its being regarded as tourist travel, which often has the aim of improving the traveller rather than being simply for enjoyment. From the seventeenth century, wealthy young European men (mainly British) would often make a Grand Tour of Europe, with at least the theoretical aim of improving their minds and completing their education by exposure to foreign art, culture and music. Similarly, later proponents of leisure travel often believed that contemplating the beauties of nature had a morally elevating effect, as discussed in the next entry. And religion can still motivate leisure travel; Muslims may undertake a pilgrimage to Mecca, or Roman Catholics visit the Vatican.

If this is a tourist guide, it was a very early prototype. The book was popular, twelve editions being published by 1522, but nothing like it followed for some time. A few guides to individual countries were published in the sixteenth century. Road books (listing routes and post roads) for tourists were available from the sixteenth century, and practical road maps for travellers began to appear in the seventeenth. But for the Grand Tour a human guide was considered essential, and tourist maps and guidebooks for leisure travel at home and abroad did not become widespread for another three centuries.

Arch. B c.25

Romantic mountains

This lovely map of Keswick and the surrounding area, in the English Lake District, was at the forefront of a new movement in the late eighteenth century – the contemplation, and ascent, of mountain scenery. The Lake District is now extremely popular with tourists and hill-walking is one of the major activities, but in 1789, when William Faden published this map in London, it was new, fashionable and exciting, and the map depicted unknown territory. Thomas West had first published his *Guide to the Lakes* in 1778, and many subsequent editions were produced over the succeeding years. The picturesque tour was becoming a popular activity; Elizabeth Bennett in Austen's *Pride and Prejudice* (begun just a few years after this map's publication) looks forward excitedly to a tour of the Lakes with her uncle and aunt. Within a decade, the Romantic poets William Wordsworth and Samuel Taylor Coleridge would be refreshing their souls amid the mountain scenery and publishing poetry about it, entranced by the beauty of this wild landscape; the Lake District was seen as a place of both aesthetic and moral inspiration. At the time this map was made, there were no recorded climbs to the summit of many of the mountains depicted; Coleridge was to make what may have been the first ascent of Helvellyn within a few years.

This map was drawn by Thomas Donald, described as 'Surveyor', and the title emphasizes that it is a new survey – *An actual topographical survey of the environs of Keswick*. It is worth bearing in mind that the Ordnance Survey of Great Britain had yet to begin; individual county maps were the best available source of cartographic information. Donald had previously published a county map of Cumberland, at a scale (like this map's) of around one inch to a mile. West's *Guide* contained, initially at least, no pictorial matter or maps; the third edition of 1784 was the first to contain a map and it showed scant detail. Other mapmakers, notably Peter Crosthwaite, were to publish maps of the area over the next few years. Scientific surveys developed alongside new Romantic ideas about the interpretation of mountain scenery. This map was engraved (by John Haywood) and published in London.

The map is beautifully coloured, the highest summits standing out in golden yellow while the valleys and lakes are in pale green and slate blue – a celebration of the lovely landscape it depicts. The town of Keswick is not shown in much detail, but dramatic hachuring emphasizes the steep mountains and ridges surrounding it. In some cases they may be overemphasized. Skiddaw, though one of the higher summits in England, has some relatively gentle slopes, and was popular with early tourists for that reason; it was even possible to ascend it on horseback. The way it is depicted here (top right) makes it appear considerably more precipitous. West's *Guide* recommends some quite elevated viewpoints and local farmers often made money by conducting visitors up this and other popular mountains – the beginning of a tourist industry in the area which has flourished ever since.

(E) C17:22 (39)

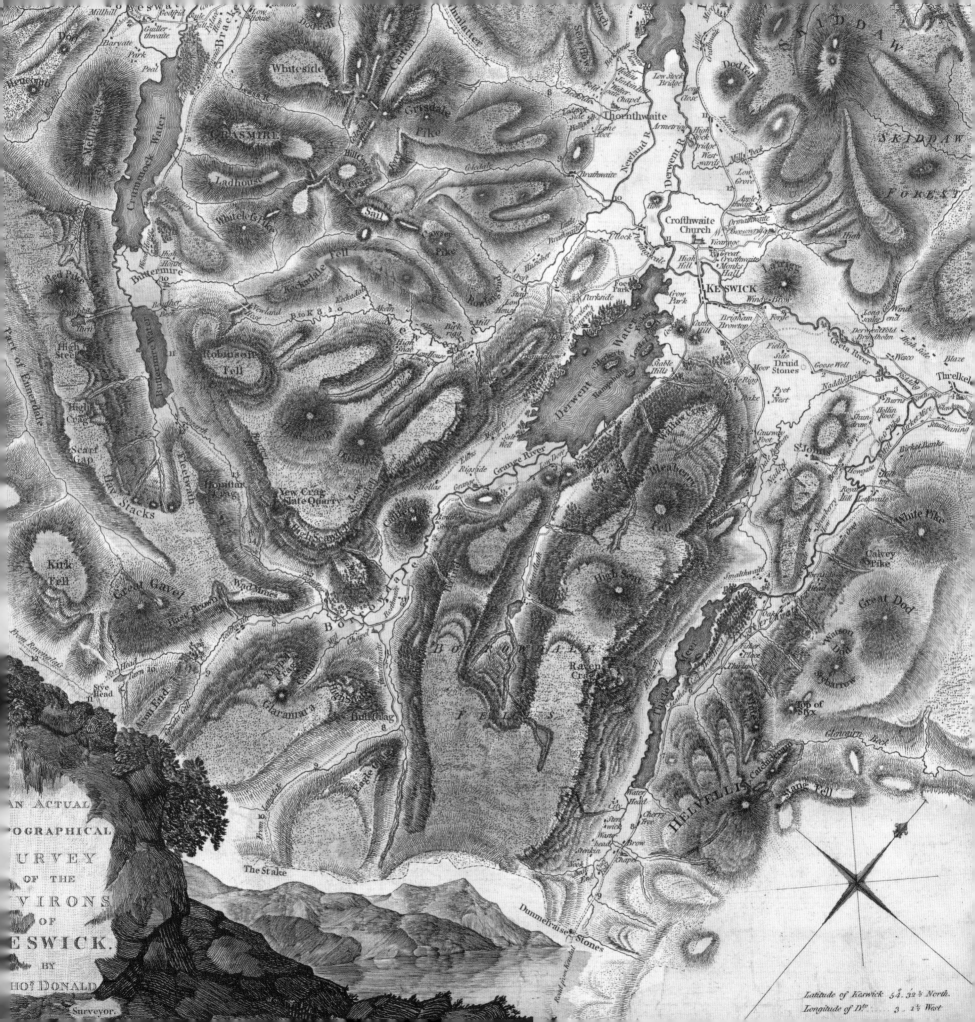

The River Thames in panorama

This beautiful panoramic view, entitled *Tombleson's panoramic map of the Thames and Medway*, was first produced in the 1830s, and ran to many editions, changing slightly in appearance and purpose over the years. The edition shown here dates from 1899, when the map had evolved from an illustration to a more serious work to a separate publication designed both to be decorative and to encourage enjoyment of the river.

William Tombleson first published the map in a book entitled *Tombleson's Thames,* a detailed topographical and historical description of the landscape through which the river flows. It followed a book of views of the Rhine that he had published a few years earlier, and was available in German and English editions. The text, written by William Fearnside, is lavish and flowery –for example: 'From its fountain-head, it is constantly acquiring importance …. What country can boast, on the bosom of a river, such power and grandeur as are displayed on passing London, the emporium of the world?' However, the work gives an enormous amount of detail; the history and local economy of the places along the river are described, as is the appearance of the landscape and a certain amount of local legend and anecdote. Tombleson illustrated the work as well as publishing it; there are engraved views of the places the river passes through in addition to the fold-out panoramic map. The views show people both working and playing on the river, and notable buildings on its banks; at this time, it was still important for transport as well as being used for fishing, watering cattle and so forth. Many views (including the example here, Temple Island near Henley) are titled in French and German as well as English, suggesting that they were available for individual sale.

The map, when published with the book, was finely engraved, uncoloured, and largely omitted practicalities such as locks. Many subsequent editions were printed without the accompanying book. The later editions are more functional, include additional place names, and give greater prominence to the railway (shown here in red); this was a map that would enable people to find their way to attractions on the river and enjoy themselves when they got there.

In one important aspect, the map is not accurate; it shows the course of the River Thames as relatively straight. Its considerable changes in direction are understated, particularly around Pangbourne, where the river turns almost by a right angle. In this respect it is reminiscent of John Ogilby's road maps in *Britannia*, where the aim is to show the route between places rather than accurately portraying their spatial relationship. The width of the river is also shown as too great, relative to its length – it is a foreshortened view to accommodate as much detail as possible. This gives a lovely sense of looking at the whole river in one view, one of the most satisfying things about a panorama.

C17:8 (153)

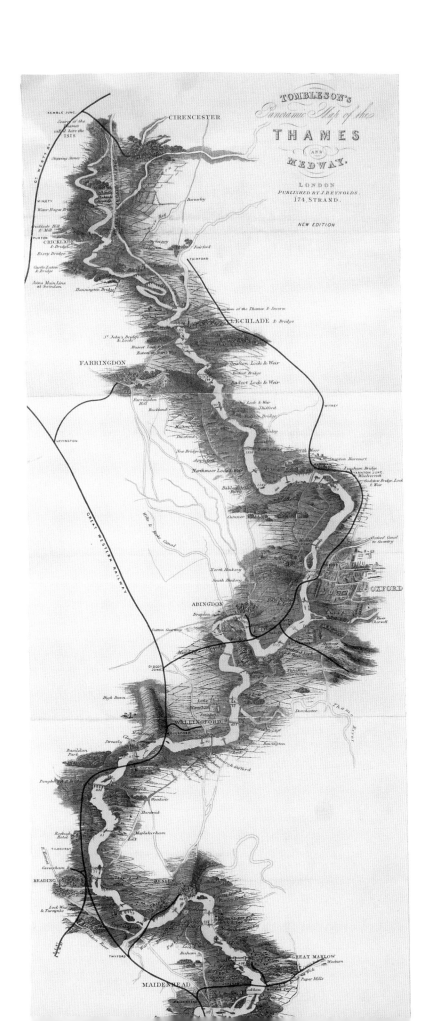

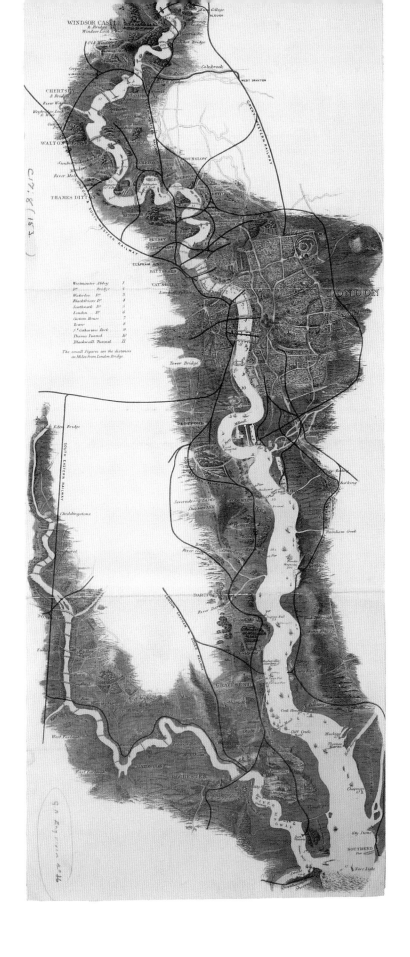

Lord Gifford's Hunt, in miniature

This map from the 1840s was produced for people going fox hunting to use. Hunting with hounds has long been a controversial subject, but at the time of this map's production (around 1843) it was enormously popular and would certainly have been regarded as a fitting activity for gentlemen (and, within limits, ladies). It is striking for its minute size – it folds into a cover less than 7 cm square, and could be easily carried in a waistcoat pocket – yet it contains a great deal of relevant information. The places where the hunt held its meets are numbered, and an eight-page booklet is bound into the cover, giving distances by road to each of them from the nearest railway station or post town. It is beautifully produced, even though diminutive. Hills are shown by delicate hachuring and county boundaries, roads and woodland are neatly hand-coloured. The tiny cover is bound with red cloth and features gold lettering and a gold picture of a horse and rider leaping over a daunting-looking obstacle.

The Lord Gifford of the title is Robert Gifford, 2nd Baron Gifford, who took over the hunt as Master in 1842 at a time of some conflict. There was a dispute with the neighbouring Old Berkshire Hunt as to exactly where the division between the two hunting countries lay. They had previously been hunted as one area, but had been divided ten years before, and the southeastern portion of the map – roughly the area between Swindon and Buscot – was claimed by both hunts. The dispute became heated in 1844 when they both tried to meet at the same place on the same day: the Old Berkshire regarded this as a breach of the peace and a warrant was issued for Lord Gifford's arrest. It may be significant that the hunt's official name – Vale of White Horse Hunt – does not appear on the map; possibly Lord Gifford was staking a personal claim. Matters were eventually resolved peacefully the following year, when a division was agreed.

The map was published by a woman, rather unusually for the time. M.A. Pittman, who also traded as Mary Ann Pittman & Son, published a number of sporting publications including *The Horseman's Manual* and the *Sporting Magazine*. The map was engraved by John Dower, who had a long and accomplished career engraving mainly county and atlas maps throughout the mid-nineteenth century.

There is something appealing about this pretty miniature map. Although there were practical reasons for its small size, the high standard of production suggests something designed as a status symbol as well. It could have been a flattering gift for a fox-hunting man, or a souvenir to pore over after a successful hunt, when the fences jumped and miles galloped grew ever greater in recollection.

C17:7 g.1

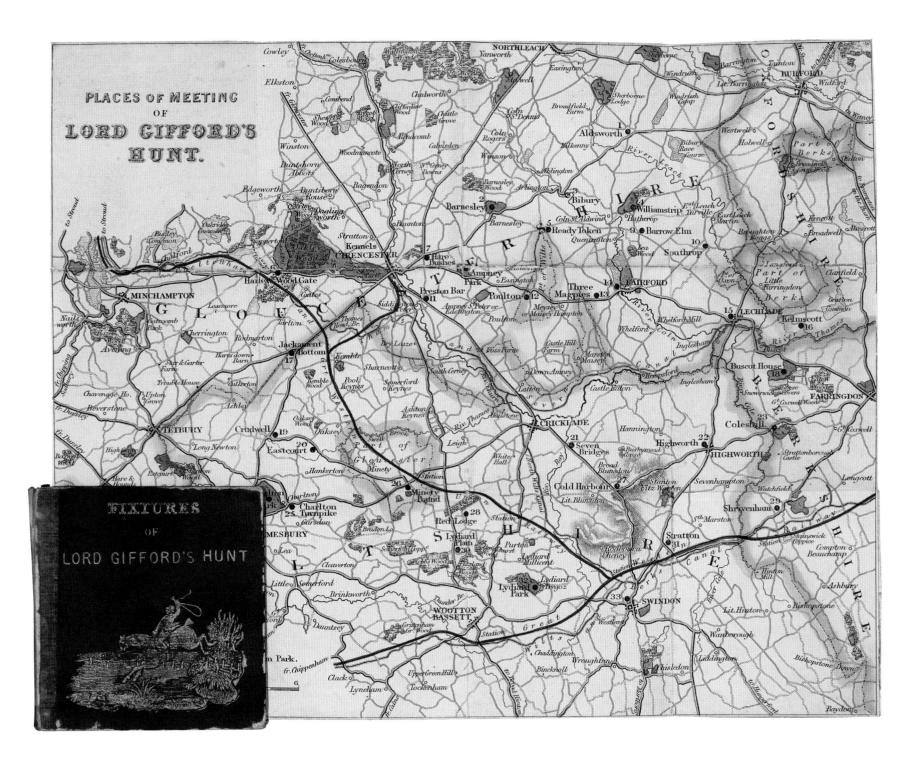

PLACES OF MEETING OF LORD GIFFORD'S HUNT.

FIXTURES OF LORD GIFFORD'S HUNT

The Crystal Palace

The *Ordnance Plan of the Crystal Palace and its Environs*, published in May 1864, was a 1:2,500 'Special' Ordnance Survey sheet, centring on the Crystal Palace in Sydenham after it had been moved from Hyde Park in the mid-1850s. The 1:2,500 scale, about 25 inches to a mile, was to become the standard scale used by the OS for their mapping of inhabited and cultivated areas across the British Isles. In size and appearance, the Palace plan (a plan is more strictly to scale, while a map takes liberties for simplicity's sake) looks like a regular 25-inch First Edition of the OS County Series. Work on the first edition had only recently begun, with some of the earliest surveys done in this area on the southern fringes of London. But the rectangle covered by the Palace sheet, straddling the Surrey-Kent-London border, did not fall neatly into the centre of a regular grid on the already established sheet-lines; a 'Special' was called for. What we have here is in effect a one-off composite, taken from six regular sheets.

Those familiar with the County Series will recognize the trade-mark hand-colouring – pale pink for grand public buildings, dark pink for stone or brick structures, grey for wooden or iron ones, cross-hatched blue for glass-houses (ordinary glass-houses, not the palatial sort), blue for water, buff for roads. They will also recognize the exquisite detail synonymous with early large-scale OS productions – free-standing mature trees individually marked, with broadleaf, conifer and orchard trees artistically distinguished; names and architectural quirks of the bigger suburban houses and villas, with their steps, flowerbeds, garden paths, ponds and sheds. The degree of detail on early sheets, including the Palace plan, surpasses in fineness that of the later ones produced when surveying had got into its stride in the 1870s and 1880s and methods had been simplified to save time. But even for its time and scale the Crystal Palace sheet pulls out all the stops, and is a work of art.

The Palace itself gets the pale-pink treatment usually reserved for cathedrals, despite its predominantly glass structure. The contents of the 'transepts' – the word is expressive – are lovingly recorded: the Assyrian Court and Renaissance Court, the Bohemian Glass Court (glass within glass), the Sculpture Gallery and Ceramic Court and Egyptian Figures, the Concert Room and Terrace Dining Room, the Queen's Apartments, staircases, indoor 'lakes' and much more. And, outside, a wonderland of fountains, water temples, music stands and archery stands, statues and flagstaffs and winding paths. There is no mistaking the surveyors', the draughtsmen's and zincographers' delight, the pride they must have felt in both Palace and plan. Never, one feels, can a theodolite have weighed less heavily on the hands.

Why was the plan produced? There is no price marked; this, and the extreme scarcity of surviving copies, may mean that the sheet was not widely printed or for sale. Richard Oliver, in his note accompanying the facsimile produced by the Charles Close Society (CCS) in 2010, suggests that the plan may have been produced as propaganda for the OS's 1:2,500. Or perhaps the simple fact that the Palace could not be viewed on a single sheet was motive enough for some to think that a few copies of a composite would be a good idea. The Bodleian Library's copy has been much consulted over the years. The CCS's facsimile, reproduced here, shows the plan as it would have appeared in its pristine state (thanks to digital cleaning and restoration by Alex Kent).

C17:8 (350)

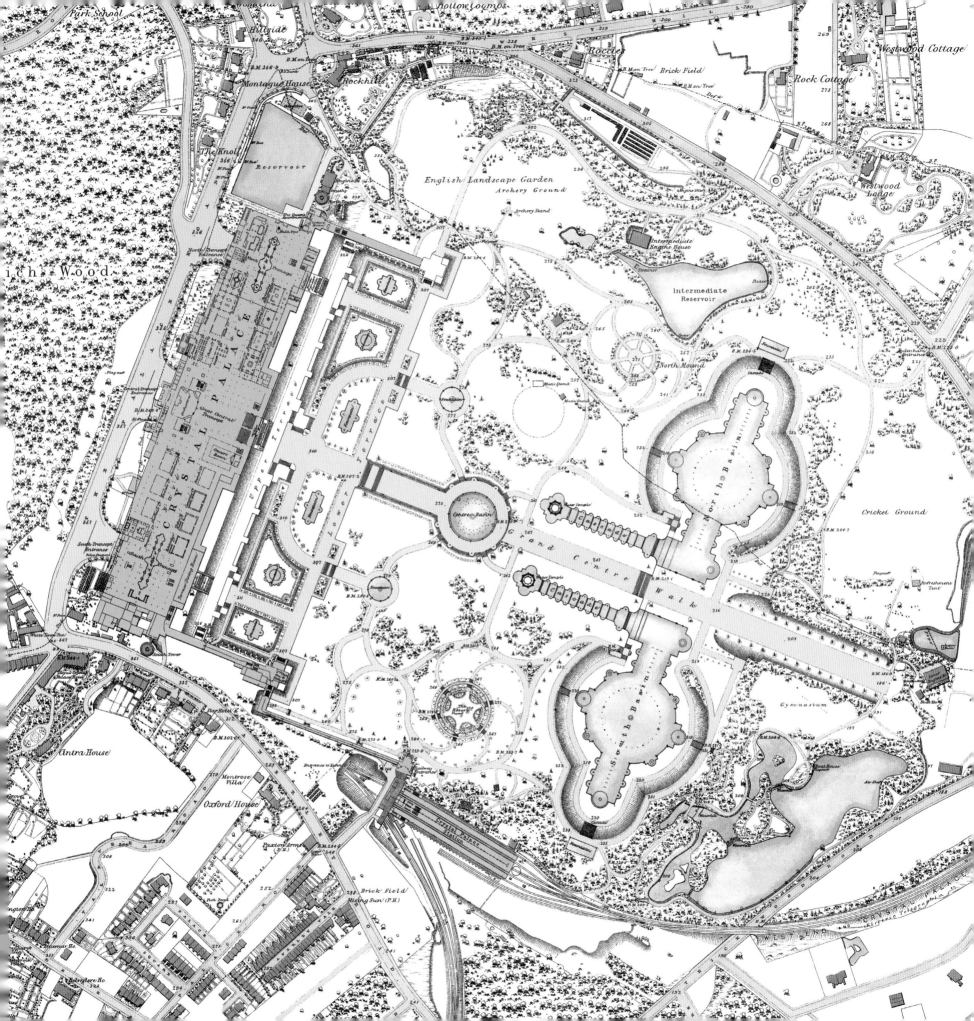

Visit Yellowstone!

This is an exceptionally sunny map. The river and rolling hills appear lit up, the bright yellowish stone that gives the area its name seems to glow in the canyon walls, and the blue sky (scattered with little white clouds) is reflected in the tranquil blue of Yellowstone Lake. Strictly speaking, it is a panorama or bird's-eye view rather than a map, showing the landscape in perspective as well as giving the layout of Yellowstone National Park. There is no visible light source, but the sky suggests a hazy sunshine, perhaps misted by the steam from Old Faithful which rises in the far distance on the right-hand side.

The inspiration behind the map can be found by looking at the foot, where a note states 'Copyright 1904 by Henry Wellge, Milwaukee, transferred to the Northern Pacific Railway Company'. Wellge produced many attractive panoramic maps, mainly of towns, from the 1880s onwards; he had his own company but in this case was working for Northern Pacific. The logo of the Northern Pacific Yellowstone Park line appears twice on the map, and the company's railway station (with 'Northern Pacific' in large letters on the roof) appears bottom right, with a train steaming into the station (just outside this extract). The map was made to promote rail travel to Yellowstone.

The park had been formally established in 1872, the first national park in the world, partly at the instigation of the geologist and surveyor Ferdinand Hayden. Hayden had mapped the park area more scientifically, if less prettily, in 1871. The construction of the railway connection about ten years later led to a considerable increase in visitor numbers. This was clearly in the interests of the railway company as well as the park authorities, especially at a time of expansion and improvement for the Northern Pacific. The map is oriented with south at the top, perhaps for artistic reasons but also putting the railway station into the foreground.

Everything about the map makes the park look inviting. Although the landscape is beautiful, the presence of civilization is clearly emphasized. The hotels are all named and marked in a fairly conspicuous red, the roads are a bright yellowish brown and outlined to make them stand out. The roads close to the station are reassuringly well populated with horses and carriages. Fort Yellowstone is shown flying the US flag. The overall effect is to show a landscape that is wild, beautiful, but not too daunting; there are steep cliffs, waterfalls and geysers, but also good roads and hotels. It is almost impossible to look at this map and not be seized by the desire to visit Yellowstone National Park – which was, of course, the idea.

F6:58 (36)

YELLOWSTONE RIVER

Mount Kenya

In 1899 a young Englishman arrived in East Africa to climb Mount Kenya, the legendary ice-cap on the Equator. Part of his object was to survey the mountain and make a map. Halford Mackinder (1861–1947) was an Oxford don, founder of the university's School of Geography, Britain's first 'modern' geography teacher. In those days geographers were expected to explore uncharted regions and make maps. So Mackinder took surveying lessons at the Royal Geographical Society and mountaineering lessons in the Alps, and obtained the Society's blessing for his venture. With two Swiss companions he reached the mountain's summit. It was no holiday climb and would not be repeated for thirty years.

Returning to camp, Mackinder unpacked his theodolite and plane table and made a survey, drafting a map and naming many of the peaks' features. It helped that he admired the mountain aesthetically. 'What a beautiful mountain Kenya is,' he wrote, 'very graceful, not stern … with a cold feminine beauty.' At the end of his survey Mackinder was gratified to find that 'the circuit had closed on the plane table with only a small error'. It was a good amateur map; the RGS published it in their *Geographical Journal* in 1900. The manuscript maps, triangulation notes, diaries and expedition photographs are now in the Bodleian Library. For the next thirty years Mount Kenya enthusiasts, their porters bearing aneroids and hypsometers, amended Mackinder's map and made discoveries. 'It is a splendid fact,' wrote one, E.A.T. Dutton, excitedly, 'that the three great mountains, Kilimanjaro, Kenya, and Elgon, form a gigantic isosceles triangle with the Equator passing through its apex.' But the need for a thorough survey and *two* professional maps, large-scale for peaks and small-scale for the whole mountain, was felt. The first need was met in 1929 by a map at 1:21,120,

compiled by the Land Survey Department of Kenya. It can be found in the back of Dutton's book *Kenya Mountain*. Revisions of the '1929' were to be a climbers' standby for the next three decades, the golden age of Kenya mountaineering, until the Mau-Mau Emergency of the 1950s, when the mountain became a guerrilla headquarters and (officially) out of bounds.

The need for a whole-mountain sheet was met by the present acclaimed 1974 1:125,000 *Map of Mount Kenya National Park and Environs*, produced by the OS in Southampton and the Survey of Kenya in Nairobi. After World War II the Colonial Office had set up its own survey organization, the Directorate of Overseas Surveys, to map the colonies. Many of these maps were printed in Southampton. 'Perhaps the finest', one OS history records, 'was the 1974 map of Mount Kenya, printed in ten colours, for which the Ordnance Survey won the Thremmy Trophy, top award in an Excellence in Lithography competition'. The '1974' is a magnificent map. Coloured in olives and greens, it looks like an annotated satellite image without a cloud in the sky. The impression of the great circular decayed volcano, with radial river valleys dropping down through ravines from an eroded volcanic plug, comes across clearly, thanks to the three-dimensional effect of shading. Contours are brown against shades of green, blue against the white glaciers. The zones through which the walker ascends are all there – tea and coffee plantations in the foothills, rain forest, bamboo forest, parkland, heath, moorland, Alpine zone, glacial zone. There are forest guard-posts, mountain huts and met stations. Even 'Icy Mike' is there, the bones of a mountaineering elephant preserved in the permafrost – probably the only animal carcass to feature on an OS map.

E10:5 (26)

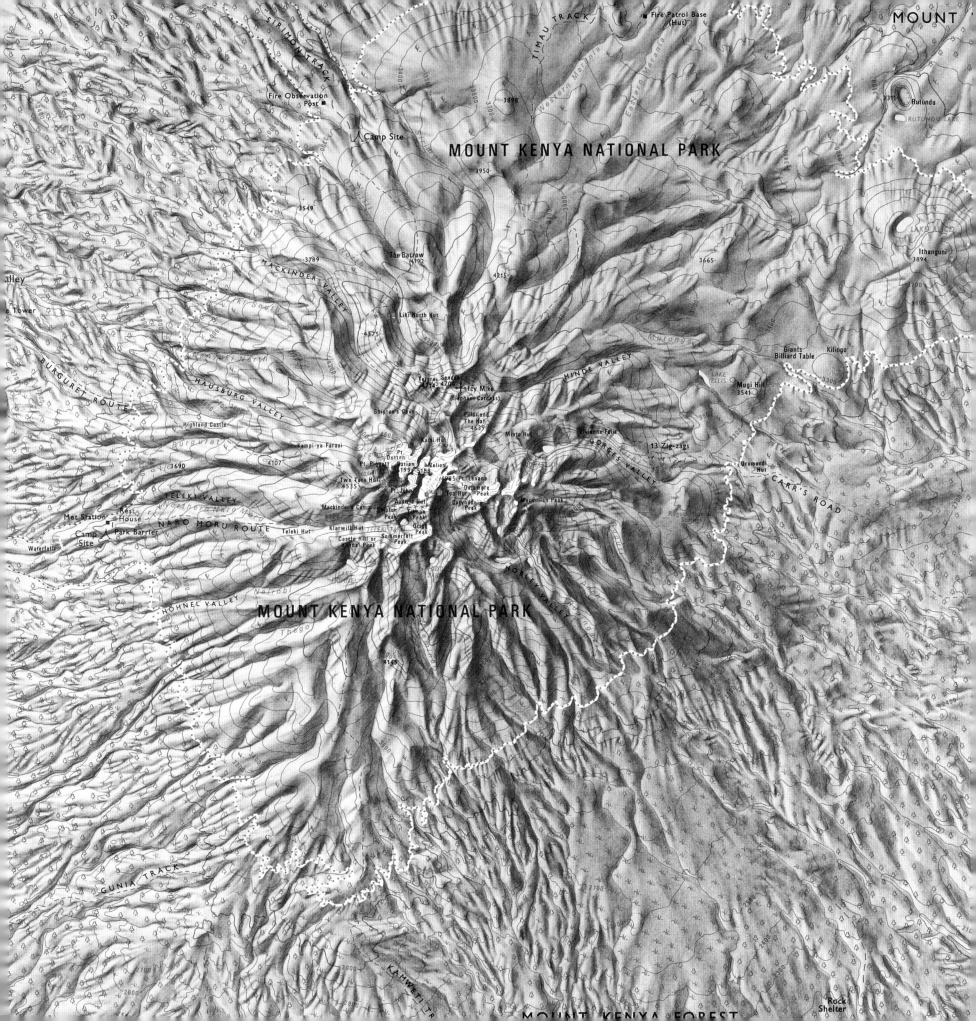

Mind the crevasse

Skiing maps have conventionally adopted one of three cartographic guises. Panoramas of mountain areas tend to represent the norm, with ski runs shown as thin coloured lines plummeting down snowy white slopes. Other options have brought into play oblique views of the pistes, or else there is the planimetric take from directly above, showing information as accurately as possible in two dimensions. All three modes, to a certain extent, endeavour to visualize the landscape and render the mountains accessible. But how practical are these maps for use in the open air?

The 3D Navigator map represents a solution to this conundrum. How does a winter sports person use a map when actively involved in an outdoor pursuit in cold conditions on potentially inhospitable, uneven terrain? The map's designers have eschewed the conventional paper map, vulnerable to moisture from melting snow and the unpredictability of wind gusts, in favour of a compact, robust and flexible format, which effectively combines key elements of a topographic map and a pop-up book. The map is printed on waterproof recyclable plastic.

Geographically, the map covers 'Les 3 Vallées' in Savoy in the French Alps, the area accessed via Moutiers on the River Isère, which lies at the foot of the three mountain valleys taking in the leading winter sports resorts of Courchevel, Meribel and Val Thorens.

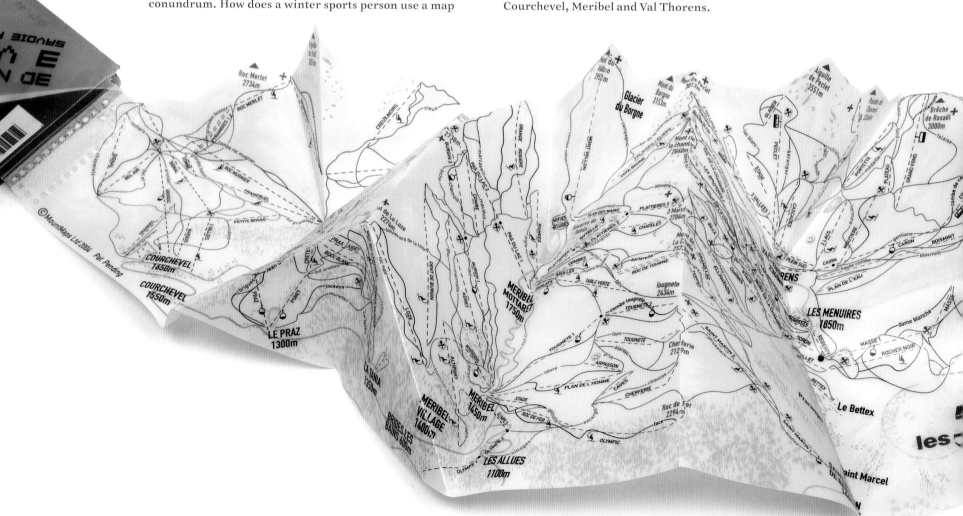

On opening out the wallet, the map itself does not look too appealing. It is folded in a bizarre fashion resembling a crumpled handkerchief (albeit made of jagged plastic). There is a clear red 'PULL' toggle nestling in the middle of the chaotic folds, and, when it is duly pulled, what resembles an Alpine panorama is revealed. Those jagged plastic edges become mountain summits, so Roc Merlet, Aiguille du Fruit, Mont du Vallon, Mont de Peclet, Aiguille de Peclet, Pointe du Thorens and Brêche de Rosaël are revealed, summits ranging in height from 2,734 to 3,551 metres. They form a backdrop to the map, which reveals the landscape in three dimensions falling away beneath them. In terms of cartographic content, pistes, graded by difficulty, are marked, along with ski lifts, cable cars, tree cover, roads, restaurants and first aid points – everything the skier would expect to need. Unfortunately the map fails to depict settlements, other than by a faint brownish stipple which somewhat resembles the green stipple used to indicate forestry. The accompanying booklet bound into the plastic wallet provides details of ski-lift opening times, transfers between ski lifts, stunning views, first aid, and other tourist information.

When folded, the map measures a snug 10.5 × 10.5 cm, easily fitting into a pocket. Once opened for consultation, the dimensions increase to 18 × 52 cm, but the robust nature of the plastic ensures that the map is windproof, and will not flap around too much when unfurled. The additional drawback of handling the map in falling snow or with icy gloves is also avoided as the map is fully waterproof. Thus, as a product designed for purpose, MountMaps have created an imaginative response to a challenging problem. MountMaps was the brainchild of Britons Stephen Brittain and Fletcher Morgan, who arrived at the idea whilst on a chairlift at another French Alpine resort, Chamonix. Their plan was to combine 'two thousand year old origami techniques and lots of mathematics and science'. This is a far cry from a paper panorama, and may require considerable interpretational initiative, but, as a response to a logistical problem, the 3D Navigator is an inspired solution. The eventual success of the design, however, may not have won over the skiing fraternity. MountMaps produced a handful of titles, and nothing since 2005.

C21:44 g.1

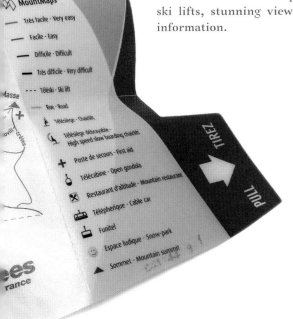

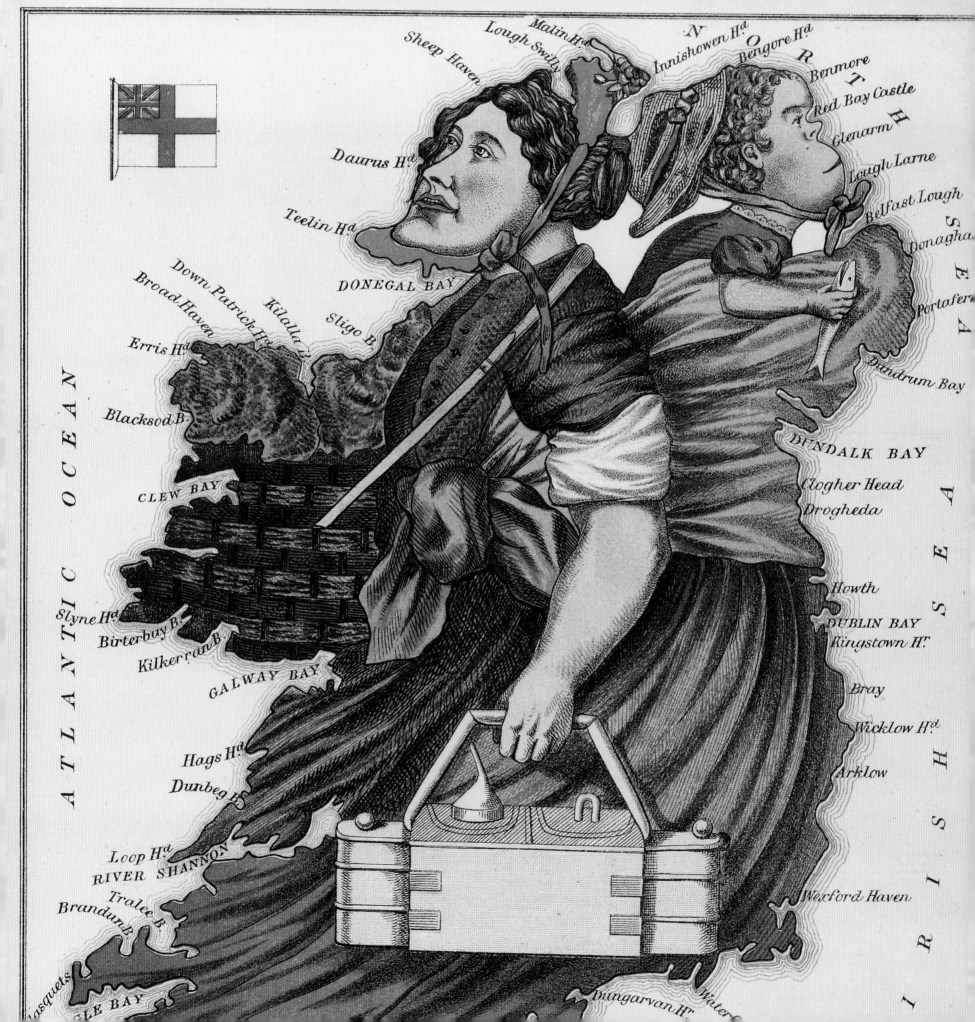

NORTH

Malin Hd.

Lough Swilly

Sheep Haven

Innishowen Hd.

Bengore Hd.

Benmore

Red Bay Castle

Daurus Hd.

Glenarm

Lough Larne

Teelin Hd.

Belfast Lough

DONEGAL BAY

Donagha

Down Patrick Hd.

Broad Haven

Kilalla I.

Portafera

Sligo B.

Erris Hd.

Dundrum Bay

Blacksod B.

DUNDALK BAY

CLEW BAY

Clogher Head

Drogheda

Slyne Hd.

Birterbuy B.

Howth

Kilkerran B.

DUBLIN BAY

Kingstown Hr.

GALWAY BAY

Bray

Wicklow Hd.

Hags Hd.

Arklow

Dunbeg B.

Loop Hd.

RIVER SHANNON

Tralee B.

Wexford Haven

Brandun B.

LE BAY

Dungarvan Hr.

Water

ATLANTIC OCEAN

NORTH SEA

IRISH SEA

CHAPTER 7

Imaginary Lands

ANY MAP IS, TO SOME DEGREE, A WORK OF IMAGINATION. THE mapmaker must select which elements of the landscape to include and how to represent them, select what to leave out, and conjure up features that are real, but intangible, like boundaries and place names. Similarly the map's users interpret the symbols on the map as real features on the ground, in order to know where to go and what to expect to see around the next corner. The maps in this section take this one step further, portraying an imagined reality. This may be intended to be fun, thought-provoking, satirical or entirely practical.

There are clear links between art and cartography; both disciplines are concerned with visual display and both may serve a decorative function. Medieval world maps were barely concerned with representing geography as we understand it. Rather, they have been described as visual encyclopaedias, showing history, mythological creatures and biblical events in a broadly geographical context. Many early printed maps were highly decorative, with illustrations of the plants and animals of the region, people in local costume, ornate borders and cartouches filled with classical references. Even for more scientific modern maps, aesthetics and visual effect are part of map design.

Some of the maps in this chapter show a real place, but represented symbolically. The *Leo Belgicus* is a famous example, and the representation of France as an oak tree, also included here, a much rarer one. Maps showing countries metaphorically, as people or animals, have been produced as occasional curiosities for hundreds of years. Earlier

FACING

The maps in *Geographical Fun* were drawn by a talented teenager, the actress Lilian Lancaster; here Ireland is shown as a cheerful peasant woman with her baby on her back.

From the eve of World War I, this is typical of political cartoon maps
of the late nineteenth and early twentieth centuries, which often showed
countries as aggressive animals or people.

examples tend to have a serious meaning. Maps of this type gained
popularity in the nineteenth century, and were often comic or politi-
cally satirical. Some are derogatory or vulgar, though the one on the
previous page, from around 1868, is rather charming. It is taken from
a book called *Geographical Fun,* written under the pseudonym 'Aleph'.
The example above, from 1914, is far more political and aggressive in
meaning. Maps are rarely used in this light-hearted way now, although
modern cartograms (showing the countries sized in proportion to
their population, for instance) or a world map with south at the top,

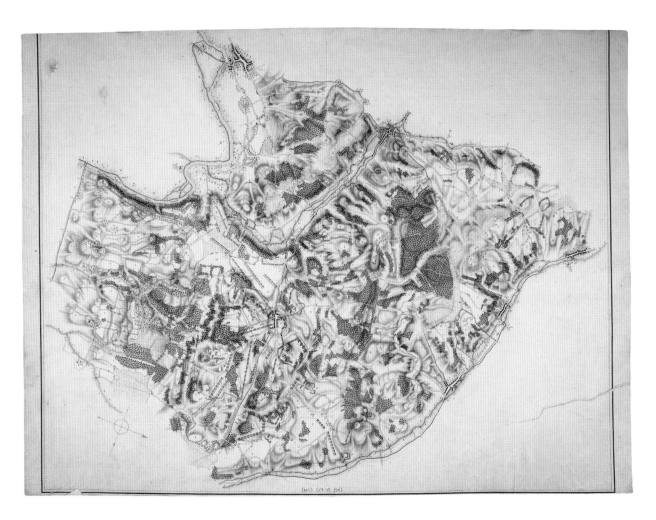

All the place names have been removed from this map, which was created
for military training. It is actually part of Buckinghamshire.

seek to challenge the assumptions contained in our conventional view
of the world.

Imaginative maps have also been created for practical reasons.
Planners have visualized improved or ideal settlements for centuries.
Some of these have come to fruition, at least in part, as in the model
villages of the eighteenth and nineteenth centuries and the new towns
and garden cities of the twentieth. John Evelyn's plan for a simpler and
more rational layout for the City of London following the Great Fire,
featured in this chapter, was doomed to failure, though later urban
planning was more successful. This chapter also includes an imaginary
landscape created for a military exercise. The map above shows a real
landscape but with all identifying features removed; it dates from the
early 1800s and was also created for military training.

As well as the links between maps and art, there is a relationship between cartography and literature, with each influencing the other. Maps are used as metaphors or literary devices: famous examples include Lewis Carroll's blank map in *The Hunting of the Snark* and Jorge Luis Borges's description of a map of countryside at a scale of 1:1; or the map may be a crucial part of the plot, as in the novel *Treasure Island*. Conversely, the creators of fantasy worlds have long felt the need to represent their imaginary geographies cartographically. The Bodleian is fortunate in possessing the papers of both J.R.R. Tolkien and C.S. Lewis, and maps illustrating the worlds of Middle Earth and Narnia are included here. There appears to be demand from fans of these and other fictional worlds to see their stories located geographically, sometimes leading to the maps being created retrospectively. As well as the fantasy maps in this chapter, the Bodleian holds many more recent maps of imaginary lands. These include a convincing street map of Ambridge (where the BBC radio serial *The Archers* is set), with advertisements for fictional local businesses in the margins. Other examples range from Sodor Island (home of Thomas the Tank Engine) to the Land of Ice and Fire of *Game of Thrones*. There is even a copy of Harry Potter's *Marauder's Map*, sadly without magical powers.

Historically, many artists have made maps, including such well-known Renaissance masters as Leonardo da Vinci and Albrecht Dürer. Since the twentieth century the number of artists working with maps has greatly increased, particularly since the 1960s. The artist Macdonald Gill made many beautiful maps in the mid-twentieth century that represented the world in a fanciful or amusing way; his *London Wonderground* is one of the best-known. Modern artists sometimes incorporate maps into their work or use the cartographic form as a work of art; one such is included in this chapter.

In some cases imaginative maps are just for novelty value: endless variants on the form of the London Underground map exist, covering subjects as diverse as local pubs, Lake District fells and medallists in the London 2012 Olympics.

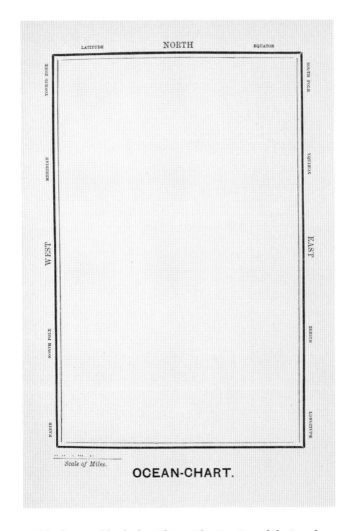

The famous blank chart from *The Hunting of the Snark*,
showing only the sea and not the land; it was popular with the
crew in the story because they could all understand it.

Drayton's Poly-Olbion

'I shall leave your whole British Empire, as the first and southerne part, delineated,' so begins Michael Drayton (1563–1631) in his dedicatory address to the *Poly-Olbion* (1612, 1622). Through Drayton's epic poetry, prose illustrations by John Selden (1584–1654) and the richly illustrated maps of William Hole (d. 1624), the *Poly-Olbion* journeys through the topographical and antiquarian highlights of the counties of early modern England and Wales. Drayton began work on the *Poly-Olbion*, meaning 'multiple blessings' or 'multiple Albion', as early as 1598, but publication did not take place until 1612, owing to difficulty securing patronage for this exceptionally expensive work. The poem, later to become so well known, was not considered a success on pub-lication, and securing funds for the second part was dealt a blow by the death of one of Drayton's main patrons, Henry, Prince of Wales, within months of the 1612 publication. The second part of *Poly-Olbion* finally appeared in 1622, but a plan to issue a third part detailing Scotland was never realised, curtailing the comprehensive survey Drayton had envisaged.

If the Page fa-tisfie not, in-quire in the Margine:

Poly-Olbion travels through the counties of England and Wales describing the topographical features, 'sto-ries, antiquities, wonders, rarities and pleasures and commodities of the same'. Unusually for maps of the seventeenth century, there is little emphasis on borders. Instead, rivers and springs are clearly present, often symbolized by a water nymph; forests are populated by hunters, hills by shepherds, and local myths and legends are featured prominently. Drayton intended to record England and Wales for a new audience, exploiting the discoveries of the Elizabethan era. The combination of the lyrical poetry of Drayton and the prose history of Selden, relatively unknown and unattributed in the 1612 printing, makes for an interesting contrast. As Drayton expands on the legends and myths of the coun-ties through metaphor, Selden brings the 'stories' of the poet down to earth with his prose illustrations.

The map pictured here is the twelfth song of the *Poly-Olbion*, 'Parte of Shropshyre on the east of Severne'. Here we can see in detail the work of the engraver, Hole, considered one of the most versatile of his profession in this era. He relied upon the atlas of Christopher Saxton (*c.*1540–*c.*1610) to reflect accurately the topography of the land while drawing on Drayton's poetry to populate the landscape with anthropomorphized features. Particular highlights of the map include the confluences of rivers and streams, where we see the water nymphs come together in an embrace; the cathedral city of 'Lychefeld' marked by a woman wearing a masonry crown; and the well at St Wilfrun's, which is marked by a woman with open arms drawing water from it. A fascinating feature of this Shropshire map is Wrekin Hill, which depicts the local legend of the Welsh giant Gwendol Wrekin ap Shenkin ap Mynyddmawr, who was tricked into creating the hill to save the town of Shrewsbury from his inten-tion to flood it.

J-J Drayton d.41 (1)

HROPSHYRE

Seuerne

Dunsmore

Manyfold

Douc

Moreland

STAFFORD

Yendon

Hans

SHYRE

Churnet

Tearne

Taine

Needwood fo:

Sow

Trent

Tre

Blyth

STAFFORD

Tearne

Penk

Wrekin   Hill

Canke fo: Alias Cankwood

LYCHEFELD

St. Wiltruns Well

Smestall

WOLVERHAMTON   Tame

Rebuilding the City of London

The disastrous and destructive fire of London in 1666 was viewed by some as an opportunity to build something more modern, something more fitting for the age. Diarist and polymath Sir John Evelyn was one of these and he produced his map for the rebuilding of the city in response to King Charles II's call.

Unlike the layout of old, Evelyn envisioned London with long, straight and impressive boulevards – much like the later Parisian style of Baron Haussmann. It would show the world that London was a place to be reckoned with, how far it had come and its ambitions for the future. In the new London there would be very few of the narrow streets that spread the fire in the first place, and the wide avenues would act as a fire break in any future conflagrations. The new London would also be built in brick and stone to minimize the risk of combustion and fire damage. The competition proved popular with the movers and shakers of the day, with other plans produced by Sir Christopher Wren and Robert Boyle, but all were ultimately rejected. The difficulties of overcoming the problem of land ownership proved insurmountable and so – although some bottlenecks were eased and street markets were relocated to market halls – the city grew up much like what it had been before, along similar street patterns. Was this an opportunity wasted?

The reconstruction of the churches was planned centrally, however. To replace those burned in the fire, fifty-one new churches were designed and built under the direction of Sir Christopher Wren. Some of these 'Wren' churches still exist in their original form, while some have been substantially altered by the passage of time and the Blitz. Old St Paul's was decaying even before 1666 and, after it had been substantially damaged in the fire, the decision was taken to rebuild it. This task was also assigned to Sir Christopher Wren, so, although his grand plan of a new London failed, he, more than any man, influenced the rebuilding of the city.

The map itself is a small affair, just 14 × 22 cm, with the principal features numbered to a key. It was issued in this form by Alexander Hogg in 1785 – a publisher and bookseller of Paternoster Row, who was best known for publishing the journals of Captain Cook – more than a century after it was originally conceived.

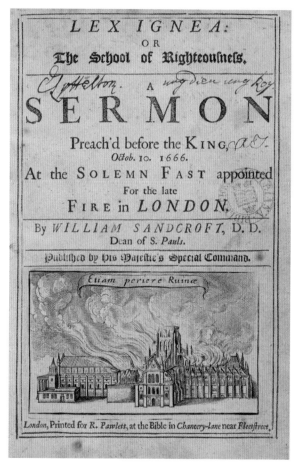

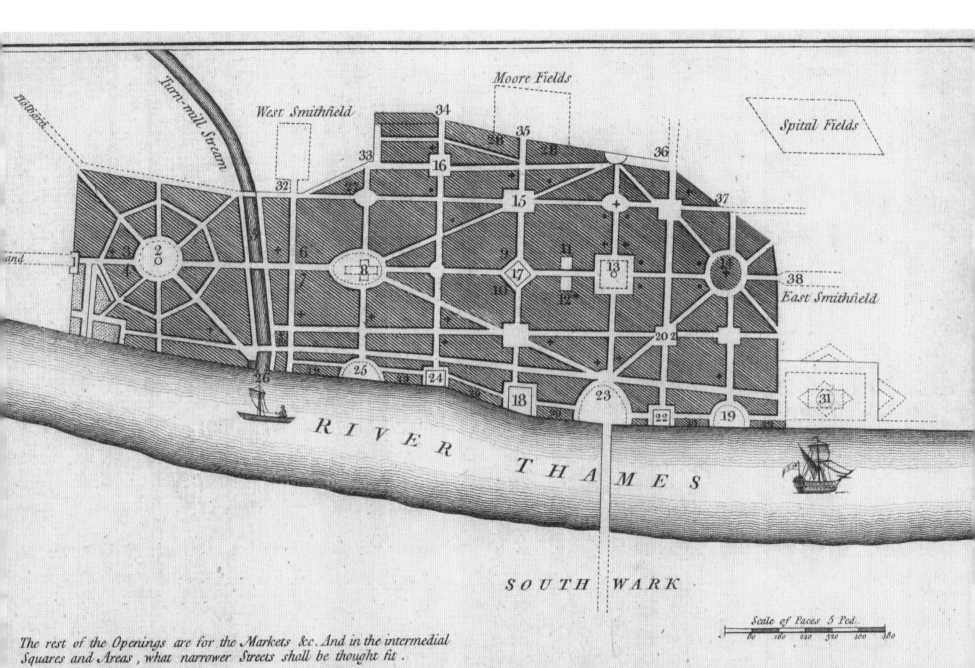

Turn-mill Stream

Holborn

and

West Smithfield

Moore Fields

Spital Fields

2

32

33

34

16

35

28

28

36

37

15

6

7

8

9

11

13

17

38

East Smithfield

10

12

14

26

25

23

24

20 21

18

22

19

31

R I V E R   T H A M E S

S O U T H   W A R K

The rest of the Openings are for the Markets &c. And in the intermedial
Squares and Areas, what narrower Streets shall be thought fit.

Scale of Paces 5 Ped.
80 160 240 320 400 480

Leo Belgicus

In 1583 the concept of the Low Countries being mapped in the shape of a lion was introduced by the Austrian baron Michael von Eytzinger, in his history of the Low Countries, *De Leone Belgico*. Not only did the geographical disposition of this region encourage comparisons with the shape of a seated lion, but thirteen of the seventeen provinces included a lion in their emblems.

This *Leo Belgicus* is a copper engraving and etching contained within the pages of an unattributed composite Dutch atlas. It looks fondly back at a short period of peace during the Eighty Years' War (1568–1648).

The Visschers were an Amsterdam dynasty of mapmakers running through four generations. Claes Jansz., born in 1587, was the first of the family to come to prominence. He began his career as an etcher and gained fame as an engraver of landscapes. It was he who published the first state of this map in around 1611. His son Nicolaus, whose name can be seen alongside the title, was born in 1618 and was producing cartographic products up to his death in 1679.

The geographical subject of the map covers the seventeen provinces, nowadays The Netherlands and Belgium, presented within the body of a seated lion. Beyond the lion's body, an idealized landscape is created, populated with contemporary and allegorical figures. The map is an early example of peace propaganda, celebrating the Twelve Years' Truce (1609–21) between the Seven United Dutch (or northern) Provinces and Spain, details of which are found beyond the cartographic representation of the Low Countries and within the landscape.

The map and imaginary landscape are framed on each side by columns featuring views of cities. To the left are ten northern settlements from the modern day Netherlands, on the right another ten, this time from today's Belgium and Luxembourg. Heading each column, the sovereignty of both areas is announced, the Stadtholder ruling the north, the Spanish Infanta Isabella Clara Eugenia, widow of Albert VII, Archduke of Austria and Duke of Burgundy, ruling the Habsburg or southern Netherlands. Coats of arms of all the seventeen provinces are ranged across the top.

Labels such as '*'t Vrije Neerlant*' (the Liberated Netherlands) and '*'t Neerlandt onder d'Aertshartogh Albertus*' (the Netherlands under Archduke Albertus) can be seen beside the two seated women, beneath whom lies the trampled figure of '*d'Oude Twist*' (the Old Conflict). The women represent the northern and southern Netherlands. Other statements developing the map's theme include '*Zeghen*' (Blessing), '*Rijckdom*' (Wealth), and '*Const en Wetenschap*' (Art and science), delivered from on high by God. '*Vailighe Tijdt*' (Safe time), '*'t Lants Welvaert*' (Prosperity of the country), '*'t Vergrooten der Steden*' (Growth of cities), and '*'t Veijlich Reijse*' (Safe travel) – all of which are indicative of good times and prosperity – are shown within the bounds of the image. The entire theme of the map is celebrated by the angel emerging from the lion's mouth, proclaiming '*Bestant voor 12 Iaer*' (Twelve-year truce).

The lion itself holds a sheathed sword. The sheath bears two seals showing seven arrows (representing the seven northern provinces) and the cross of Burgundy for the southern provinces. The seals each bear a statement, '*Voor twaelf jaren*' and '*Duodecim annos*' (For twelve years). The same insignia for the north can be seen in the right hand of one of the seated women; the other woman holds on to the southern provincial emblems. To the bottom right we see a resting figure, '*Slapende Oorlogh*' (Sleeping war). The Low Countries are at peace.

Map Res. 34

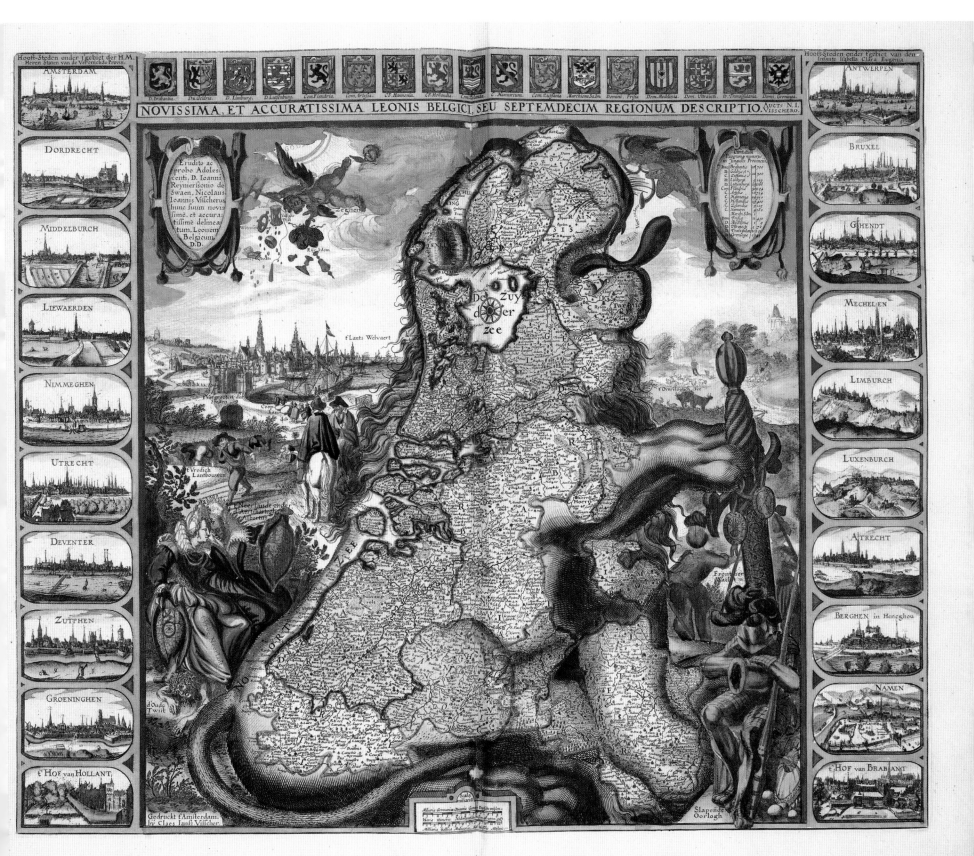

Hooft-Steden onder 't gebiet der H.M. Heren Staten van de Vereenichde Provin.

- AMSTERDAM
- DORDRECHT
- MIDDELBURCH
- LIEWAERDEN
- NIMMEGHEN
- UTRECHT
- DEVENTER
- ZUTPHEN
- GROENINGHEN
- 't HOF van HOLLANT

Hooft-Steden onder 't gebiet van den Infante Isabella Clara Eugenia

- ANTWERPEN
- BRUXEL
- GHENDT
- MECHELEN
- LIMBURCH
- LUXENBURCH
- ATRECHT
- BERGHEN in Heneghou
- NAMEN
- 't HOF van BRABANT

D. Brabantia. Du. Geldria. D. Limburg. D. Lutzenburg. Com. Flandria. Com. Artesia. Co. Hannonia. Co. Hollandia. Com. Zeland. c. Namurcum. Com. Zutfania. Marchiona. Sa. Im. Domini. Frisia. Dom. Mechlinia. Dom. Ultraiect. D. Transisulana. Domi. Groninga.

De Zuyder zee

t' Lants Welvaert

Gedruckt t'Amsterdam by Claes Iansz. Visscher

Slapende Oorlogh

France as an oak tree

Students of geography may recall being told that maps should not only answer questions but help identify questions to ask. This map of France, published in Britain during the French Revolution, raises a question of authorship. The handwritten imprint gives an address but no name: 'Published as the act directs June 28 1796 By the author No.49 Great Portland Street'. Who is this masked author? An examination of his work provides some clues to his identity.

The map and legends are neatly side-framed by typeset text detailing the events of the French Revolution. It seems the author possessed a fine eye for proportion and design. However, the name of each country is engraved in a different script – an excessive ornamentation that might indicate a florid character.

The map itself shows the various administrative divisions and centres of France – political, religious, educational and judicial – and some of the sites of major confrontation between royalists and republicans. The *département* divisions are keyed to a legend.

The texts and map title reveal strong monarchist sympathies. Just one of many examples is the entry for the town of Vans, describing the events of 14 July 1792: 'Nine priests massacred …. Among that number was M. Téron; the barbarians recollecting that he had a son about 10 years old, fetched him to be the witness of his father's death, who expired amidst the tortures of these wretches, and the piercing shrieks of his unhappy child.' Such vivid details might not withstand rigorous scrutiny, but a cursory check confirms that clashes took place around some of the dates chronicled.

An oak tree is superimposed on the map. The title cartouche has an explanation: the 'branches extend towards those countries where the Present Anarchists have endeavoured to further their infamous principles'. The author was probably aware of the metaphorical *Leo Belgicus* maps, and the idea of representing France as an oak may have been inspired by an essay on liberty trees by the Abbé Henri Grégoire – a prominent bishop, scholar, abolitionist and revolutionary. Liberty trees are historic in origin but their appeal to the Revolution was more contemporary – they were a symbol of freedom during the American War of Independence. Perhaps more fancifully, the author may have heard the story of the *Chêne chapelle* (Oak chapel) in Allouville-Bellefosse. A Revolutionary mob wanted to destroy a hollow oak containing a chapel. They were placated when they learned that the tree had been renamed the 'Temple of Reason' and was now a symbol of the new thinking.

The British Library holds a companion map by the same author entitled *The Kingdom of France is represented in the form of a Ship*. This is more satirical than metaphorical and is a forerunner of the kind of cartoon cartography popularized by Fred Rose's 1877 map of Europe. In the text to this map, the author asserts that he 'had the honour of attending the king' when, in July 1789, Louis XVI was conducted to the Paris Town Hall by Lafayette, the Commander of the National Guard.

William Doyle, Professor of History at Bristol University, finds it intriguing that this confirmed royalist 'accepts the Revolutionary division of the country into departments, rather than cleaving to the old provinces'. The author might have been presented with a familiar cartographic dilemma: should one show political divisions de facto or de jure?

We do not have a name for the mysterious mapmaker of Great Portland Street; he appears to have been brave enough to express his views but sufficiently cautious to conceal his identity.

The map invites more questions. Could this cartographer and chronicler of current affairs, a man of fine taste, living or working from a fashionable address in London, also have been a satirist, and a dandy – perhaps even a Pimpernel?

(E) C21 (114)

ENGLAND

GERMANY

ENGLISH CHANNEL

SWABIA

Bay. of BISCAY

SWITZERLAND

ITALY

SAVOY

The KINGDOM of FRANCE

Being one of the most Antient
in Europe is represented as an
Oak whose Branches extend
towards those Countries where the
Present Anarchists have endeavour'd
to fix their infamous principles.
The Monarchy began under Pharamond
in the Year 420, since which time
there have been 67 Kings to the
Unfortunate Louis 16, born at Versailles
August 23, 1754. Crowned June 11.
1775. Married May 16.th 1770, to
Maria Antoinette, Archdutchess
of Austria born at Vienna,
Nov.r 29.
1755.

BORDEAUX

SPAIN

MEDITERRANEAN SEA

CORSICA

Leagues of 2280 Toises 25 to a Degree

London Wonderground

This map, drawn to promote the London Underground, shows a strange and imaginative view of the city. It is the work of MacDonald 'Max' Gill, brother of the famous sculptor Eric Gill. Already known as an artist, architect and designer, MacDonald Gill was asked to design the map by Gerard Meynell, the printer and graphic designer who had been commissioned to produce a map poster for the London Underground in 1913. It was published the following year, and Gill went on to produce a number of very distinctive maps in similar style throughout his life.

The aim was to encourage use of the London Underground, for pleasure as well as business. It is a beautiful example of a pictorial map, a modern interpretation of the bird's-eye views of cities that preceded it. The map's charm comes from the way it is covered with little pictures of buildings, people, animals, birds and scenes of action all over London, some realistic and others more whimsical. It includes some stations that were not yet open: Queen's Park and Kilburn, for instance, appear with 'Opens 1915' across them on banners; the text was removed in later printings. Writing around the colourful border in the original version read: 'By paying us your pennies, you go about your businesses, in trams electric trains, in motor driven buses, in this largest of all cities, Great London by the Thames'.

The map is visually striking, with its bold colour scheme and elegant typeface. The border lettering and coats of arms suggest a patriotic pride in the hub of the empire. A closer examination of the detail reveals a wonderfully quirky view of London, with many jokes. Some were topical, and are rather baffling to the modern viewer, but many will still raise a smile. There are puns (such as the Bricklayer's Arms pub – '2 per person!'). The Harrow Road is being harrowed (by a farmer who comments, 'Harrowing work, this!' to be sure that we get the joke). The first three verses of Blake's famous poem 'The Tyger' are reproduced next to the London Zoo, with a giraffe superciliously commenting, 'This is the kind of thing that makes me tired!' while a passerby offers him a bun. There is also an appreciation of the traditions of London – the words of Oranges and Lemons, and other traditional rhymes and songs, appear across the map in various guises. It emphasizes London's position in the world: a town crier to the west points out the route to 'Kew, Windsor, Oxford, Gloucester, Wales, Ireland, U.S.A.'. It was clearly designed for entertainment rather than navigation when displayed on the station platform, and was so popular that, according to contemporary reports, passengers happily missed their trains so that they could go on studying it. A folded version was soon made available for individual purchase. The writing in the border was replaced with 'The heart of Britain's empire here is spread out for your view. It shows you many stations and bus routes not a few. You have not the time to admire it all? Why not take a map home to pin on your wall!' This is the map reproduced here.

Gill went on to produce many other pictorial maps of London and the world, often for promotional purposes. They included a famous map of steamship routes in 1927 to promote trade across the British Empire, a map showing how 'Tea revives the world' in 1940, and many private commissions. Some were in the form of murals, in institutional buildings and even on board ships.

C17:70 London (219)

Exercise Surprise Packet

The start of the Cold War in the late 1940s, and Britain's involvement in the Korean War soon after, led to an increase in training involving large-scale troop movements in the British Army during the 1950s, with names such as 'Exercise Hereward', 'Exercise Father Tiber' and 'Exercise Noah's Ark'. Ordnance Survey maps were used to plan and carry out these mock engagements.

'Exercise Surprise Packet' took place in October 1951, with the premise that Britain is joined to Europe by the Anglian Peninsula. The northern part of Britain, called 'Fantasia', is an authoritarian state with plans to invade the democratic 'Southland', and seize an atomic stock-pile stored at Broad Hinton, just south of Swindon in the 'Midland zone'.

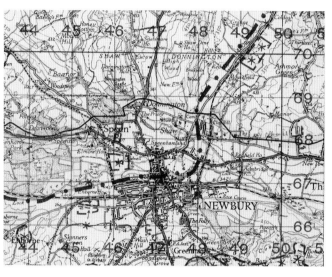

In the exercise the intention was for the Midland zone to join with the United Nations against Fantasia but instead the Midlands joined with their northern neighbours and took part in the attack on Southland. Despite large numbers of airborne troops being deployed and the 'bombing' of southern cities, Southland were able to hold off the attack by the movement of large numbers of troops to key areas.

The detailed mapping for Exercise Surprise Packet was over-printed on maps from the Ordnance Survey one inch to a mile New Popular Edition, as shown in the extract below, with imagined troop positions, made-up boundaries and in some cases names. The thick blue dot and dashed line just to the north of Newbury is the imagined international boundary between Southland and the Midlands. In addition to all these features maps produced for the Surprise Packet exercise included a large lake around Tidworth in Wiltshire and marsh and bog areas.

The map shown opposite, *Exercise Surprise Packet – Sketch Map 'A'*, was specially produced for this exercise by the Geographical Section, General Staff, the cartographic branch of the War Office. While appearing at first to be a conventional outline map of England, on closer inspection unusual things become apparent. District names are not what you would expect, Southland and Fantasia, the Midlands spreading over into Wales. There is also an area of inundation (flooded land) in the area around Colchester north of London. Strangest of all is the image in the inset at the top right-hand corner of the map. It is here that the peninsula joining Britain with Europe can be seen, linking the country to the Continent in a way not seen since the rising of sea levels at the end of the last Ice Age, around 10,000 years ago.

C17 (532) [1]

EXERCISE
SURPRISE PACKET

SKETCH MAP
"A"

ANGLIAN PENINSULA
(SOUTH)

FANTASIA

MIDLAND

SOUTHLAND

SCALE
10 5 0 10 20 30 40 50 MILES

Geographical Section, General Staff, (Misc.) 1540
1650/9/51.

Drawn and reproduced by Ordnance Survey, 1951.

LEGEND
TOWNS..•
AIRFIELDS..⊙
AIRFIELDS UNDER CONSTRUCTION..........○
GROUPS OF AIRFIELDS............................▨

There and back again

The Hobbit, or There and Back Again tells the story of a journey. The hobbit in question, Bilbo Baggins, travels from his snug hobbit-hole in the quiet backwater of Hobbiton over the Edge of the Wild into Wilderland in order to steal back the dwarves' treasure from the fearsome dragon Smaug. On the way he grows in courage, cunning and diplomacy. Such a journey required a map.

All I remember about the start of *The Hobbit* is sitting correcting School Certificate papers in the everlasting weariness of that annual task forced on impecunious academics with children. On a blank leaf I scrawled: 'In a hole in the ground there lived a hobbit'. I did not and do not know why. I did nothing about it, for a long time, and for some years I got no further than the production of Thror's Map.

In this letter to the poet, W.H. Auden, recently elected Professor of Poetry at Oxford, and avid fan of *The Lord of the Rings*, Tolkien wrote of the unexpected appearance of the hobbit, and perhaps unusually for a writer, of his compulsion to draw a map.

'Thror's Map' is the treasure map at the heart of the story, but, as the tale grew and the hobbit and his companions journeyed into new regions, new maps were required. The creation of maps was always central to Tolkien's story-telling and to the verisimilitude of his imaginary lands. He used them as an aid whilst he was writing to ensure that the journey was believable and indeed accurate within its own bounds. Some maps were brief sketches, others were more fully envisaged, produced specifically to share with the reader.

His finished map of Wilderland is a beautiful pictorial map designed to appeal to children. Packed with detail, the map rewards the attentive reader with glimpses of the giant spiders lurking in Mirkwood and of the huts of the Woodmen nestled in the forest further south, whilst the menacing form of Smaug flies over his lair in the Lonely Mountain.

Many of the key places in the story are pinpointed on the map. In keeping with its fairy-tale nature, most of the place names are simple and descriptive, turning common nouns and adjectives into place names – the Lonely Mountain, the Misty Mountains. However, some Elvish names appear, such as Esgaroth (Lake Town) and Mount Gundabad, which are derived from an early form of the Elvish language, Sindarin. This was the language chiefly spoken by the Elves in *The Lord of the Rings*, the sequel to *The Hobbit*. Although it began as a stand-alone story, *The Hobbit* was 'drawn into the edge of' the vast creative endeavour of Middle-earth, which was brimming with Tolkien's invented languages and which he had been working on for twenty years.

The Hobbit was published in 1937 with two maps, which literally book-end the text – Thror's Map as the front endpaper and the map of Wilderland as the back. Although Tolkien drew the maps in blue and black ink, his publisher, George Allen & Unwin Ltd, chose to print them in a more eye-catching red and black. *The Hobbit* has been in print since its first publication and has been translated into fifty-six languages. Although many different illustrators have been employed, with varying degrees of success, Tolkien's two maps have been a constant feature of the book – an inseparable part of the original work.

MS. Tolkien Drawings 35

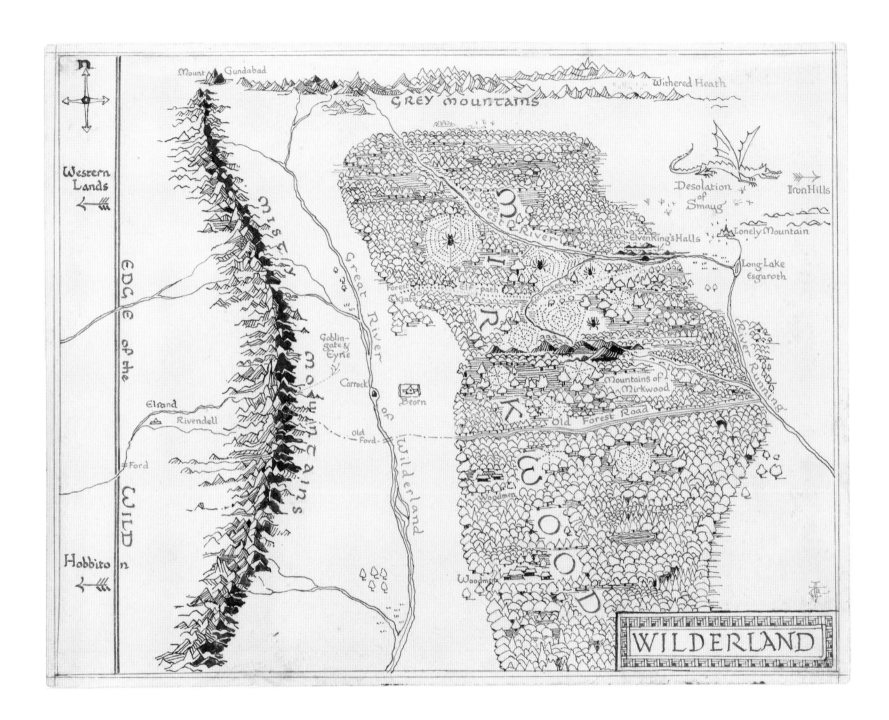

N

Western Lands ←

Edge of the Wild

Hobbiton ←

Mount Gundabad

GREY MOUNTAINS

Withered Heath

MISTY

Forest River

Desolation of Smaug

Iron Hills

ElvenKing's Halls

Lonely Mountain

Long-Lake Esgaroth

Great River

Goblin-gate & Eyrie

MIRKWOOD

Forest Gate

Elf-path

Carrock

Beorn

of Wilderland

Mountains of Mirkwood

River Running

Elrond

Rivendell

Old Ford

Old Forest Road

Ford

MOUNTAINS

Woodmen

Woodmen

WILDERLAND

The magical realm of Narnia

Although C.S. Lewis had been an enthusiastic artist as a child, he never went on to illustrate his own books for publication, unlike his friend Tolkien. The map of Narnia is a rare example of his adult artwork. It depicts the magical realm as it appears in *Prince Caspian* (1951), the second of the seven novels that make up the series 'The Chronicles of Narnia' (1950–56). Lewis apparently derived the name of his imaginary kingdom from *Murray's Small Classical Atlas*, which gives the Italian town of Narni in its Latin form, as Narnia (see extract below). But in conception, Lewis's Narnia is based on the landscape around his Belfast home with its view of the Mourne Mountains, which 'made me feel that at any moment a giant might raise his head over the next ridge'. In his cartography County Down is transformed into the mountains and forests of Narnia, where the sea is not to the west, as is common in myth and fantasy fiction, but to the east, as it is in the earth-bound geography of Northern Ireland.

The map was never published in Lewis's lifetime. He had been introduced – possibly by Tolkien – to the work of Pauline Baynes, who was just beginning her successful career as an artist and illustrator. Lewis appears to have sent the annotated map to her (the creases where he folded it can still be seen), writing in a letter of 5 January 1951 that 'My idea was that the map should be more like a mediaeval map than an Ordnance Survey – mountains and castles drawn – perhaps winds blowing at the corners – and a few heraldic-looking ships, whales and dolphins in the sea'. Baynes, who illustrated all the 'Narnia' books, redrew the map for *Prince Caspian*. A famously laconic entry in her diary reads 'Met C.S. Lewis. Came home. Made rock cakes'.

MS. Eng. lett. c. 220/1, folio 160

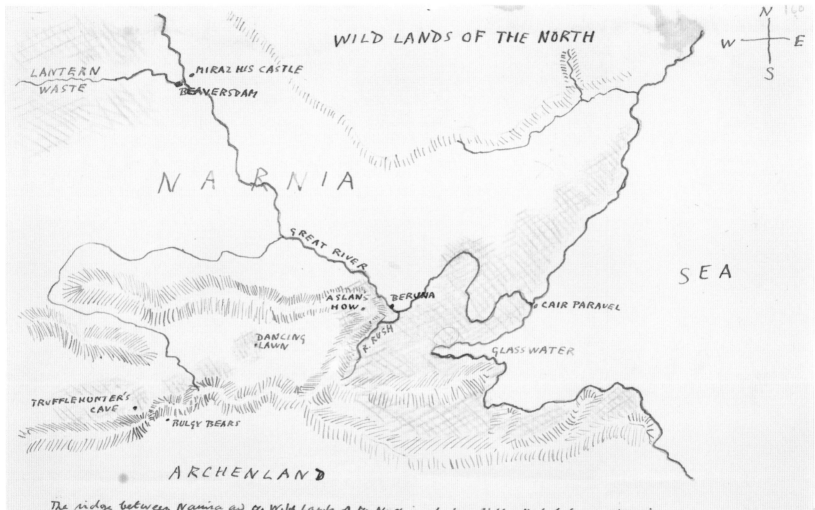

WILD LANDS OF THE NORTH

N 160
W—E
S

LANTERN
WASTE

MIRAZ HIS CASTLE

BEAVERSDAM

N A R N I A

GREAT RIVER

SEA

ASLANS
HOW

BERUNA

CAIR PARAVEL

DANCING
·LAWN

R. RUSH

GLASS WATER

TRUFFLEHUNTER'S
CAVE

·BULGY BEARS

ARCHENLAND

The ridge between Narnia and the Wild Lands of the North is only low hills: that between Narnia and Archenland, real mountains.

Aslan's How is on a moderate hill: but the range of which it is the Eastern end gets higher as it goes Westward.

Green = major woods.

A future story will require marshes here. We needn't mark them now, but must not put in anything inconsistent with them!

Cartography or art?

What might at first glance appear to be a topographic map of Tyne and Wear in the northeast of England transpires to be something altogether different. It is a map to intrigue, challenging all Geordies, Mackems and displaced Smoggies to view their home area in an alternative yet vaguely reassuring light.

A map or a work of art? Artist Layla Curtis, who grew up in the northeast and has family connections with the area, created this collaged map by taking extracts from a variety of topographic maps. The originals were published primarily in Australia and the United States, although, for those looking carefully, there is some British, Canadian, Irish, Jamaican and New Zealand cartography on view. Her work has been described as 'exploit[ing] the psychogeographical and political power of place names and map making'. Segments of mapping have been extracted from existing sheet maps and skilfully reassembled to create a cartographic 'landscape' which is instantly familiar, yet so very different from the geography on the ground.

Curtis's initial forays into cartography took place in Japan, where she first set about creating an imaginary landscape by way of collage, the underlying intention being to impose the unfamiliar on to the familiar, inviting the observer to question their understanding and expectation of the mapscape laid out before them. As an artist, she endeavours to explore the notion of borders and boundaries, both physical and metaphorical.

This map was commissioned by Newcastle-based Locus+, a visual arts commissioning agency that works with artists on the production of socially engaged, collaborative and temporary projects. The collage used to create the print is a diptych; one part is the map, and the other, reproduced on the back, forms the index, collaged from tourist guides to Newcastles and Sunderlands around the world. It was reproduced as a limited edition digital pigment print, whilst 30,000 copies of the double-sided, folded print version of *NewcastleGateshead*

were distributed free across the UK to coincide with NewcastleGateshead Festival of the Visual Arts 2006.

The collage portrays the existing, familiar structure of Newcastle, Gateshead and the surrounding area. The North Sea coastline is reasonably close to how we might expect it to look, and Curtis has made provision for the area's two key river estuaries, the Tyne and the Wear, as well as mirroring built-up development by populating those locations where the observer looks to find Newcastle and Sunderland with urban activity.

There are fifty-two Newcastles or New Castles (and even a correctly pronounced New Cassel) marked on the map, along with Newcastle Emlyn and Newcastle-under-Lyme; there are also twenty Northumberlands, seventeen Dudleys, fifteen Washingtons, twelve Whickhams, eight Shields (plus one North Shields), six Sunderlands, five Heatons, four Durhams and even two Middlesboros; there are also ten North Easts. Finally there are numerous references to the region's former economic driver, Coal, and the real gem on view for the quintessential Newcastle experience is a spot called Shearer Point, in honour of Newcastle United's all-time record goalscorer.

Many of these places can be found exactly where one might presume them to be – Birtley, Dudley, Dunston, Heaton, Ryton, Sunderland, Sunnyside, Wallsend, Walker, Washington and Whickham, for example. Some are completely displaced, such as Berwick, Carlisle, Durham, Gosforth, Hexham, Jesmond Dene, Middlesboro (sic), Morpeth and Prudhoe, whilst the only Gateshead to be found on the map is a mystery island out at sea. To illustrate the map's artistic credentials, however, Baltics Corners is placed precisely where one might expect to see the Baltic Art Gallery.

In the words of Matthew Hart, Curtis is 'forcing us to ask how maps construct places and people, inviting us to think about what happens in the moment of cartographic reinvention'.

Contributors

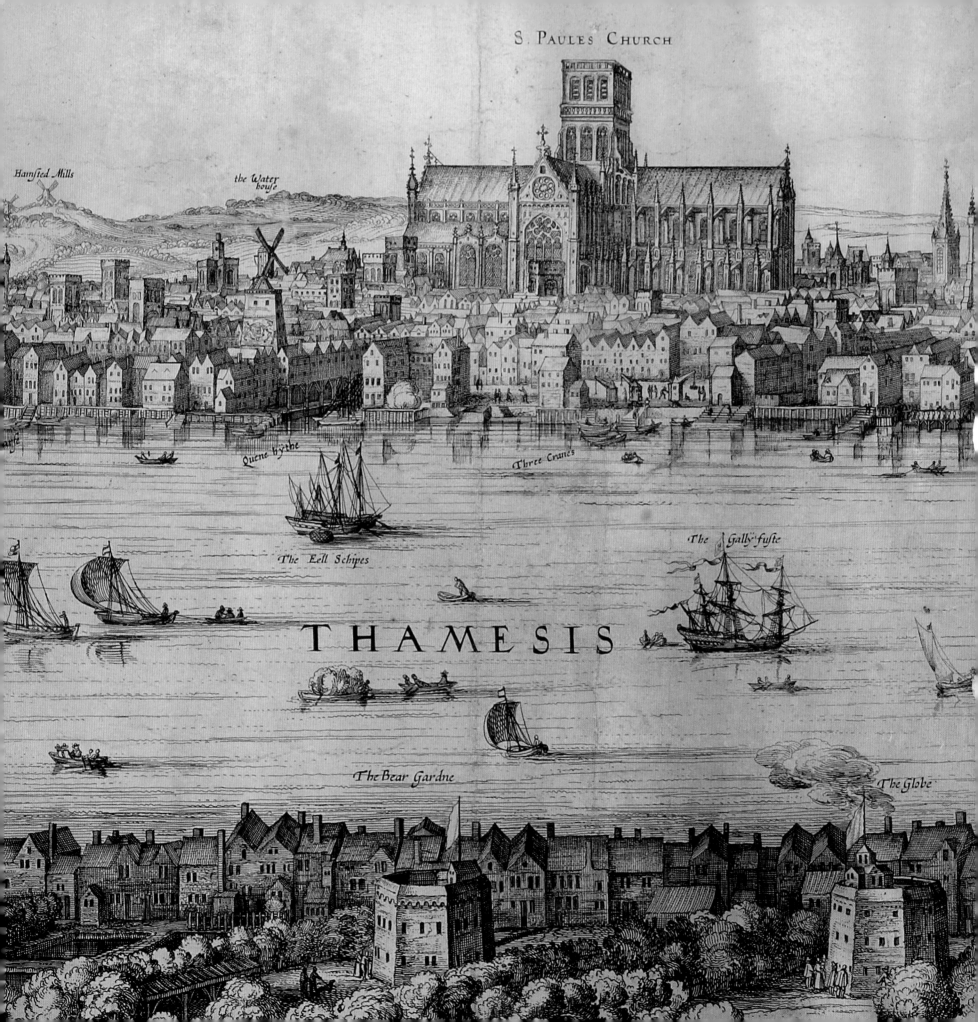

S. PAULES CHURCH

Hamsted Mills

the Water house

Quene-hythe

Three Cranes

The Eell Schipes

The Gally fuste

THAMESIS

The Bear Gardne

The Globe

Image sources

1. Travel and Exploration

p. 12 *Recreational map, United States at c1:9,500,000* [On reverse of] *Sinclair road map, New Jersey.* Chicago: Rand McNally, 1936. F6:38 (3)

p. 14 *The end of the Peutinger table restor'd as far as it relates to Brittan*, by W. Stukeley, [1720]. Gough Maps Great Britain 1

p. 15 *[Portolan chart of the eastern Mediterranean], by Bartolomeo Oliva. [Venice]: 1559.* MS. Can. Ital. 143, fol. 4

p. 16 *A plan of the intended navigable canal from Chesterfield to the River Trent near Stockwith*, J. Varley and T. Kitchin. [S.l.]: T. Kitchin, 1769. Gough Maps Derbyshire 5

pp. 19, 20–1 *[Map of Great Britain, known as the Gough Map]. c.1360.* MS. Gough Gen. Top. 16

p. 23 *[Map of the Holy Land]. c.1390.* MS. Douce 389

p. 24 'Typus orbis terrarum' from the *Geographia*, by Claudius Ptolemaeus Alexandrinus, trans. Jacobus Angeli, ed. Nicolaus Germanus. Ulm: Johann Reger, for Justus de Albano, 21 July 1486; with the maps from the edition of Ulm, Lienhart Holl, 1482. Arch. B b.19 (Bod-inc. P-529 (2))

p. 27 *[Selden Map of China]*. [16--?] MS. Selden supra 105

p. 29 'Map of the road from London to Aberystwyth', from *Britannia, volume the first* ... London: John Ogilby, 1675. Vet. A3 b.10

p. 31 *Virginia, discovered and discribed by Captayn John Smith; graven by Wiliam Hole.* [1612] MS. Ashmole 1758 13v-14r

p. 33 *[The second part of the Oriental Navigation]*, by John Thornton, 1682. Map Res. 117

p. 34 'The Kangooroo', from *The Voyage of Governor Philip to Botany Bay with an account of the establishment of the colonies of Port Jackson & Norfolk Island.* London: John Stockdale, 1790. 20675 c.4

p. 35 'Sketch of Sydney Cove, Port Jackson, in the County of Cumberland, New South Wales. July 1788', from *The Voyage of Governor Philip to Botany Bay... ibid*

p. 37 *Map of the inland navigation, canals and rail roads with the situations of the various mineral productions throughout Great Britain, from actual surveys, projected on the basis of the trigonometrical survey made by order of the Honourable the Board of Ordnance, by J. Walker, land and mineral surveyor of Wakefield. Dedicated to the King's most excellent Majesty.* Wakefield and London: Published by Richard Nichols, bookseller, Wakefield; Longman, Rees, Orme, Brown and Green, 39 Paternoster Row, and G. & J. Cary, 86 St James Street, London, 1830. (E) C16 (138)

p. 38 Extract from *Eastern Archipelago, Sunda Strait and its approaches...1885.* London: Admiralty, 1885. Admiralty Chart 2056

p. 39 *Sunda Strait from a Dutch Govt. Chart 1862.* [Inset on] *Eastern Archipelago, western portion, including the Java Sea and the Southern Passages to China...1867.* Published at the Admiralty, under the superintendence of Captain G.H. Richards, R.N., F.R.S., Hydrographer. London: Admiralty, 1867. Admiralty Chart 941a

p. 40 Inset from *Khartûm and environs, Intelligence Branch No. 282.* London: [War Office] Intelligence Br., 1883. E4:20 Khartoum (1)

p. 41 *Route from Suakin to Khartoum, March 17th, 1874.* MS. E4:1 (19)

p. 43 *[Sketch maps of the Sese Islands, Lake Victoria, Uganda]. [c.1910].* 752.11 t.1 (24)

2. Knowledge and Science

p. 44 *This chart with equidistant and streight lined meridians, parallels and rumbs ... sheweth the longitudes, latitudes, courses and duistances of all places, as truly, as the globe itself can doe ... I first published... in my former edition of Errors in Navigation... William Kip sculpsit.* [S.l.]: Edward Wright, [1610]. As published in *Certaine errors in nauigation ...* (E) B1 (1047)

p. 46 *Amerique septentrionale* par N. Sanson ... par G. Sanson. Paris: Pierre Mariette, 1669. Map Res. 87, pl. [8]

p. 48 Extract from Warwickshire XLIV-6. From Ordnance Survey County Series 1:2,500. 1st edition. Southampton: Ordnance Survey, 1889

p. 51 *Analyse géographique des Départements de la France.* Par Barrut-Lemerrie auteur et editeur. Paris: Bourrut-Lemerie, [1820-1839?] Vet. E6 f.372

3. Pride and Ownership

p. 141 Bruges from *Civitates orbis terrarum* as above

p. 142 Extract from *Oxonia antiqua instaurata sive urbis & academiae Oxoniensis topografica delineato olim a Radulpho Agas impressa. A.D. 1578 nunc denuo aeri incisa A.D. MDCCXXVIII. A. Ryther delin.* [*Facsimile engraved by R. Whittlesey*]. [S.l.]: R. Whittlesey, 1728. Gough Maps Oxfordshire 2

p. 143 *Celeberrimæ Oxoniensis academiæ avlarvm et collegiorvm ædificiis totivs Evropæ magnificentissimis cvm antiquissima civitate coinvnctæ elegans simvl et accvrata descriptio Radulpho Agaso avtore ano dni 1578. Augustinus Ryther anglvs deliniavit 1588.* [S.l.]: Ralph Agas, 1588. [Map Room]

pp. 144–5, 209 *London*, C.J. Visscher delineavit. Amsterdam: Jodocus Hondius, 1616. Douce Prints a.53 (2)

p. 146 [Oxford] from *The Theatre of the Empire of Great Britaine.* London: John Sudbury and George Humble, 1612. Map Res. 74

p. 147 *Oxforde as it now lyeth fortified by His Ma[jes]ties forces, 1644.* Wood 276b (30).

p. 149 *A Geometrical Plan and West Prospect of Stoke Town in the County of Devon with His Majesty's Dock Yard and Ordnance Wharfe*, John Milton. [S.l.]: T. Milton [i.e., J. Milton], 1756. Gough Maps Devonshire 8

p. 151 *A plan of the city of Bath in the County of Somerset. Copied from the Original Survey of Mr John Wood of Bath, Architect, Anno Dom. 1735.* [Bath]: J[ames] Leake, 1736. Gough Maps 28, fol. 46

p. 153 *A plan of Boston and its Environs, shewing the true Situation of His Majesty's army and also those of the Rebels, drawn by an engineer at Boston, October 1775.* London: Andrew Drury, Duke's Court, St Martin's Lane 12 March 1776. (E) F6:60 Boston (1)

p. 155 'Calcutta,' from *Maps 1845–47 of the Society for the Diffusion of Useful Knowledge.* London: Chapman and Hall, 1844. 2027 b.37

p. 157 *Liverpool 1:500.* Southampton: Ordnance Survey 1890. C17:79 Oxford (15). ©Protinus Holdings. Images supplied courtesy of Rod Adkins, Protinus Holdings

p. 158 Map extract from *On the mode of communication of cholera*, by John Snow. London: John Churchill, 1849. Photo courtesy of Giles Darkes

p. 159 *A Map of Oxford showing the localities in which cholera and choleraic diarrhoea occurred in 1854, and cholera in 1832 & 1849.* [London: J. Churchill; Oxford: J. H. and J. Parker, 1856]. C17:70a.230

p. 161 *A balloon view of London.* London: Edward Stanford, 1859. C17:70 London (327)

6. Maps for Fun

p. 162 *The chain of Mont Blanc, from an actual survey in 1863-4,* by A. Adams-Reilly. London: published under the authority of the Alpine Club, by Messrs Longman & Co., 1865. C21:44 (5)

p. 164 *Visitor's panoramic map of the neighbourhood of Brighton. Drawn from nature by Saml. Johnson.* London: Gall & Inglis, [1901]. C17:58 (36)

p. 165 [Cover from] *Bacon's new cycling road-map of Oxford and district* . London: G.W. Bacon & Co., 1910. Dunston F 662

p. 167 [Cover from] *The Trossachs and Loch Lomond.* Southampton: Ordnance Survey, 1920. Ordnance Survey Map Covers 1 (39)

p. 167 [Cover from] *Ordnance Survey "One Inch" Map, Truro and St Austell.* Southampton: Ordnance Survey, 1933. Ordnance Survey Map Covers 1 (23.2b)

p. 167 [Cover from] *Ordnance Survey District Map London (North)*. Southampton: Ordnance Survey, 1922. Ordnance Survey Map Covers 1 (29)

p. 167 [Cover from] *Ordnance Survey "One Inch" Map, District map series. Dorking and Leith Hill.* Southampton: Ordnance Survey, 1929. C17 (29g) [14].

p. 169, pp. 170–1 [View of Jerusalem and the Holy Land] from *Peregrinatio in Terram Sanctam* . Mainz: Erhard Reuwich, 1486. Arch B c.25

pp. 173 *An actual topographical survey of the environs of Keswick*, Thomas Donald. London: Wm. Faden, 1789. (E) C17:22 (39)

p. 174 'Island near Henley', from *Tombleson's Thames.* London: Black & Armstrong, 1834. G.A. Gen. Top. 4. 25

p. 175 *Tombleson's Panoramic Map of the Thames and Medway.* London: J. Reynolds, 1899. C17:8 (153)

p. 177 *Places of meeting of Lord Gifford's hunt.* [London: M.A. Pittman, 1843]. C17:7 g.1

p. 179 *Ordnance plan of the Crystal Palace and its environs: from sheet VIII.10, 11, 14, 15 of the county of Surrey and sheets VII.10 and VIII.11 of the county of Kent.* Southampton: Ordnance Survey, 1863. Facsimile (made from the Bodleian's copy) C17:8 (350). © The Charles Close Society for the Study of Ordnance Survey Maps and Protinus Holdings. Digital restoration by Dr Alexander J. Kent. Reproduced by permission of the CCS; image supplied courtesy of Rod Atkins, Protinus Holdings

p. 181 *Yellowstone National Park.* [S.l.: Northern Pacific Railway], 1904. F6:58 (36)

p. 183 *Tourist Map of Mount Kenya. National Park & Environs.* [Tolworth]: Directorate of Overseas Surveys for the Kenya Government, [1974]. E10:5 (26)

p. 184 *3D Navigator: Les 3 Vallées Savoie France.* MountMaps, 2004. C21:44 g.1

7. Imaginary Lands

p. 186 'Ireland' from *Geographical fun: being humourous outlines of various countries. With an introduction and descriptive lines. By 'Aleph'.* London: Hodder and Stoughton, 1868. C1 d.69

p. 188 *Hark! Hark! The dogs do bark!: with note by Walter Emanuel.* London: G.W. Bacon & Co., [c.1914] 17075 b.6

p. 189 *[Military map of South Buckinghamshire]* Royal Military College, High Wycombe, *c.*1801. MS C17:15 (54)

p. 191 'Ocean chart' by Henry Holiday, from *The Hunting of the Snark: an agony in eight fits* by Lewis Carroll. London: Macmillan, 1891. 280 e.3905, p.17

pp. 192–3 [Map of Shropshire]. Taken from *[Poly-Olbion]. A chorographicall description of all the tracts, rivers, mountains, forests, and other parts of this renowned isle of Great Britain, with intermixture of the most remarkeable stories, antiquities, wonders, rarities, pleasures, and commodities of the same. Divided into two bookes; the latter containing twelve songs, never before imprinted. Digested into a poem by Michael Drayton. Esquire. With a table added, for direction to those occurrences of story and antiquitie, whereunto the course of the volume easily leades not.* London, Printed for Iohn Mariott, Iohn Grismand, and Thomas Dewe, 1622. J-J Drayton d.41 (1)

p. 194 Title page from *Lex ignea: or The school of righteousness*, a sermon, by William Sancroft. London, [1666?]. Vet. A3 e.219

p. 195 *Sir John Evelyn's Plan for Rebuilding the city of London after the Great Fire in the year 1666.* London: A.Hogg, 1785. (E) C17:70 London (1165)

p. 197 *Novissima, et accuratissima Leonis Belgici, seu Septemdecim Regionum description or The Seventeen Provinces as a sitting lion*, N[icolaus] I[oannis] Visscher. [S.l.]: Claes Jansz. Visscher, [c.1650]. Map Res. 34

p. 199 *The Kingdom of France Being one of the Antient in Europe is represented as an Oak whose Branches extend towards those countries where the Present Anarchists have endeavourd to fix their infamous principles. The Monarchy began under Pharamond in the Year 420, since which time there have been 67 Kings, to the Unfortunate Louis 16, born at Versailles August 23d, 1754, Crown'd June 11, 1775, Married May 16th, 1770, to Maria Antoinette, Archdutchess of Austria, born at Vienna, Novr, 29, 1775.* No.49 Great Portland Street [London]: by the author, June 28 1796. (E) C21 (114)

p. 201 *The Wonderground map of London town.* Drawn by MacDonald Gill. London: The Westminster Press, 1914. C17:70 London (219)

p. 202 Extract from *England and Wales New Popular Edition one-inch map, G.S.G.S. (Misc.) 1560/6. Sheet 158 Oxford and Newbury.* London: Military Survey, 1951. C17 (532) [1]

p. 203 *Exercise Surprise Packet – Sketch Map 'A', G.S.G.S (Misc) 1540.* London: Military Survey, 1951. C17 (532) [1]

p. 205 *Map of Wilderland*, drawn by J.R.R. Tolkien for *The Hobbit* (London, 1937). MS. Tolkien Drawings 35 © The Tolkien Estate Limited, 1937

p. 206 'Italia', Plate 8 from *Murray's Small Classical Atlas.* London: J. Murray, 1904. 2023 c.13

p. 207 *[Map of Narnia for Prince Caspian, by C.S. Lewis].* MS. Eng. lett. c. 220/1, folio 160. © copyright C.S. Lewis Pte. Ltd. 1951

p. 209 *NewcastleGateshead visitor* by Layla Curtis. 2005, collaged road and topographical maps (detail). O1 (21). Reproduced courtesy of Layla Curtis

Select bibliography

General

Brotton, J., *A History of the World in Twelve Maps*, Allen Lane, London, 2012

Parry, R., Perkins, C.R., *World Mapping Today*, Bowker Saur, London, 2000

French, J., Scott, Valerie, and Tooley, R.V., *Tooley's Dictionary of Mapmakers*, Map Collector Publications, 1999

Vaisey, D., *Bodleian Library Treasures*, Bodleian Library, Oxford, 2015

Wallis, H., Robinson, Arthur Howard, *Cartographical Innovations: An International Handbook of Mapping Terms to 1900*, Map Collector Publications, Tring, 1987

Travel

Akerman, J., 'American Promotional Road Mapping in the Twentieth Century', *Cartography and Geographic Information Science*, 29 (3), 2002, pp. 175–92

Akerman, J. 'Introduction', in J. Akerman (ed.), *Cartographies of Travel and Navigation (Kenneth Nebenzahl, Jr., lectures in the history of cartography)*, University of Chicago Press, Chicago, 2006

Arad, Pnina 'Pilgrimage, Cartography and Devotion: William Wey's Map of the Holy Land', *Viator: Medieval and Renaissance Studies*, 43 (1), 2012, pp. 301–22

Baynton-Williams, Ashley, 'Biography: John Ogilby'. *MapForum*, Issue 1, 1999, www.mapforum.com/01/magazine.htm (accessed 12 Feb. 2015).

Campbell, Tony, 'The Jansson-Visscher Maps of New England', in R.V. Tooley (ed.), *Mapping of America*, Holland Press, London, 1985

Chesterfield Canal Trust, http://www.chesterfield-canal-trust.org.uk/index.php (accessed 29 April 2015)

Davenport-Hines, Richard 'Gordon, Charles George (1833–1885)', *Oxford Dictionary of National Biography*, Oxford University Press, 2004, online edn, Jan 2008, www.oxforddnb.com/view/article/11029 (accessed 30 April 2015)

Davey, Francis, (ed. and trans.), *The Itineraries of William Wey*, Oxford, Bodleian Library, 2010

Delano-Smith, Catherine 'Milieus of mobility: itineraries, road maps and route maps,' in J. Akerman (ed.), *Cartographies of Travel and Navigation (Kenneth Nebenzahl, Jr., lectures in the history of cartography)*, University of Chicago Press, Chicago, 2006

Dickinson, G., 'Britain's First Road Maps: The Strip-Maps of John Ogilby's Britannia, 1675', *Landscapes*, 4 (1), (2003), pp. 79–98

Harley, J.B., *John Ogilby: Britannia*. (Theatrum Orbis Terrarum series of atlases in facsimile; 5th ser., v. 2 Y). Theatrum Orbis Terrarum, Amsterdam, 1970

Frostick, Raymond, *The Printed Maps of Norfolk 1574–1840: A Carto-Bibliography*, Raymond Frostick, Norwich, 2011

Harvey, Paul D. A., *Medieval Maps of the Holy Land*, British Library, London, 2012

Millea, Nick, *The Gough Map: The Earliest Road Map of Great Britain?*, Bodleian Publications, Oxford, 2007

Morgan, Gwenda, 'Smith, John (bap. 1580, d. 1631)', *Oxford Dictionary of National Biography*, Oxford University Press, 2004, www.oxforddnb.com/view/article/25835 (accessed 29 April 2015)

Pächt, Otto and Alexander, Jonathan J.G., *Illuminated Manuscripts in the Bodleian Library Oxford*, (Vol. 3: British, Irish and Icelandic Schools), Clarendon Press, Oxford, 1973.

Queen's University, Belfast, *Mapping the Realm: English Cartographic Constructions of Fourteenth Century Britain*, www.qub.ac.uk/urban_mapping/gough_map/ (accessed 10 April 2015)

Röhricht, Reinhold, 'Die Palästinakarte des William Wey', *Zeitschrift des deutschen Palästina Vereins*, 28, 1904, pp. 188–93

Tyacke, Sarah, and Huddy, John, *Christopher Saxton and Tudor Map-Making*, British Library, London, 1980

Knowledge

Baigent, Elizabeth, 'Quin, Edward (1794–1828)', in *Oxford Dictionary of National Biography*, Oxford University Press, Oxford, 2004, www.oxforddnb.com/view/article/22958 (accessed 18 Feb. 2015)

Bendall, Sarah, 'Speed, John (1551/2–1629)', *Oxford Dictionary of National Biography*, Oxford University Press, Oxford, 2004, online edn, Jan 2008, www.oxforddnb.com/view/article/26093 (accessed 26 April 2015)

Crane, Nicholas, *Mercator: The Man who Mapped the Planet*, Weidenfeld & Nicolson, London, 2002

Gent, Robert H. van, and Taschen, Benedikt, *The Finest Atlas of the Heavens = Der prächtigste Himmelsatlas = L'atlas céleste le plus admirable*, Taschen, Hong Kong and London, 2006

Hannas, Linda, *The English Jigsaw Puzzle, 1760-1890*, Wayland Publishers, London, 1972

Harley, J.B., and O'Donoghue, Yolande, *The Old Series Ordnance Survey Maps of England and Wales: Scale: 1 Inch to 1 Mile: A reproduction of the 110 sheets of the survey in early state in 10 volumes*. Harry Margary, Lympne Castle, Kent, 1975

Herries Davies, G., *Sheets of Many Colours: The Mapping of Ireland's Rocks, 1750–1890*, Royal Dublin Society, Dublin, 1983

Hodson, Yolande, *An Exhibition to Celebrate the Bicentenary of Ordnance Survey*, Ordnance Survey, Southampton, 1991

Ireland, H.A. 'History of the development of geologic maps', in *Bulletin of the Geological Society of America*, 54 (9), 1943, pp. 1227–80

Krogt, P.C.J. van der (ed. and comp.), *Koeman's Atlantes Neerlandici*, HES, 't Goy-Houten, 1995

Rapoport, Yossef and Savage-Smith, Emilie, 'An Eleventh-Century Egyptian Guide to the Universe: The 'Book of Curiosities', edited with an annotated translation', in *Islamic Philosophy, Theology and Science, Texts and Studies*, vol. 87, Leiden, Brill, 2014

Secord, J.A., 'Beche, Sir Henry Thomas De la (1796–1855)', in *Oxford Dictionary of National Biography*, Oxford University Press, Oxford, 2004, www.oxforddnb.com/view/article/1891 (accessed 25 March 2015)

Shefrin, Jill, *Neatly Dissected for the Instruction of Young Ladies and Gentlemen in the Knowledge of Geography: John Spilsbury and Early Dissected Puzzles*, Cotsen Occasional Press, Los Angeles, 1999

Smith, Thomas R., 'Manuscript and printed sea charts in seventeenth-century London: the case of the Thames School', in Norman J.W. Thrower (ed.), *The Compleat Plattmaker*, University of California Press, Berkeley, Los Angeles and London, 1978

Skelton, R.A., *Atlas; or, A geographicke description of the world, Amsterdam 1636*, (Theatrum Orbis Terrarum series of atlases in facsimile; 4th ser., v. 2 Y), Theatrum Orbis Terrarum, Amsterdam, 1968

Whitaker, Ewen A., *Mapping and Naming the Moon*, Cambridge University Press, Cambridge, 2000

Winchester, S., *The Map that Changed the World: A Tale of Rocks, Ruin and Redemption*, Penguin, London, 2002

Wulf, Andrea, *Chasing Venus: The Race to Measure the Heavens*, William Heinemann, London, 2012

Pride and ownership

Baynton-Williams, Ashley, 'John Speed: The Prospect of the Most Famous Parts of the World', *MapForum*, Issue 3, 1999, www.mapforum.com/03/march.htm (accessed 26 April 2015)

Bendall, Sarah, *Dictionary of Land Surveyors and Local Map-Makers of Great Britain and Ireland, 1530–1850*: British Library, London, 1997

Goss, John, *Blaeu's The grand atlas of the 17th century world*, Studio Editions, London, 1997

Kain, R., & Baigent, Elizabeth, *The Cadastral Map in the Service of the State: A History of Property Mapping*, University of Chicago Press, Chicago and London, 1992

Marsden, Luis, 'The adventure of the copperplates', in *Colonial Williamsburg: The Journal of the Colonial Williamsburg Foundation*, Colonial Williamsburg Foundation, Williamsburg, Virginia, 1987, pp. 5–18

Oxford University Gazette, May 2, 1893, pp. 426–7, p. 485

War

Black, J., *Maps and Politics*, Reaktion, London, 1997

Bond, Barbara, 'Escape and evasion maps in World War II and the role played by MI9', *The Ranger*, 2 (19), Summer 2009, pp. 28–32, www.defencesurveyors.org.uk/Images/Ranger/Ranger%20Volumes/Ranger%20Summer%202009.pdf (accessed 3 April 2015)

Clout, H., and Gosme, C., 'The Naval Intelligence Handbooks: a monument in geographical writing', *Progress in Human Geography*, 27 (2), 2003, pp. 153–73

Collier, P., 'The Impact on Topographic Mapping of Developments in Land and Air Survey: 1900-1939', *Cartography and Geographic Information Science*, 29 (3), 2002, pp. 155–74

Godfrey, J.H., 'General preface to the Geographical Handbook series', in *Iraq and the Persian Gulf*, Naval Intelligence Division, London, 1944

Hall, Debbie, 'Wall tiles and Free Parking: escape and evasion maps of World War II', *MapForum*, 4, 1999. www.mapforum.com/04/escape.htm (accessed 3 April 2015)

Postma, Johannes, *The Dutch in the Atlantic Slave Trade, 1600-1815*, Cambridge UP, Cambridge, 1990

Rado, John, *History of fabric map production* www.silkmaps.com/history.html (accessed 3 April 2015)

Wilson, Leonard S., 'Some Observations on Wartime Geography in England', *Geographical Review*, 36 (4), 1946, pp. 597–612

Hochschild, Adam, *Bury the Chains*, Pan, London, 2012

Kinross, J., *Fishguard Fiasco: An Account of the Last Invasion of Britain*, Logaston Press, Little Logaston, 2007

Weetman, W.C.C., *The Sherwood Foresters in the Great War, 1914-1919, 1/8th Battalion*, Thos. Forman & Sons, Nottingham, 1920

Royal Geographical Society, *A Gazetteer of the World*, RGS, London, 1856

Cities

Füssel, Stephan, and Taschen, Benedikt, *Civitates orbis terrarum = Cities of the World: 363 Engravings Revolutionize the View of the World: Complete Edition of the Colour Plates of 1572–1617*. Taschen, Köln & London, 2008

Hyde, R., *Gilded Scenes and Shining Prospects: Panoramic Views of British Towns, 1575–1900*, Yale Center for British Art, New Haven, Connecticut, 1985

Macray, William Dunn, *Annals of the Bodleian Library, Oxford: With a Notice of the Earlier Library of the University*, Bodleian Library, Oxford, 1984

Millea, N., *Street Mapping: An A to Z of Urban Cartography: An Exhibition in the Bodleian Library, February–April 2003*, Bodleian Library, Oxford, 2003

Ristow, Walter W., 'Cartography of the Battle of Bunker Hill', *Revista da Universidade de Coimbra*, 27 (1979), pp. 263–79

Scouloudi, Irene, *Panoramic Views of London 1600-1666 with Some Later Adaptations: An Annotated List*, Guildhall Library, London, 1953

Wellsman, John, *London Before the Fire, A Grand Panorama*, Sidgwick & Jackson, London, 1973

Recreation

Bainbridge, S., 'Romantic writers and mountaineering', *Romanticism*, 18 (1), 2012, pp. 1–15

Brodsky-Porges, E. , 'The grand tour ….', *Annals of Tourism Research*, 9 (4), 1982, pp. 585–6

Browne, John Paddy, *Map Cover Art*, Ordnance Survey, Southampton, 1990

Carlson, J., 'Topographical Measures: Wordsworth's and Crosthwaite's Lines on the Lake District', *Romanticism*, 16 (1), 2010, pp. 72–93

Hyde, R., *Panoramania!: The Art and Entertainment of the 'All-Embracing' View*, Trefoil, London, 1988

Levet-Labry, E., and P. Schut, 'Sport and Tourism – An Effective Cooperation: Canoeing and Mountaineering in France before the First World War', *Sport in History*, 34 (2), 2014, pp. 276–94,

Mackinder Halford J., and Barbour K. Michael (ed.), *The First Ascent of Mount Kenya*, Ohio University Press, Athens, Ohio, 1991.

'Peregrinatio in Terram Sanctam' by Bernhard von Breydenbach http://www.nls.uk/collections/rare-books/collections/breydenbach (accessed 26 June 2015)

Towner, J., (1984). 'The grand tour: Sources and a methodology for an historical study of tourism', *Tourism Management*, 5 (3), pp. 215–22

The V.W.H. Hunt http://www.vwh-hunt.co.uk/about-us/history/ (accessed 23 Oct. 2014)

Imagination

Cosgrove, D., 'Maps, mapping, modernity: Art and cartography in the twentieth century', *Imago Mundi*, 57 (1), 2005, pp. 35–54

Doyle, William, University of Bristol (author of *The Oxford history of the French Revolution*, etc.). Personal correspondence

Harden, J. David, 'Liberty Caps and Liberty Trees,' *Past and Present*, 146, 1995, pp. 66–102

Hill, Gillian, *Cartographical Curiosities*, British Museum Publications, London, 1970

Schilder, Günter, *Monumenta cartographica Neerlandica*, Uitgevermaatschappij Canaletto, Alphen aan den Rijn, 1986

Woodward, David (ed.), *Art and Cartography: Six Historical Essays*, University of Chicago Press, Chicago and London, 1987

Layla Curtis, www.laylacurtis.com (accessed 6 Feb. 2015)

MacDonald Gill, www.macdonaldgill.com (accessed 15 Feb. 2014)

Poly-Olbion, www.poly-olbion.exeter.ac.uk/ (accessed 2 April 2015)

Chêne Chapelle, www.en.wikipedia.org/wiki/Chêne_chapelle (accessed 8 May 2015)

Index